BRINGING HOME ANIMALS

Bringing Home Animals

Religious Ideology and Mode of Production of the Mistassini Cree Hunters

Adrian Tanner

ISER

Institute of Social and Economic Research

First published in the United Kingdom
by C. Hurst & Co. (Publishers) Ltd.
1-2 Henrietta Street, London, WC2E 8PS

ISER Books gratefully acknowledges the assistance of the Faculty of
Arts, Memorial University of Newfoundland.

National Library of Canada Cataloguing in Publication

Tanner, Adrian, 1937-

Bringing home animals : religious ideology and mode of production of Mistassini Cree hunters

(Social and economic studies ; number 23)

Bibliography: p.
Includes index.
ISBN 0-919666-34-5

1. Mistassin Indians -- Hunting. 2. Indians of North America -- Quebec (Province) -- Hunting. 3. Mistassin Indians -- Rites and
ceremonies. 4. Indians of North America -- Quebec (Province) --
Rites and ceremonies. 1. Memorial University of Newfoundland, Institute of Social and Economic Research. II. Title. III. Series: Social
and economic studies (St. John's, Nfld.) ; number 23

E99.M683T36   1979   971.4'00497   C80-003652-2

Published by ISER Books - Faculty of Arts Publications
Institute of Social and Economic Research
Memorial University of Newfoundland
St. John's, NL A1C 5S7
Printed and bound in Canada

To the memory of
Alys Ada Tanner
(1902-1977)
and
Herbert Gabriel Tanner
(1899-1971)

Contents

Figures

Maps

Tables

Plates

Preface

This is a book about the Cree Indian hunters and trappers who live at Mistassini, some 350 miles north of Montreal, Quebec. My eighteen months living with them, both in their village and out on the trap-lines and in the hunting camps, was an extremely pleasant period, but because I am concerned in this study with other matters I do not try to give even the flavour of this experience. The easy-going companion-ship as part of a Cree family and the direct encounters with the natural wonders of the sub-arctic boreal forest were made possible for me mainly through the generosity and skill of my Indian hosts. Yet, as a prelude to the study, something must be said about this personal experience. In part this is to pay tribute to the Mistassini Indians; it is also to show how I was drawn into undertaking this research, and how my experience itself influenced the way I have come to formulate some of my conclusions.

One of the basic assumptions upon which this study is based is that the Mistassini have a unique culture of their own, and that a non-Cree person who wishes to comprehend their behaviour must cross over a gap which exists between his own assumptions about the world and theirs. The existence of such gaps between groups of people — gaps which require some special effort and some kind of technique to bridge — is one of the guiding concepts of anthropology. The cultural gap plays a significant part in the personal encounter which ethno-graphic work entails.

In my own experience the cultural gap has not always been so clear cut, since my work in Canada has been with native groups who have a considerable history of interaction with European cultures. Moreover, as a student of northern Indian and Inuit studies I noticed a trend among anthropologists towards placing less emphasis on indigenous cultural factors in their work. Instead they demonstrated a growing amount of direct influence over the lives of native people which came from outside the group. Many of the external influences were traced to the larger White North American society, from which the researchers themselves came. Native cultural traditions were seen to be losing some of their relevance in the modern world, as they were over-whelmed by the more powerful external influences. At the same time, some studies found that unassimilated native groups continued to exist by adapting to changes from the outside, but the implication was that the continuity of native culture was in these cases subject to controls not in the hands of the group itself.

Much of this emphasis on external factors concerned the idea that

Indians and Inuit had become minorities within Canada. Even native communities with expanding populations were being surrounded by a larger and faster-developing non-native population. At the same time criticisms were being levelled at the Canadian government against the policy of maintaining native reservations, because it was based on the false assumption that native communities could enjoy a degree of social and economic independence from the surrounding non-native society, and this would supposedly shield them from the worst effects of European contact. The system of reservations, far from providing a solution to the problems of culture contact, was seen as compounding the difficulties. The reserves, as they are apologetically called in Canada, were revealed to be a sordid archipelago of dispossessed bands whose powerlessness had turned to self-destructive social pathologies, including internal bickering, petty crime, heavy drinking and suicide. On or off the reserve it appeared that a further depressing chapter was being written in the saga of the disappearing Indian.

I therefore felt that I faced two options in planning a doctoral research project: either I could undertake a study of an Indian or an Inuit group, under the qualification that it was a part-culture on its way to becoming another ethnic minority in the Canadian cultural mosaic, or I could go to a third world country and undertake a study of a more isolated and culturally autonomous group. I found this latter alternative difficult to accept, in part because I had first been drawn into the study of anthropology as a result of some experiences I had had whilst working in the arctic, getting to know Inuit hunters and trappers who had retained full control over large parts of their land, over their productive activities and over large areas of their culture. However, I decided to go abroad.

In 1967, while preparing to do this, I took a short summer job with a research team, the McGill-Cree Project, studying social and economic change among Cree Indians in Quebec. I was to interview Indians living in tents and shacks on the outskirts of the mining towns of Matagami and Chibougamau. These people had a mixed economy which included hunting and trapping along with casual labour and welfare payments. I also paid a quick visit to Mistassini Post, an Indian village about 50 miles north of Chibougamau. Although our study found some indicators suggesting that these Cree were being drawn into the dominant society as a sub-group of the working class, and also that recent industrial developments in the area were having some adverse effects on their freedom to hunt and trap, my attention was also caught by the very active hunting and trapping sector of the economy. A large proportion of the population was engaged full-time in these pursuits, living in camps that were physically and cultur-ally distant from the influences of the dominant White society. Moreover, the apparent vitality of the hunting and trapping way of life was also the basis for a strong sense of identity and values shared by all

Cree people in the area, even by those who had considerable contact with Whites.

Some of the general characteristics of hunting and trapping at Mistassini were familiar to me from previous studies in the north, and from historical material on the fur trade. Up to then my own interest in the fur trade had been as an historical era, or as only a marginal activity among contemporary native groups. I saw the fur trade as a factor of great importance in the process of the colonization of North America. Even though the trade was the result of European and later Canadian industrial enterprise, it had a unique set of traditions and assumptions, which had apparently been formed as much in response to the concerns and necessities of the native groups who participated in the trade as by the demands of the institutions which initiated the trade and which controlled its operations. Moreover, the relative autonomy enjoyed by Indians and Inuit within the fur trade during stable periods was in part due to the role of this trade in the colonial strategy. The fur trade was arranged so as to enable the colonizing state to exploit a natural resource without using a large capital outlay, by leaving the organization of production largely in the hands of native people. At the same time the colonial power was also able to conduct an imperial 'holding operation', maintaining at minimum expense the bare bones of a sovereignty claim over a vast area until such time as European settlement could take place. In these circumstances the native groups were for the most part left in control over the lands they hunted.

My summer's experience among the Cree started me on a re-examination of my doubts regarding the possibilities of an anthropological study of an autonomous North American native culture. I was aware that no cultural group in the world is entirely independent; it is more a question of the degree of autonomy. As far as Mistassini was concerned, I concluded that the degree of cultural autonomy was significant, and as a result I changed my mind and decided to conduct research there.

I was particularly interested, from a theoretical perspective, in work being conducted relating to the cognitive aspects of culture. I was critical of some of what I saw as crude attempts to relate these aspects to material factors, such as the ecosystem, or the economy. It seemed to me unlikely that the problem of the relation between material and cognitive aspects of culture could be solved by theoretical argument alone. In particular, I was impressed by an empirical approach to a similar problem by Marcel Mauss and H. Beuchat, written as long ago as 1904-5 (Mauss 1966). Using mainly the accounts of explorers, they show that there is an important relationship in Inuit groups between the sharp summer-winter seasonal climatic contrast and the economic, religious, legal and moral aspects of Inuit culture. However, the contrasts found at the cultural level do not have a direct material cause.

There is, instead, a form of symbiosis between the Inuit and their major game animals, such that they follow the concentration and dispersal patterns of these species. This pattern is elaborated at the level of social structure, so that, effectively, there are two seasonal forms of social organization. It is this contrast in 'social morphology', as the authors call it, which in turn determines other aspects of the culture. Having read Speck's work on Montagnais-Naskapi religion (1935), in which material factors are given almost no attention, I became interested in trying to see if a further study of this kind of phenomenon and its relationship to material factors was still possible.

In the early summer of 1969 I travelled to Mistassini, and with the help of the chief, Smally Petawabeno, I was offered accommodation in the house of a widow, Josephine Rabbitskin, with her four teen-age children. They belonged to the Nichicun sub-group, a formerly separate band whose territory was to the north of Mistassini. Many of the Nichicun families spent the summer in one section of the village, most of them at that time living in tents. Since two previous anthropologists had lived with hunters in groups belonging to the Mistassini proper, I decided to try and stay with a Nichicun hunting group for the winter, in order to extend data to include this northern sub-group.

During the first summer I worked on the language, having previously made a short study of the Albany dialect of Cree with Professor C. D. Ellis, and I conducted interviews on a variety of topics, including genealogy, mythology and the magico-religious aspects of hunting and trapping. My results with the latter subject were at first uneven, and I continued to have problems until after I had the experience of observing hunting rites in actual use. It was not that the elders were reluctant to discuss these questions with me. My first impression was that most of them did not consider the question of religious exegesis particularly interesting or important. Questions about practices reported by previous ethnographers in the Quebec-Labrador region were often greeted with denials that anything of the sort existed. In fact, it was only later that I was able to observe the Mistassini version of many of these practices, so it turned out that much of my problem had been in making my questions intelligible. I seldom came across any reluctance to answer questions due to Christian teachings, but there was a tendency to see some subjects as inappropriate or dangerous to speak about in the village context. This was in part due to the suspicion in the minds of some Cree people that the ability to perform hunting magic indicated a knowledge of sorcery techniques. Also those younger Cree persons who were aware of the contrast between Cree and White views of the world sometimes tended to play down the significance of Cree religious practice in an effort to reduce tensions arising from this contrast.

Many of my early difficulties in obtaining data about Cree religion arose from my limited fluency with the language, and the need to use interpreters who were not themselves familiar with the practices being discussed. Although I found it relatively easy to elicit and control noun terms for certain religious concepts, semantic analysis of these terms by themselves was not sufficient to discover the principles underlying the organization of religious categories. As will be seen, for example, in my discussion of a term like *Mistaapew* (see Chapter 6), in the Cree language a number of distinct connotations may be entailed in a single noun term. Informants may not all employ a term in exactly the same way. Distinctions between various possible meanings are often contained in other parts of an utterance, for instance in particular semantic elements of the verb, particularly roots and medials. The subtle distinction between such concepts may well be established by the regular use of the noun phrase in a particular verbal context. I suggest this as a result of instances in which an informant had previously been unable to assist me with a problem when it was phrased in one way, although an alternate phrasing of the question produced quite different results. Since I never became fully fluent in all complexities of the verb in Cree, I found that questioning about religious practice was most fruitful in cases where I had already observed the details of the practice.

By August, when the hunting groups were being formed at Mistassini for the following winter, I let it be known that I wanted to spend the year with one of the Nichicun groups. I was lucky that my first invitation came from Willie Jimiken. He and his wife were no longer as physically active as they had once been, and were for the most part restricted to hunting within a mile or two or their camp. However they had three unmarried adult children, Charlie, who is a skilled and energetic hunter, and Louise and Dinah, who are both active with much of the heavy work around camp. This family had decided to send only one child, the youngest daughter, to school, so that the others could concentrate on learning the bush skills. Although Dinah had learned English at school, she never used it in speaking to me over the whole winter. The other family who joined Willie Jimiken's hunting group was Johnny Rabbitskin, with his wife and three small children. Nobody in that family spoke English either.

I have very warm feelings about the winter that I spent in the bush with the Jimiken group. Because of the nature of this study, I do not deal with this particular experience, but with what is generally true about hunting groups. However, the fact that I have chosen to concentrate my study on hunters and trappers living in the bush, to the neglect of other aspects of Cree life, is no doubt due in part to my fond recollections of life with this group, as well as my later experience with groups led by Clarence Rabbitskin and Alfred Coon Come.

Living in an Indian hunting camp never fails to excite me with its mixture of powerful impressions. My awareness and interest in the natural environment of the wilderness is heightened by following whatever captures the attention of the Indians. Gradually the eyes become trained to pick out the significant details from the dark green of the forest and the white of the snow. The land and the water are revealed to be alive with animals. In a small way I am able to share in the work, hunting or carrying loads as best I can. Constant activity brings both excitement and exhaustion. The warmth, the food and the comfort of camp at the end of the day become goals of immense proportions. One of the most notable features of life in a Cree bush camp is the relative absence of expressions of hostility. In this small cluster of families each person lives very much in contact with all of the others, and very much dependent on them. This dependence, emotional as well as physical, is, however, accompanied by the emphasis of its opposite, that is, by a strong awareness and consideration given to the independence and the autonomy of each individual. Within this careful balance between individual autonomy and the reliance on others my own presence must have added particular strains. This was probably especially the case in the early months of my stay, before I had learned what to expect; however, if I did upset the equilibrium of the group I was not sensitive enough to be aware of it, and I never observed signs of anger, frustration or hostility among group members during the whole winter.

My living arrangement began with my eating meals with the Jimiken family, and sleeping in my own tent. I attempted to buy all extra items that had to be bought because of my presence, and in fact I tried to pay more than my share. But the cash sector of the economy is of limited significance in the bush, and I found that much of what was required had to be made by the Indians out of the resources they gathered from the bush. Some of these I purchased, but many were given to me as gifts. Most of my diet came from the animals killed by the Indians. Meat was almost always available in abundance, but I was totally unable to repay adequately either with purchased food, or with my efforts at hunting, or by helping with chores around the camp.

After a few weeks, as soon as the group arrived at their hunting territory, I was incorporated into the Jimiken family in the role of the youngest son, and gave up maintaining my own dwelling. I then began to experience the patient training in some of the fundamental bush skills by Willie and Charlie. My small achievements, most of which were within the capability of any adolescent Cree boy, were generously praised. The Cree themselves are aware of the difficulties of training a mature person who has not been brought up in the bush, even in the case of a Cree child who has grown up in residential school. I did not learn enough to hunt or trap independent of the direction of others. My role as mainly an onlooker and helper in productive activities happened to fit in well with my task as an ethnographer, but I must have been something of a liability to the group.

The inadequacy of my physical condition, compared to that of the other group members, became immediately apparent in our first week in the bush as we travelled by canoe and portaged our supplies between lakes, although I did improve in time. Portaging requires both the skill to assemble and tie the load properly and the strength to lift it. It also requires considerable stamina to carry several hundred pounds for a mile or more. As I discovered later, these same kind of physical qualities are called for in many aspects of hunting and trapping. One must often keep snowshoeing for hours on end. Often on hunting trips large amounts of food are not carried, and one must continue without meals until camp is reached, sometimes while dragging heavy toboggan loads. Such feats are the stuff of the heroism which is idealized in our own Canadian-Anglo-Saxon culture, but our heroes need only make such efforts on a handful of occasions during a lifetime. For the Cree hunters it is part of everyday life.

Cree hunters have a mental attitude towards these privations such that they are able to suppress feelings of hunger and exhaustion. The training for this was explained to me by a young Mistassini man, Rene Neeposh, when I visited the hunting group of his father, John Neeposh, and Clarence Rabbitskin. Rene was at that time in his third year as a hunter and trapper, after he had finished residential school. He described his first year as an exhausting experience, when it was all he could do to keep up with the adult hunters, even when carrying little or no load. If he complained about his tiredness or hunger he suffered the embarrassment of having people stop and let him rest, or of telling him to stay behind in camp. He learned not to complain. His father taught him to ignore tiredness, and to keep going when he felt he could not go on. As he became able to do this he found he could go on longer and longer trips. During his second year he began trapping on his own, and, at the time I was visiting his camp, he said that he finally felt confident of being able to handle himself in any situation in the bush. He had by then experienced several emergencies, when it had been necessary to go without food, or to travel day and night hauling a sick person by toboggan.

The summer months spent at Mistassini Post, and in the fishing or berry-picking camps in the vicinity, were in strong contrast to the hunting group life. For one thing, the social world was so much larger, and it was difficult to keep track of everything of importance that was going on. While I continued to live and share day-to-day experiences with many Cree families, I was also engaged in more formal interviewing for much of the time. I received the help of many people, including Phillip and Anne Marie Awashish, the Reverend Ken Blaber, Alfred Coomshish, Eddie Jolly, the Reverend Tom DeHoop, Jimmy Gunner, George and Glenna Matoush, Edward Matoush, Jimmy Matoush, Emmet McLeod, Robert Metawashish, Edna Neeposh, Rene Neeposh, Smally Petawabeno, John Rabbitskin (Jr.) and Glen Speers. A full list of all those who answered my questions would be unmanageably large, so that I will restrict myself to mentioning the following: Sam Blacksmith, Charlie Etap, Eva Etap, Evadney Gunner, Robie Gunner, Bally Husky, George Loon, William Matoush, David Neeposh, Matthew Neeposh and Walter Wapachee. At different times I stayed in many Cree households, including those of Alfred and Harriet Coon Come, Bally and Hattie Husky, Willie and Jane Jimiken, John and Annie Neeposh, Clarence and Margaret Rabbitskin and Josephine Rabbitskin. At Nichicun I was shown various kindnesses by the men of the Ministry of Transport Aeradio and Radiosonde Station, not the least by the cook Pierre, whose last name I never did learn.

In writing up my work as a doctoral dissertation I relied a great deal on the advice and criticisms of my committee at the University of Toronto, and in particular on my supervisor, Professor E. G. Schwimmer, now of Laval University, Quebec. Time and again, over countless beers and numerous cups of coffee, he probed the obscurities of earlier drafts, bolstered my confidence when it was dented by his high standards of work and sent me back to my fieldnotes with renewed determination. I also had the good fortune at Toronto to work with some of the most eminent scholars to have made major contributions to the study of the Northern Algonkian Indians: Professor R. W. Dunning, Professor R. Knight and Professor E. S. Rogers. It was their insistence on the ecological basis for the study of hunting societies that became my own starting point. During the stage when I was preparing my research proposal I benefited from comments on my work from Professor T. McFeat and Professor S. Nagata.

I would like to acknowledge with gratitude the financial support of the Canada Council and of the University of Toronto Committee for Arctic and Sub-arctic Research which my research received.

Revision of the manuscript for publication benefited from the comments of earlier drafts by Professor Judith Adler, Professor Jean Briggs and Professor Elliott Leyton, all of Memorial University of Newfoundland, as well as by Professor Rémi Savard and Pierre Grégoire, of the University of Montreal. Some of the individuals who answered specific questions or provided data from their own studies were: Dr. Alan Cooke, Professor David Cooter, Professor Peter Denny, Professor Harvey Feit, Ignatius LaRusic, José Mailhot, Toby Marantz (Ornstein), Professor Roger Pothier, Professor Richard Preston, Professor Peter Sindell and Mary Ann Sindell. Assistance with the drawings was generously provided by Ann McLean.

I also am indebted to Marguerite MacKenzie, who shared with me her skill as a Cree linguist and her experience and her intimate knowledge of the Mistassini people and their culture.

This book has been published with the help of a grant from the Social Science Federation of Canada, using funds provided by the Social Sciences and Humanities Research Council of Canada.

A Note on the Orthography of Cree Words

In this study I have attempted to employ the Cree orthography which has been developed, along Bloomfieldian lines, by Ellis (1973). The system is designed for use with an ordinary typewriter keyboard as a standard orthography for several of the Cree dialects, although I will only deal here with its use for the Mistassini dialect.

This system is not entirely phonetic, but what Ellis calls 'morphophonemic', meaning that a single morpheme is always spelled the same, even though in speech its pronounciation may vary somewhat, according to the adjacent sounds in the utterance. Not only does this simplify the spelling, but it allows for visual recognition of the 'same' morpheme in various positions.

For a non-speaker of Cree to pronounce correctly words written in this orthography would require knowledge of a number of simple rules stating the conditions under which certain sound shifts are made, just as he would also be required to know a number of rules giving the correct intonation pattern. However, these features almost never carry any meaning in Cree. My purpose in using Cree terms in this study is (a) so that a term can be reused in the text without having to give the English definition a second time, (b) so that Cree speakers and researchers who are studying the Mistassini or related groups can recognize the terms I have referred to, and (c) so that equivalents can be established between terms used by me and terms used by previous ethnographers who have used their own phonetic transcriptions. As it happens, all of these purposes can be served without using a more detailed orthography that would be required to mark allomorphic variations, or the details of the stress pattern.

Vowels

	Front	Back
High	i	u
Mid	e	
Low		a

All vowels except *e* have a long form and a short form. The long form is marked in the orthography by a double letter. However *e*, which is always long, is written with a single letter.

Where Ellis has used *o*, I employ the letter *u*, following the usage by MacKenzie (1972), Mailhot (1976) and Mailhot and Lescop (1977), for the dialects of Quebec-Labrador.

Consonants

	Bilabial	*Alveolar*	*Palatal*	*Velar*
Stops	p	t	c	k
Fricatives		← s →		
Nasals	m	n		
Semi-vowel	w		y	

In speech all stops may be either voiced or unvoiced, but this is not phonemic. The phoneme *s* may be realized as alveolar (š) or palatal (s). None of this is marked in the orthography.

1
Mistassini

1. Introduction

The North American Subarctic is an extensive and remarkably uniform geographic region. Apart from the great intrusion of Hudson Bay from the north, it is an uninterrupted belt of predominantly spruce forests, lying immediately south of the tundra zone, a belt which curves down from Alaska and the Yukon, through the southern part of the Northwest Territories and the northern parts of the prairie provinces, reaching its southern apogee on the northern shore of the Lake Superior, from where it bends eastwards to cover most of central Quebec and Labrador. It is marked by a southern boundry which is at times very sharp, and which marks the northern limit of commercial agriculture, leaving the subarctic as a region still largely untouched by development except for pulp wood operations and mines located in small towns isolated from each other and attached to the nearest large metropolis to the south. Most of the zone is considered to have the legal status of 'unoccupied crown land'.

For the Amerindians, the native people of America, the subarctic was also a uniform ecological zone, inhabited in the west by the Northern Athapaskans and in the east by the Northern Algonkians, two linguistically unrelated groups who, however, shared much in common in terms of basic technology and social life. For example, they shared the use of the snowshoe, the toboggan and the birch-bark canoe. They both had an economy based on fishing, large and small game hunting, used regional groups which were separated for most of the year into small multi-family hunting groups, with seasonal gatherings at places of resource concentration, and had shamanistic religions largely concerned with the control of forces in the natural environment.

While some of these groups moved onto the plains and became horse-mounted hunters, many remained in the subarctic forest and with the coming of the Europeans they underwent a somewhat different experience of contact from those Indians further south, although the contact was hardly less rapid than in the areas of intensive European settlement. At first the Europeans had no intention of alienating the subarctic Indians' land or dispensing with their services. On the contrary, the Indians were seen as potential allies, as trappers for the growing fur trade, and as middlemen in that trade. Few Europeans were interested in settling in the subarctic, so it was necessary for them to use Indian labour to trap the furs, and to transport the supplies.

1

This situation continued for a long time after the fur trade had run its course in other areas. By the time Canada became a nation in 1867, the fur trade was a spent economic force for the country as a whole, but in the subarctic and the arctic it remained, in most places, the only means of producing a marketable commodity. Although compared with more modern industrial enterprises its methods were hopelessly archaic, as long as the subarctic remained isolated from the industrial centres of Canada the fur trade was able to continue using a system of production and trade changed only in detail from its hey day.

The final decline of the northern fur trade, or its transformation and modernization, have been both mourned and celebrated. The community which is the subject of this study, Mistassini, Quebec, might well be viewed from the perspective of a former fur trade post now undergoing transition to some other economy, such as that of industrial wage workers, or recipients of government subsidies. However, I have chosen merely to note the forecast of the imminent disappearance of the fur trade and subsistence hunting as an economic base at Mistassini, and to describe and analyse the society as a functioning economic and social system. I do this because, regardless of how realistic the forecasts are, or how archaic the present system is, it is a system that fully involves most of the population. Moreover, I am particularly concerned with the adult population, who, while hoping that education will bring a better life for their children, do not see themselves as giving up the bush for a job or for the life of a welfare recipient. Circumstances may prove them wrong, but my purpose is to examine a fur trade community before that change — if it does come soon — takes place.

Another reason why the focus of my interest in this study is directed at what Mistassini society is, and what it has been, rather than what it may well be in the process of transforming into, is that the Indian fur trade community, as one example of a type of colonial encounter, offers some interesting insights and questions regarding the social and economic formation that can arise in this particular kind of colonial enterprise. Because of the nature of fur-bearing animals, the production of wild fur cannot be industrialized. Moreover, because it was the Indians who already possessed an efficient technology and the skill to harvest these animal species, the fur trade began with a dependence on a non-European technology, a technology which itself was based within a complex non-European tradition, one which was part of a non-European social structure and religious ideology. Upon this starting point were added techniques with a European origin, or techniques developed in the context of the North American fur trade, but the final form taken by these innovations could not be imposed unilaterally on the Indians by the European traders. The fur trade was thus somewhat different from some other types or phases of European colonial activity. For example, it is to be differentiated from plantation agriculture, in which the Europeans controlled all aspects of production, and where the colonized population were used as a labour commodity; and it is also different from the situation where the colonized group could play no useful role in the colonial enterprise, and where, consequently, the colonial group paid no heed to the interests and welfare of the subordinated aboriginal population.

In many parts of the subarctic the twentieth century saw the end of the fur trade, as well as a shift to an 'internal colonialism' within Canada by the metropolis over the hinterland, and the decline of many native communities into a position of irrelevance. For several reasons, which we will discuss later in this chapter, in a few centres such as Mistassini the fur trade remained relatively important, even while the trade itself lost its position within Canada as a whole. Recent new attempts to industrialize the arctic and subarctic have again focused national attention on the area and its inhabitants and have allowed native people to regain some measure of importance through pressure on the government to recognize their title to the land, and settle their claims based on that title (Sanders 1973).

Because Mistassini is a functioning fur trade community, with most of its population living the nomadic life of hunters and trappers in small scattered hunting groups for most of the year, and because their trade relations are still conducted through the Hudson's Bay Company, using a system of credit which has been the core of this relationship for many generations, this study can be used to enquire into some of the special theoretical problems raised by attempts to understand what happens when two quite different economic systems interact and exchange. One of these problems is the identification of boundaries between units of analysis. That is, what criteria should a theorist use to define clearly the units of study which go to make up the particular social system model that his work employs, and how are these criteria arrived at? Secondly, there is the difficulty of the application of social theory models in cases of regular and sustained interaction with members of an entirely different group, a group which cannot be analysed as sharing the same social structure, or even one having a separate system of economic production which is nevertheless basically similar to that of the first group.

The Indian fur trade communities illustrate these problems. As soon as the fur enters into the sphere of the fur trade controlled by the trader, it is treated as a market commodity. The fur is marketed, processed and manufactured as a commodity, by merchants who buy and resell at a profit, and who employ wage labour. But to get the fur as far as the trader's door involves a technical and social process of an entirely different nature. The complex labour operation which this production of wild furs involves is not performed by wage labourers employed by the merchant. The Indian producers, moreover, control the means of production and, the most important of these, the land. This might suggest that we need a model which recognizes two systems of economic production, with material inputs and outputs arriving and leaving where the two modes articulate. However, the process of interaction itself is not without social and ideological consequences, and moreover there appears, on the surface at least, to be an imbalance of power between the partners of the exchange. For example, once the Indians are dependent on this exchange they cannot withdraw from the transaction, while the Hudson's Bay Company, and the fur market in general, have several competing sources of fur, and an unstable demand for the commodity. The Indians usually have only one source for their imported supplies and a relatively inflexible demand for them.

In an earlier study of the history of the fur trade in one part of the Canadian subarctic, the Yukon Territory, I suggested that this problem might be solved by introducing a third model, one which involved a set of institutions which were marginal to both the trader's and the Indian's society, but which, in the context of trade, served to enable transactions to take place between the two social groups (Tanner 1966). However, such a solution underplays the influence of the inequality of the two participants in the transactions. A more common approach is through the use of the concept of domination, with the assumption that where there is an articulation between two social systems the relationship of domination enables one of them to impose its conditions of existence on the other. To what extent, however, must the subordinate system alter its character? Is it sufficient that it merely removes the most obvious contradictions between the two social systems, but is able to retain its autonomy in areas irrelevant to the operation of the dominant system? The more thoroughgoing implications of a dominance model of the articulation between two systems of production is that in all spheres the dominant society tends to impose its own conditions on the subordinate one, whether or not this is necessary to the continued functioning of the dominant one.

Another approach to this question is to recognize the existence of more than one system of economic production in use within those native communities which are involved in the fur trade, by stressing the distinction between one system which applies to the subsistence production and another to the production of furs for the market. Since market production in this model is seen as entirely within the Indian society, it is not necessary to assume that it must have a dominant position over the subsistence activities. In other words, in external exchange relations using the open market the Indian has an overall subordinate position *vis à vis* the merchant, but within his own society production which is directed towards the market itself is kept subordinate to the demands of subsistence production. This kind of model of the articulation between the European merchant and industrial economic system and the Amerindian subsistence-based economy points towards a necessary contradiction between the two, particularly in regard to the production of fur. The European system has a dominant power position with respect to market trade, but at the same time market trade is also subordinate to the demands of subsistence production. Moreover, the European economy cannot entirely dominate subsistence production. The production of furs, however, continues despite the contradictory pressures upon it. Such an explanatory outline requires a careful examination of the actual internal relationships between subsistence production and market production. The following study, with data limited to a few years and to a small sample, cannot settle this question for the fur trade as a whole, but at this late date a start must be made on the empirical level.

A second issue, this time outside the sphere of economics, arises in the context of the study of fur trade colonialism. This concerns the ideology of the colonized group. Here we are faced with two theoretical directions, again based on which social unit is chosen as the significant unit of study. The reality within the shifting walls of which men live is a production of their own thought processes. In the colonial situation, while many of the elements of thought by which that reality is constructed are passed down from an historical tradition and exemplified in language, new external elements are now more freely available. Moreover, economic and political subordination create problems of understanding, in addition to material contradictions, and these problems demand changes in the traditional understandings. Colonialism can lead to ideologies which proclaim the colonized person's inferior status and past, and lead to attempts to emulate the perceived model of the colonizer's society; on the other hand it may lead to various kinds of ideologies of rejection and opposition to the colonist, stressing the incompatibility of the situation, and the solution through the eventual elimination of the colonizer, either by force or by supernatural means. It may also lead to the holding of mutually contradictory ideologies, which in some situations stress the underlying equality of the colonized to the colonizer, and therefore the injustice of their material differences, while at other times stress the moral or spiritual superiority of the colonized, in which case his lack of relative material prosperity is explained as a matter of choice.

The Mistassini appears to be a case that does not fit neatly in to any of these types. Instead there has emerged a clear separation between two kinds of social situation, one appropriate for those living in the settlement of Mistassini, or within the European sphere of influence, and another quite different one which is used by hunters who spend much of their time in the bush. In the former context there are many of the symptoms of culture loss and feelings of inferiority associated with the first type of ideology mentioned above, which has been adopted by some colonized peoples. However, the second context, that of the bush camps, can be seen as a confrontation only with the forces of nature, and hunters, in this context, turn their backs on the dominant European group and the contradictions entailed in colonial subordination. Moreover, many adults regularly alternate between the two contexts on a seasonal basis. If my treatment of the ideology of hunting sounds close to the romantic idealization of the bush by a White man, it should be added that the Mistassini themselves consistently hold up this bush way of life as ideal, even those individuals who have faced starvation in the past when hunting has failed. In this study I have tried to curb my own romantic feelings about my experience in the bush, since I am writing about the Mistassini Indians and not myself.

If the ideology of Mistassini hunters overlooks their situation of political subordination, it may well be a reflection of relationships established within that situation, of which we have noted one aspect, in the economic sphere, where, within the system of production used by hunters, it is the organization of subsistence production which establishes the framework within which furs must be produced, and not the other way around. Since the economic spheres of market exchange and subsistence production and sharing are kept within quite separate social contexts, the latter can operate as if the conditions of existence were religious and outside in the natural world among the animals. If this means that this ideology is only part of a larger framework of thought — one which contains internal divisions and contradictions — we ought not to be too surprised, since the colonial situation itself can hardly avoid contradiction in one guise or another.

2. *The problem*

Mistassini is both the name of a village and the name of a band of Cree Indians for whom the village is either a permanent home or a seasonal gathering, trade and administrative centre. The village is located on a large lake, called Lake Mistassini. The name, meaning 'big rock', and originally referring to a large rock part way along the western shore of the lake, was used since early times to refer to the Indians who inhabited the whole region. As the fur trade developed and a permanent trade post was opened on the lake a more defined group of Mistassini Indians emerged, at least as far as the traders were concerned. These were the regular customers who returned each year to the post. It may have been that such a group was descended from a precontact group which used to assemble seasonally, but we have little prehistoric information on this point. As the system of debt trade became institutionalized the Mistassini group, or 'band', became well defined, although movement between bands was common. Today the term 'band' also refers to an administrative unit of the Department of Indian Affairs.

My own work in the area began in 1967 (Tanner 1968) and most of the observations for the present study were made between 1969 and 1971. The use of the present tense in this book refers to that time period.

Despite the interest that several observers have paid to the Mistassini Cree, their isolation during winter while hunting and trapping was such that for a long time anthropologists relied on summer interviews for information on the way of life during the winter.[1] In 1953/4 E.S. Rogers conducted the first ethnographic field work with a Mistassini hunting group, and before my own research began in 1969, he published a monograph on hunting territories and hunting groups (1963) and another on the material culture (1967), as well as a number of articles (e.g. Rogers and Rogers 1959, 1963). Since then he has continued to publish other findings based on the data he collected in 1954 (1972, 1973). Field work with subarctic hunters who live scattered in small groups presents special methodological problems, however. Since it is impractical to spend the winter moving from group to group, the ethnographer is restricted to observing in detail only one or two groups. The present study, then, places our general first-hand knowledge of the Mistassini hunters on a somewhat broader basis than previously, at the same time as looking at the more specific problem of religious ideology.

One of the areas of the culture of Mistassini hunters which, from early ethnographic accounts, appears to have had a particularly close relationship to hunting activities is religion (Speck 1935). In his descriptions, Rogers refers several times to religious activities (1963:64-7, 1967:5, 1972:128-32, 1973:10-15). He stresses the relationship between these religious activities and economic production, but relies on Speck's monograph (1935) for an analysis of the religion (Rogers 1967:4-5).

It is open to question, however, if the relation between the religious practices of the Mistassini and their productive activities have yet been satisfactorily established, either by Speck or by the other anthropologists who have written on the religion of Northern Algonkian hunters. A review of this literature suggests two somewhat opposed kinds of explanation. Speck and Hallowell point to cognitive factors as the link between religion and productivity. Religious practices depend on religious beliefs, which conform to a unique view of reality. This same world view also informs and influences hunting activities. Thus both productive activities and religious activities spring from the same source, which is cognitive. Speck, who was less of a theoretician than Hallowell, never expounded on the principles of this view, as the latter did (e.g. 1955), but his treatment of Montagnais-Naskapi religion can be shown to be based on assumptions such as these. On the other hand, more recent theorists, dealing with Algonkian religion in a more piecemeal fashion, have explained particular religious practices

as filling particular ecological or socio-economic functions (e.g.
Dunning 1959; Henriksen 1973; Moore 1957; Park 1963). According
to this approach, hunting and trapping, as practised by the Northern
Algonkians, imposes certain restraints on the activities of individuals
or of groups. Particular religious activities have the effect either of
influencing hunting behaviour in a manner which results in greater
productive efficiency (e.g. Moore 1957), or legitimizes, and thus helps
to maintain, the system of social relations on which efficient hunting
depends.

Speck's treatment of the social institutions of Northern Algonkian
hunting and trapping groups have come under attack from several
quarters, on the general grounds that he failed to take into account the
fact that these groups were no longer in their pre-European contact
situations, but were by then under the dominant influence of Euro-
Canadian contact agents. These agents consisted of the fur trade, the
missionaries and the government. While much of this debate ostensibly referred to Speck's claimed discovery that hunting territories
existed in pre-contact times, the result of the critique of Speck's work
was that a new picture of boreal forest Indian society began to emerge.
Northern Algonkian hunters were now seen as a subordinate, dependent group whose social institutions, environment and ecological
adaptation had been altered or destroyed, and who were undergoing a
process of acculturation under the influence of external White sources.

Although no re-examination of the religious material of the northeastern Algonkians in the light of this new approach has been undertaken, the postulated change of Algonkian society from one based on
subsistence hunting by multi-family groups to one based on production, by individuals, of fur for the market, on some wages and on
government transfer payments, might lead us to the expectation that
the place of ideology, and religion in particular — especially the rites
and beliefs surrounding hunting and trapping — would have undergone a concomitant change.[2] The model of Canadian Indian
communities under fur trade conditions which has increasingly gained
acceptance — as, for example, has been provided by Leacock (1954)
(based on a study of the Montagnais) — does not deal with ideological
change. This approach was stated as a general theory by Murphy and
Steward (1956), and it provides us with a useful starting point in our
re-examination of Algonkian religion.

The central influence of the introduction of fur trapping to the
Montagnais, according to Leacock, was a shift from 'production for
use' to 'production for exchange' (1954:7). She argues that the availability of imported foods, particularly flour and lard, broke down the
dependence upon the sharing of game between families, so that 'the
individual family becomes self-sufficient' (ibid.). Economic ties
between families were replaced with ties to an external agent, the
trader, with the result that the individual's 'objective relation to other

band members changed from the cooperative to the competitive.' Finally, the shift from 'production for use' to 'production for exchange' involved a change from an economy geared to supply explicit and limited subsistence needs which were known in advance, to one in which individuals produced fur as exchange value, to satisfy material needs which become, in theory, limitless (ibid.).

Leacock's analysis proceeds by identifying two contradictory socio-economic patterns within the fur trade communities of eastern Quebec and southern Labrador, one based on hunting for game, which is a continuation of past patterns, and one based on trapping of fur for trade, introduced from the dominant society. Historical changes in the region are seen as evidence of the gradual replacement of the first pattern by the second. Although different communities are said to be at different stages in this historical process, as Murphy and Steward note, 'the stages ... are not presented by ... [Leacock] as clearly distinguishable periods during which cultural stability was achieved' (1956:338). Within any one community a clear distinction is made, according to Leacock, between hunting and trapping, and, in the historical process, trapping inevitably becomes more important than hunting. The culmination of this process, towards which some Indians are being forced reluctantly, is for them to emulate the White trapper who has his own trapline which he exploits by himself year after year, using a network of permanent overnight cabins. In the interests of efficiency the White trapper leaves his family behind, and uses mainly store food, rather than relying on subsistence hunting. The adoption of trapping thus, according to Leacock's analysis, leads to an individualization of both the production groups and the pattern of holding rights to resources. Murphy and Steward believe that the historical process described by Leacock is of general significance in similar contact situations, and leads to 'the structure of native culture being destroyed' (1956:353), and to a culmination stage when the Indians 'learn the national language, intermarry extensively with non-Indians, and acquire many of the non-Indian values and behavioural patterns' (ibid.:350).

In examining Leacock's and Murphy and Steward's theories our purpose is not merely to question Leacock's conclusion that the Mistassini, along with other groups in the western part of the peninsula, have completed a process of adjustment to trade so that trapping has become 'economically prior to hunting' (1954:36). For if it can be shown that this is not so it might be possible to explain any individual exceptions to the proposed effects of the fur trade acculturation process by reference to special local environmental and historical circumstances. Instead, by starting with the observation that the Mistassini have reached some degree of accommodation to the fur trade, we ask in what way this 'culmination' is different from that predicted by the above theories? More important, in this respect, than whether or not this culmination involves land or wild animal resources being considered 'private property' (but see Chapter 9), is the assumption by Leacock of a conflict between *subsistence hunting*, requiring multi-family production groups and communal rights to resources and production, and *trapping for trade*, which requires individual (family or solitary trapper) production, and individual rights to resources and production. Is such a conflict in evidence at Mistassini, or has it been resolved?

On the more general question of the breakdown of Indian culture, it is always difficult to find objective criteria for such an assessment. However, I do not believe this to be the case for the Mistassini who have managed to retain control of their major economic base, the land. In this study I will show that there has also continued to exist a religious system of some complexity, with a systematic ideology. Since this system is not part of the non-Indian pattern, this suggests a considerable degree of cultural autonomy and cultural continuity. In the present study I feel that a convincing case can be made both that the economy does not exhibit the hypothesized tendency to individualization, and that the religion does not exhibit the acceptance of the non-Indian world view. These two demonstrations alone suggest that we stop looking at the Mistassini as a group in conflict between traditional and modern elements, or between the contrary demands of hunting and trapping, and try to understand it as a social form in its own right.

As we have seen, Leacock's analysis begins with the most useful insight that a distinction exists between those groups which have a system of 'production for use', and those with a system of 'production for exchange'. This distinction originates with Marx, who, as Sahlins has recently pointed out (1971:30-1, 1972:82-6), did not make the assumption, implicit in Leacock's model, that a system of production in which some of the items produced are subsequently exchanged must thereby be classified as engaged in 'production for exchange'. The important distinction here is between a system in which production is undertaken for the purpose of acquiring 'use value' for the group that does the producing (whether or not this includes acts of exchange) and a second system in which a person or a corporation, by using capital, brings together the forces and the means of production of a commodity, which can then be sold at a profit, thereby acquiring 'exchange value'. Such systems constitute different modes of production. The concept of a mode of production, as developed in an anthropological context by Friedman (1975), Godelier (1973, 1975), Sahlins (1972) and Terray (1972), derives also from Marx, and refers to the particular combination of the technical conditions and the social relations of production, where it is recognized that the concept of production includes an economic, a juridico-political and an ideological level.

While it is clear that the fur trade enterprise, as represented, for example, by the Hudson's Bay Company (H.B.C.), operates on the basis of the second, or capitalist, mode of production, it is also clear that in organizing the trapping of raw fur by Indians, the H.B.C. adapted its capitalist methods so as to be able to interact with the Indian system of hunting production which was (and, I will argue, still is) based on entirely different principles. Leacock's analysis suggests that a conflict between these two systems was introduced into Indian life. In other words, when an Indian was hunting, he was involved in the first mode of production, while as a trapper he was subject to the entirely contrary presumptions concomitant with his participation in the capitalist mode of production. The conflict between the two, and the ultimate dominance of the fur trapping (capitalist) mode both explain for Leacock the dilemma in which Indian communities are involved, and indicate to her the direction in which change must take place. However, Leacock's contention that production for trade broke down the links of sharing and dependency between hunters and led to private acquisition and accumulation of wealth (or, in other words, that the Indians adopted the essentials of bourgeois economic motivations) (1954:7; cf. Murphy and Steward 1956; Hickerson 1967) is questionable on both empirical and theoretical grounds. The reluctance which is sometimes demonstrated by the native people to give their assent to this process lies outside the theory, and must be put down to a vague residual factor, like Leacock's reference to 'resistance to changing basic patterns of everyday existence' (1954:9).

Terray has also made use of the idea that in the colonial situation (which the H.B.C. situation resembles in most respects) the colonist's sector of the economy dominates over that of the colonized. The term 'dominates' is defined by Terray as the condition where the mode of production in question subjects the other modes of production to the requirements of its own reproduction (1975:91). But, as Terray also points out, each mode of production transforms and shapes the other, so that the dominant mode itself is altered and comes to depend upon the subordinate mode, just as the other way around.

At Mistassini, then, we find two modes of production: a capitalist one found mainly in the settlement, which includes industrial wage work, the local H.B.C. operation, and the activities of the local government agencies; and a second mode, that of the hunting group, a 'domestic' mode of production (Sahlins 1972), based on subsistence hunting and fur trapping. The settlement economy dominates over that of the hunting group, primarily because of the dependence on the H.B.C., but aided recently by the presence of government agencies. The capitalist fur trade, on the other hand, in adapting itself to the local situation and to assure its own reproduction as a major organizer of the hunting group's activities, has been forced to adopt 'non-capitalist' methods. This system will be described in more detail in Chapter 3.

In addition to the foregoing opposition between the modes of production of the settlement and of the hunting group, a second distinction can also be drawn within the hunting group itself between subsistence production and production for the market. But in this case neither the concept of mode of production nor the concept of domination is helpful in clarifying the distinction. If we take the three logical possibilities for the relationship between hunting and trapping — hunting but no trapping, mixed hunting and trapping, trapping but no hunting — we find historical instances of all three arrangements. Aboriginal Cree Indians did not trap for the market, and little trapping was done in some historical periods, when fur-bearers were scarce. The present day Mistassini Cree both hunt and trap. Most White trappers do little or no hunting while they are trapping. These cases have taken place under similar, or identical, environmental and technical conditions. Material conditions of living in the bush do not by themselves determine the relationship between subsistence and market production. In order for the hunting group mode of production to continue a basic minimum of both subsistence and market production is required, and production in either sphere and beyond this minimum depends partly on local ecological opportunities. However, the particular emphasis of production depends also on the set of established social relations, the values which circulate within the social system, and the content of the ideological system. At the ideological level the Cree hunting group is oriented towards subsistence hunting and fishing. Rituals and myths are based on an assumption of the primacy of hunting, and within the hunting group religious ideology acts to a large degree to determine the social relations of production within the group.

Thus, even though the hunting group is subordinate to the capitalist mode of production and to the Hudson's Bay Company, it is still in a position of relative autonomy. This autonomy is, in part, the result of material conditions — the need to hunt for subsistence as well as to trap for purchased goods, and the necessity for groups to be scattered and thus isolated from the settlement and direct means of control — but it also derives from the requirements for the maintenance of hunting group social relations, as well as the operation of systems of land tenure and religious ideology, both of which are closely related to the process of production in the hunting group. Despite this relative autonomy, however, it is essential, in attempting to understand the hunting group mode of production, to take into account the fact that this process of subordination by external capitalist influence has its own history. The autonomy of the hunting groups results not from the ability of the hunting sector of the economy to *resist* this historical process of externally-caused change, but to *modify* its mode of production in a way that enables the hunting group to retain control of the means of production, and ensure the conditions for its own reproduction despite the existence of these powerful external influences.

In this study I will concentrate on establishing the technical and economic aspects of the hunting and trapping mode of production at Mistassini (Chapters 2 and 3), and on outlining details of the ideological level (Chapter 4 to 8), in order to demonstrate the interrelation of the two. By limiting my focus to the relationship between ideology and economy, I do not attempt to give a fully balanced view of the social and juridico-political level of this mode of production, although towards the end I will turn to the specific question of hunting territory ownership and hunting group leadership, in the manner of a test case, showing the relationship of these levels to the economy and to the ideology (Chapter 9). The study deals with social relations of production only as part of the above focus, and thus neglects two important topics which would be included in any overall description of the hunting group mode of production. These are (1) the structure of social relations beyond the short-term formation and operation of the hunting group, and (2) the way that the social relations of production are reproduced through time. Both of these issues are relevant in particular to the 'test case' in Chapter 9, where we examine the land tenure system. For the most part, however, the analysis of the operation of the hunting mode of production during the summer season, when it is in closest touch with the capitalist mode, and when the wider social relations are reactivated, is neglected in favour of a deeper analysis of the situation during the winter.

3. *Mistassini: the historical background*[3]

The history of the Mistassini band, as found in the documentary sources, is almost entirely the story of the fur trade. Besides the traders, White contact agents and agencies have been few, and have only begun to have any influence quite recently, with the arrival of missionaries and government representatives at the time of the Second World War. Moreover, the story of the fur trade is remarkably stable in form; that is, the major changes introduced by the fur trade took place relatively quickly and without apparent opposition, and from then on the year by year pattern appears to have been remarkably similar and relatively free from sudden breakdowns in what became the standard pattern of doing things. At the heart of this stability lies two factors, both of which are functions of the geographic location of the Mistassini territory. First, the Mistassini land is located in a marginal, or hinterland, area with respect to the nearest fur trade centres, and second, the territory is located in an area of the overlapping interest of two competing trading systems, that of the east coast of James Bay and that of the Saguenay River.

That either of these factors should be the cause of relative stability

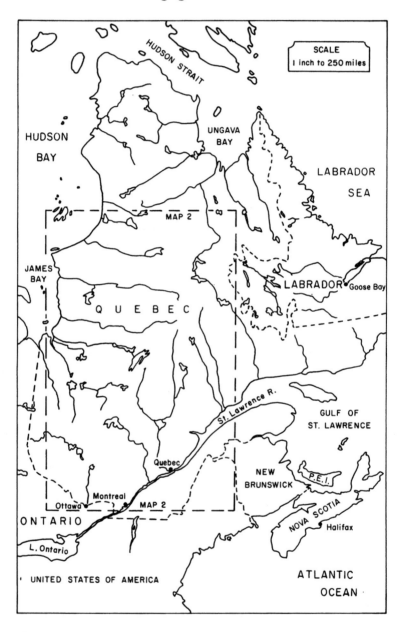

Map 1. Quebec

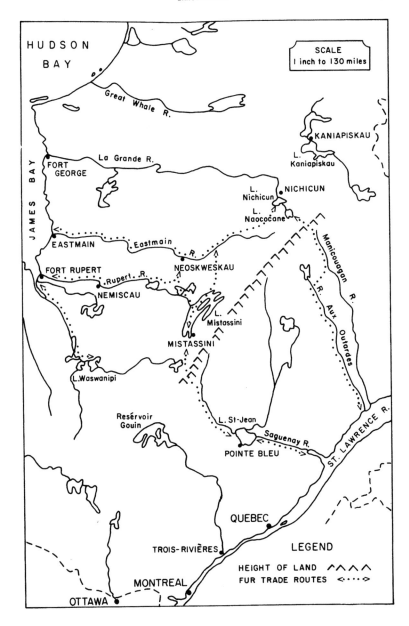

Map 2. Fur trade posts and routes of the Mistassini region

is perhaps ironic. In theory, marginal operations are the least stable, and the spatial factors that make the region marginal (in the case of Mistassini, the distance and the difficulty of the overland route to tidewater) have acted as dampers on the operation of other economic forces. As long as the fur trade was relatively isolated from direct head office control, and relatively isolated from direct market forces, then local and non-economic factors could determine how the trade was conducted. For example, Cooke has shown that in the nineteenth century the 'Ungava Venture' of interior posts in northern Quebec and Labrador was abandoned largely because of the perceived difficulties of the operation, and even though the scheme was — unbeknown to the Company — making money (Cooke 1969). In the Mistassini case the trade was carried on, usually on a small scale due to the limited transport facilities, as part of a continuing rivalry, rather than with any clear knowledge of the relative profitability.

This brings us to the second factor, that of the on-going rivalry between the traders of the Saguenay and those from James Bay. Mistassini and what is now its northern outpost, Nichicun (the specific area of the Mistassini territory where much of my fieldwork with hunting groups was conducted), are two of a number of posts in the area which straddle the height of land between the St. Lawrence and the James Bay drainages. Both posts are actually near the height of land, and are about equally accessible for traders arriving from either of these directions by canoe, using the rivers as supply routes. By the same token, before the posts were established, Indians from these areas could travel down the rivers on either side of the height of land, and just as easily reach the posts on James Bay or the Saguenay River. Although the French entered the area first, after 1668 the English controlled the James Bay side, while the St. Lawrence River side was controlled first by the French, later by the Northwest Company, and, after 1821, by a number of independent traders. The people of Mistassini themselves also look in both of these directions (west or south) for their external ties with other Indian groups; there are few ties to the north or to the east. Intermarriage between bands is largely to the west, with the James Bay communities between Rupert House and Great Whale River, or south to Lac St. Jean and the community of Pointe Bleue. The geographic height of land remains, roughly speaking, the dividing line between the areas of influence of the French and English cultures. The result of this trade rivalry between two regions, which can be seen as lasting for about two hundred and fifty years, resulted not in cut-throat competition, but in the operation of a system of posts that remained open through most of the periods of market fluctuations, and ended only with the replacement of the canoe brigades by modern transportation.

From 1600, with the founding of Tadoussac at the mouth of the Saguenay River, until 1713, with the Treaty of Utrecht, the major influence over the whole region was that of the French, who introduced missionaries and traders licenced by the French Crown. As early as 1603 Champlain was told of the overland route from the St. Lawrence to James Bay, via the Saguenay River and Lake Mistassini. Indians described in mission records as belonging to the Mistassini 'nation' are first mentioned at Tadoussac in 1640, and were first visited by Guillaume Couture in 1663. After the beginning of British influence in James Bay with the founding of Charles Fort (later Fort Rupert or Rupert House) in 1668, visits were made to Mistassini by French missionaries to counter this threat, and by 1676 a trading post was established at Lac St. Jean to the south, closer to Mistassini than James Bay, although in both cases the canoe routes are difficult. The first trader at Mistassini was Louis Jolliet, who established a post in 1679, but only short trading visits were made by the French until the fall of New France in 1760. Instead, in 1682, a more aggressive policy of military and commercial confrontation against the English in James Bay itself was begun, and by 1697 all the English posts in the area except Fort Albany were closed. After these posts were returned to the English by the Treaty of Utrecht, the region of Mistassini was still in a disputed zone, claimed by both sides. An attempt was made to negotiate a boundary between the Hudson Bay Company's territory and the area covered by the French *Domaine du Roi*. The *Domaine* was an area covered by a monopoly of trade licenced by the French Crown. The H.B.C. attempted to have the height of land made the boundary, which would have put Mistassini just inside the H.B.C.'s territory, but the French insisted on a boundary closer to James Bay, and negotiations broke down. The issue was not settled until 1763, when the English took over the operation of the *Domaine*, under the name of 'The King's Posts'. English and Scottish traders began to visit Mistassini regularly each summer, although they did not establish a permanent post or winter there until the nineteenth century.

It is not clear when Indians from Mistassini first visited the English posts on James Bay, but by 1730 some Mistassini were going there while others were travelling to Lac St. Jean. During the 1780s the H.B.C. engaged local Indians from the James Bay coast to travel inland with presents for the so-called French Indians, in order to lure them to the coast to trade. The H.B.C. policy of establishing inland posts was not begun in earnest until 1778, with the first attempt to reach Lake Mistassini, where it was known that rival traders were operating. The lake was finally reached from James Bay after several failures in 1790, at which time there began a period of direct competition between the H.B.C. and the Northwest Company who, in 1788, had purchased the rights to the King's Posts. Neither side appears to have been really certain of where the boundary between the King's Posts and the area granted to the Hudson's Bay Company by its charter lay; in this area the height of land is not a natural barrier, such as a mountain range.

In the main, the competition faced by the H.B.C. at this time in the interior of Quebec-Labrador was with adversaries whose locations were not well known — usually summer trading expeditions which followed different patterns from year to year. This situation of competition continued throughout much of the nineteenth century. Although the H.B.C. absorbed the Northwest Company in 1821, the Company was outbid for the lease to the King's Posts in the following year. By 1831 the H.B.C. was forced to buy out these rights to the King's Post for much more than the original price, but foreign trappers and free traders had already entered the southern part of the region from the southeast, and reached as far as Mistassini. In 1904 a free trader from Lake Ashwamouchoun made a trading trip to Mistassini (Wilson 1952: 88), and sporadic competition in fur buying has continued since, particularly in periods of high fur prices.

This continual threat of competition made it necessary for the H.B.C. to keep open a line of posts on the height of land between James Bay and the St. Lawrence, from Waswanipi through Mistassini to Nichicun, even after it had become uneconomic to keep other interior posts open, in order to protect the valuable trade of this region. Thus it was the insecurity of the H.B.C.'s hold over the area that resulted, ironically, in relatively stable trade conditions, since any tightening of the terms of trade, or closing of a major post, would merely have driven the Mistassini south to trade.

The opening of the post at Lake Nichicun 260 miles northeast of Mistassini by the H.B.C. in 1816 was part of an overall plan to carry the fur trade to the Naskapi Indians of barren lands of northern Quebec and Labrador. This was undertaken, even though the Company had grave doubts about the productive potential of the area, because it was feared that direct or intertribal trade between these groups and rival traders would divert furs from the rich country inland to the immediate south of the Naskapi. This fear was increased when, in 1814, two Moravian missionaries published an account of a journey made from the Atlantic coast of Labrador to Ungrava Bay. At the same time, there were also numerous rumours of rival posts in the interior, many of these to the northeast of James Bay. The factual basis for these stories seems to have been thin. However, in 1814 the Northwest Company did move its post at Mistassini to the vicinity of Lake Albanel, to be closer to the hunting grounds of its customers. Voorhis states that, from 1725 on, there was a French fort at Nichicun (1930:126), but this early date seems very doubtful. Yet an identifiable Nichicun band of Indians probably existed well before the establishment of a post in the area. An adult of the Nichicun 'nation' is mentioned in baptismal records as early as 1684 at Rivière Assumption (Larouche 1972:50). This river is a tributary of the Rivière aux Outardes, itself a tributary of the St. Lawrence. Furthermore, the Nichicun band were shown in approximately their present location on maps starting from 1794 (Speck 1931:567).

At the time when Nichicun first became a Hudson's Bay Company post the area was being trapped by hunting groups trading at James Bay posts such as Eastmain. However, it was also at the edge of the hunting grounds of migratory hunters of the large herds of barren ground caribou. By 1893/4, when Low visited the area, the woodland caribou had been practically exterminated, and the large barren ground herds were much reduced. Starvation resulted, and the post was forced to put aside supplies of salt fish for emergencies (Low 1896: 100-1, 318). At that time there were thirteen families who traded at the post, while others from the area went each summer to Rupert House, on James Bay, and Bersimis and Sept Iles, on the St. Lawrence to trade (ibid.:101). After the post closed in 1919 Speck met some Nichicun who had joined the Sept Iles band (Speck and Eisley 1942), but the present group is descended from others who continued to trade on the James Bay side. The group continued to gather each summer at Lake Nichicun, and some years the women and the old people remained all summer in this locality, while the men visited one of the posts to the southwest, usually Rupert House, by canoe. During the 1920s and 1930s a post was open at Neoskweskau, located inland on the Eastmain river, where the Nichicun would go each summer.

Starting about 1937 competition again forced the H.B.C. to reopen Nichicun Post. A former employee of the then-defunct Revillon Frères Company of Paris, which had competed with the H.B.C. on James Bay and elsewhere from 1901-34, began to use aircraft to fly to Nichicun in the spring to purchase the Indian's winter fur catch. After the Second World War another trader took up this practice, and a free trader operating from Mistassini also made trips overland to the area. Also, in the late 1930s, Indians from Pointe Bleue, on Lac St. Jean, began to trap in the area of Nichicun and further north. They arrived from Lac St. Jean by canoe, and trapped very much in the style of White trappers. They were not accompanied by their wives or families, they brought large amounts of store food with them, and compared to the Nichicun Indians they were very industrious trappers who concentrated only on the species that gave the greatest cash return, such as marten and mink. They were suspected by the H.B.C. of trading with the Nichicun Indians, but my own informants such as Williams Rabbitskin deny this, and say that the strangers were generous with gifts of game meat. To meet the threat of competition the H.B.C. reopened Nichicun as an outpost of Neoskweskau. A local Indian, William Edward, looked after the store at first, followed by a succession of White managers. After the Second World War the supply of Nichicun shifted to Mistassini from Neoskweskau, and the management of the post was put in the hands of Indian employees of the H.B.C. from Mistassini. At the same time the Nichicun Indians went for the first time to Mistassini during the summer, to carry their own furs, and to transport supplies back to the post by canoe. In the

mid-1940s a weather station was opened at Lake Nichicun. Starting in
the late 1950s the H.B.C. outpost was operated as an unmanned store,
and was stocked with basic supplies. Nichicun Indians would visit this
store and take what goods they needed, leaving behind a list of things
taken, the cost of which was later added to their accounts at Mistassini.
This honour system of trade remained in effect during my visit in
1969-70.

4. *Mistassini: the ethnographic setting*

The Mistassini band is a community composed of a majority of hunters
and trappers who are scattered in small hunting groups for most of the
year, and who gather for a few summer months at the village at the
southeast end of Mistassini Lake. As is shown in Table 1, since 1940
the population has grown enormously, due to (*a*) a process of band
consolidation, as neighboring bands were added on when their trading
posts closed, and (*b*) factors causing the general demographic growth
of the Indian population (Romaniuk and Piche 1972).

Table 1.   POPULATION GROWTH

	Mistassini	*Nichicun (& Kaniapiskau)*	*Total East Cree*[7]
1857[1]	200	155	1,610
1881[2]	150	180	1,430
1894[3]	25 families	more than 13 families	
1911[2]	170	70	1,474
1915[2]	169	65	1,792
1919[4]		15 families	
1924[4]	159	(Neoskweskau 140)	1,720
1952[5]	450	(included with Mistassini)	2,544[8]
1970[6]	1,401	"	5,451

Notes:
[1] Canadian Government Blue Book, quoted in Hind 1863
[2] Department of Indian Affairs, Annual Reports
[3] Low 1896
[4] Speck 1931:598
[5] Rogers 1962:23
[6] Salisbury 1972a
[7] Includes the East coast of James Bay, plus Great Whale River, Nichicun,
Neoskweskau, Nemescau, Mistassini and Waswanipi
[8] Estimate, based on 1951 census

Some idea of the relative operation of these two factors can also be
obtained from Table 1. The column on the right, showing the total
East Cree population, can be taken as representative of the overall
demographic growth of the region. Comparatively little immigration
or emigration has taken place for the region as a whole. The combined

totals of the other two columns give some indication of the growth in the total population in the region which has now become consolidated into the single settlement of Mistassini (i.e. Mistassini, Nichicun and Neoskweskau). Thus the change in the population of Mistassini from 1924-52 (159 to 450) reflects this process of consolidation. The most recent rise in the Mistassini population to 1,401 in 1970 is faster than the already speedy rise of the rate of population increase for the whole of the East Cree, and may reflect in part the further consolidation by individuals from the Waswanipi and Chibougamau bands to the south. Since 1970 an even further population jump has been caused, if temporarily, by the closing of the H.B.C. post at Nemescau.

Hunting and trapping has remained a major form of economic production for the community. Some Mistassini were drawn into wage labour, starting in the 1940s primarily in pulp cutting, mineral exploration and mining. In the 1950s several mines were opened in an area 50 miles south of Mistassini Post, and the town of Chibougamau was founded there. Some men obtained work in the mines. For most, however, work was only short term and part of a cycle that included brief hunting and trapping trips (La Rusic 1968, Tanner 1968). Since 1970 many of the Indians who inhabited the Chibougamau area, whose hunting territories were spoiled for hunting and trapping purposes by the mines, found themselves being harassed on their grounds by the game wardens, and have left Chibougamau for Mistassini. The town remains a centre for casual employment of Indians, but the Indian community in Chibougamau, in contrast to that of Mistassini, remains unstable and without a steady population increase.

Those people who are full-time residents of Mistassini Post, as well as the hunters who reside there during the summer, depend for their livelihood for the most part either on employment with one of the community services (house construction, band administration, school, church, store or guiding) or on transfer payments of various kinds. During the summer, and occasionally in winter, some younger men leave the village for employment, for example to Montreal, northern Ontario, or Vermont, mostly of a casual and often short-term variety.

Production within the winter hunting group varies slightly according to the time of year. In the fall, and again in late winter, large game, either moose or caribou, are hunted, and in the late spring there is considerable reliance on geese and ducks. At other times during the period from November to May, when the lakes and rivers are frozen and snow is permanently on the ground, the central activity is trapping. Beaver is the most important animal trapped; it brings in most of the income which comes from fur, and a large percentage of the subsistence food. Unlike the larger game, beavers are usually caught at least every few days, and thus are a staple food all winter long. Fish also play an important role in the winter diet of some

Plate 1. Mistassini Post: Government-built houses, and tents. Note the
uniform orientation of the doors.

hunting groups. Purchased food, particularly flour and lard, makes up
a small portion of the diet, but is eaten with almost every meal, and
also serves as a reserve food supply in case of failures in hunting or
trapping. The economy of the entire group of hunters is coordinated
by the manager of the Hudson's Bay Company, and controlled by
means of a credit account with each individual.

The hunting groups are composed of from two to five commensal
units, which are generally nuclear families. The sequence and location
of winter activities are usually well planned, and based on knowledge
of the areas suitable for particular kinds of hunting and trapping at a
particular time of the year. It is necessary for the whole group to move
camp several times each winter, and this limits any heavy material
items that the group may want to carry. In trapping, men, individually or in pairs, cover sectors around the main camp, and may spend
nights away from the main camp as they move further afield. Hunting
for food is conducted in one of two ways; either it is ancillary to these
trapping journeys, or it is organized into communal hunting expeditions which are highly planned and timed, with special regard for the
place and the time where large amounts of game can be most easily
killed and transported. When a major move is undertaken, both as a
result of a change of campsite, and when meat of big game is moved to
camp, the whole group works together. In spring, some trapping,
such as for otter and muskrat, and some hunting for waterfowl, are
undertaken communally by the men, if these animals are found in
sufficient concentrations.

The whole of the Mistassini land is divided into hunting territories,
each of which is associated with an individual who has usufructuary
rights by inheritance, by gift, or by establishing long-term occupancy.

Cases of all of these ways of establishing rights are given in Chapter 9. This system has been used by the provincial government as the basis for a system of quotas limiting the number of beaver which are allowed to be caught in each territory, with the size of the quota depending on the number of beaver lodges reported by the title holder the previous year. The quota is shared by the members of the hunting group, which varies considerably in its membership from year to year.

Ideally, the hunting group has a core of closely related families. In fact, in its composition there is a normative and a statistical preference for kin — both primary and more distant kin, particularly affines. Great care is taken to avoid overt interpersonal hostility within the group during the winter. Leadership resides formally with the hunting territory owner, but strong deference is also generally paid to age and to reputation for religious power. During the mid-winter period when the group often lives together in one dwelling, and when considerable time is spent there, because of the short daylight period, the hunting group takes on the character of a household unit focused around the women and children. At the beginning and end of the hunting season the unity of the hunting group is based more on male communal labour and on frequent exchanges of food gifts.

In a number of important ways the summer period at the village contrasts with the winter period in the bush. Summer is both the time of leisure and of lean supplies of bush food. Some subsistence production of fish and berries takes place in camps away from the summer settlement, but the economy is mainly based on cash, while food consists mainly of starchy imported products, which are disliked as a steady diet. Summer is also the period of intense sociability, of courting, of adultery, of community feasts, of dances and of weddings. It is also the period of interaction with White culture, with regular church attendance, and equally common beer parties. Unlike the winter, during this period there are occasional open expressions of interpersonal hostility. The very intensity of summer social life makes the stability of winter bush life which follows attractive (cf. Mauss 1966: 473-4).

During this summer period there are relatively few productive activities. Apart from subsistence production, food and supplies are purchased with money from a number of sources, including fur from the previous winter, wages, and transfer payments. In addition to the payments received by everyone (family allowance, pensions) welfare is given to two categories of people: those requiring only temporary assistance, and those defined as permanently indigent. In Mistassini this follows the distinction between families who are thought to be able to support themselves by wage work, if any is available, and those who are not. Men over the age of about forty, whose only employment experience has been in the canoe brigades, tend to be defined as unemployable, although in fact among this group there is a wide variety of attitudes towards wage work. Some younger men get employment as fishing guides, in mineral exploration, wood cutting and construction, but generally spend at least part of the summer on temporary relief. During the summer hunters and trappers manufacture craft items for sale, and spend some time repairing trapping equipment and assembling their supplies for the coming winter.

Because of the relative lack of productive activities, social life during this period revolves around visiting and gossiping in public places like the store and outside the church. In summer the realignment of families between hunting groups takes place, in preparation for the following winter. This occurs towards the end of the summer, as leaders discuss with owners of adjacent territories where they intend to go. In the past, when most people stayed in tents while at the village, it was possible to observe some continuity between the region of winter residence and the relative positions of summer residential tent clusters. At present, as most people are to some extent randomly scattered in houses which are spread out, the summer social groupings are more noticeable in fish camp and berry camp formations, in visiting patterns, and in meeting arrangements at feasts, dances, church and band meetings. The most common summer social group is composed of same-sex age mates. Such groups form at almost any age level above eight or ten years, and adolescents spend much of the summer daytime in these groups. Thus in the summer the nuclear family loses some of its function as a commensal unit and as a strong focus of orientation.

Summer leadership similarly presents a contrast to that of the winter. In winter there is a single nominal leader in each hunting group, while political power is diffuse and consensual. In summer there are several powerful individuals in the settlement, both nominally and in fact, but each has charge of a special sphere of interest. Most of these individuals are either members of the small dominant group of Eurocanadians, such as the Hudson's Bay Company manager, the ministers of the Christian churches, the school principal, the administrator of beaver conservation, and the nurse, or are Indians who, like the above, are dependent on outside institutions for their power. These native leaders include the elected band chief and the Anglican catechists, as well as those with permanent jobs who have the power to hire others. There are also a number of small entrepreneurs, who run taxis, a restaurant, and, most recently, a fishing camp. As has been reported by Pothier (1967) and has been noted in many other places, the band chief has, since the 1940s, acted principally as an agent in a system of indirect rule by the Department of Indian Affairs; however, in the past few years, the present chief and the group of full-time band employees have gradually also gained some real power, through control of housing, jobs in house construction, the issuance of

Plate 2. Summer wedding at Mistassini Post: after a group ceremony, five couples shake hands with the whole community outside the church.

welfare, and by means of the passing of band council resolutions, which under some conditions are politically effective. One of the formerly separate bands, Chibougamau, has a leader who has managed to maintain his position as spokesman for that group, and, during the fieldwork period, part of the Nemescau band joined Mistassini after the H.B.C. store in that settlement was closed, and their chief similarly continued to function as the spokesman of the Nemescau subgroup. The other clearly recognizable subgroup, the Nichicun, say they have had no chief since their last powerful shaman died. There is in fact a subtle competition for power among several of the elders.[4]

Religious practice changes from winter to summer, also, and to some extent follows the pattern of political leadership. In the settlement a minister and a few lay catechists officiate at most rites. All persons are members of the Anglican church, although two rival Protestant sects are now beginning to proselytize in the area. The majority attend Sunday services, baptisms and weddings at which the minister and one or more Indian catechists officiate. Religious activity based on non-European beliefs is limited in summer principally to two or three major feasts, gossip about suspected sorcery, and a rare 'shaking tent' performance. These 'traditional' practices are usually accompanied by declarations either that the true practice has actually died out, or that they ought really to be conducted in the bush and in winter. In summer, religious activities, both of European and of

Indian origin, take the form of special events strongly differentiated from everyday activities. In winter the balance between European-based and Indian-based religious sources is reversed with the latter becoming most common, while religious activity generally becomes a normal part of everyday life. Specific details of the religious practice of a few hunting groups, which were not selected on the basis of any special reputation for their religious activity, follow in later chapters. Christian-based religious practice is not only limited in winter; it is altered in character, and consists mainly in the conduct of rites, principally involving the carrying, display or reading of religious books stored in a decorated bag, and the observance of taboos on Sundays and at the Easter period, failure in which is believed to effect individual hunting success.

During the winter period, day to day activities include a number of rites, references to knowledge derived from legends and other symbolic activities. Many of these rites are barely noticeable, and by themselves seem trivial superstitions. However, they can be shown to be parts of a system that has the organized purpose of controlling, predicting and explaining the behaviour of game animals, and the behaviour of imaginary beings which are believed to influence the animals, or are identified with particular natural phenomena. These rites are part of a single system in the additional sense that the effectiveness of all of them is subject to a linked set of native explanatory principles, although these may not be fully known to all Cree participants. I also believe it can be shown that these rites are part of a single ideology. For these reasons the hunting rites, together with the symbolic knowledge on which they are based, constitute an institution which falls within most anthropological definitions of a religious phenomenon.

2
The Ecology of Hunting

1. *Climate*

The kind of ecological conditions in which subarctic hunters work have been described in considerable detail in several studies, and in particular for the Mistassini Cree (Rogers 1963, 1969, 1973; cf. Knight 1968), material which has recently been reanalysed by Feit (1969). Martijn and Rogers (1969) have also presented prehistoric material on the region. I will not repeat the total breadth of the earlier findings. In this chapter I wish to show that the hunting economy is not dominated by chance, and that productivity is not determined entirely by uncontrollable forces of nature, but also involves a good deal of calculation. In this environment there are, however, strict limits on the range of possible adaptive procedures open to any human group. There are indications of a considerable degree of economic planning. Day-to-day magic continues along with a day-to-day use of empirically-based calculation, even in the absence of major day-to-day risks. Finally, in this chapter, I wish to draw attention to the special ecological and economic conditions of the Nichicun local band, a northern subdivision of the Mistassini, as they differ from the region as a whole.

Objectively, and for the Cree themselves, the Mistassini climate is neither harsh nor mild, except in the sense that it causes the total biomass to be comparatively low. There are relatively few species compared with places with milder winters, the 'ecological balance' is relatively unstable, and these features are determined to a large extent by the climate. In this section we cannot deal with the degree to which the climate sets limits on the Cree, but merely with how those limits operate as they impose themselves on Mistassini hunters.

(*a*) *Seasons*. The freezing point of water can be said to be a critical temperature in the annual climatic regime. At Mistassini Post, as shown on Fig. 1a, the average temperature rises above freezing in April, and falls below again around the end of October. At Nichicun Lake[1] the dates are on the average about two weeks later and two weeks earlier, respectively. However, the significant changes resulting from these temperature shifts take place some time afterwards, with freeze-up and break-up. At Nichicun, the earliest freeze-up in the past thirty years was October 25, and latest was November 19. The earliest break-up was June 2, while the latest was June 25. Freeze-up at Mistassini Post is only slightly later than at Nichicun, but break-up is considerably earlier, between mid-May and June (Feit 1969:37). The

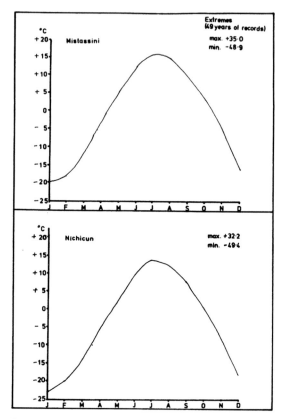

Source: Wernstadt 1972

Fig. 1a. Mistassini and Nichicun mean monthly
temperatures

significant event associated with freeze-up is the day that the large
lakes freeze over. This usually takes place after several days of cold
weather, when the smaller lakes have already become frozen and
suitable for travel. By this time snow usually covers the ground, and
toboggans are in use. However, there are some years when freeze-up
occurs before the arrival of permanent snow. In the case of break-up,
the significant event is the final clearing of ice from water routes. This
takes place earlier along rivers than on large lakes, but since large lakes
make up significant portions of travel routes, as well as being a
common place for spring camp sites, the date on which the ice clears
from large lakes is most important in making this change in seasons.

The division of the year into seasons by the Cree utilizes two levels
of classification. First, there is binary division into the period of open

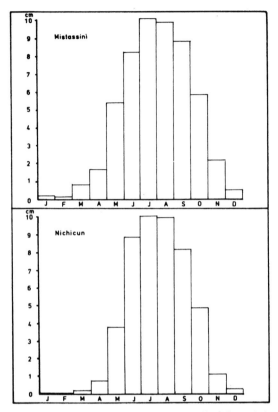

Note: Winter precipitation (Oct. to April) falls mainly
as snow, and is roughly ten times the amount of water
equivalent shown here.

Source: Wernstadt 1972

Fig. 1b. Mistassini and Nichicun mean monthly
precipitation

water (*niipin*) and the period of frozen lakes and rivers (*pipun*). At a
second level there are six sub-divisions, depending on informants
(Rogers 1963:47) (see Table 2). There are important practical distinctions between *niipin* and *pipun* (or 'summer' and 'winter', as we may
refer to them for convenience) (see Table 3). First, for a basically
nomadic people, the change of major seasons marks the change in
methods of transportation; by snowshoe, with toboggan or sled, in the
winter, and by canoe and portage in the summer. Some extended
walking is done during summer, while hunting bear or moose, or
picking blueberries, but otherwise summer travel is by water. The

Table 2.   MISTASSINI CREE SEASONS

Year			*Pipun*			
Two major seasons	*Pipun* 'winter'				*Niipin* 'summer'	
Minor seasons	*Miicis-kaasic* 'late fall'	*Pipun* 'winter'	*Siikun* 'early spring'	*Miiyuskamuu* 'late spring'	*Niipin* 'summer'	*Tahkwaacin* 'early fall'

period of change from summer to winter is relatively short: hunters may be using the canoe one day, when only the ice at the edge of large lakes presents some problems, while at the same time the ice on smaller lakes may be fit to walk on. During the break-up period there is a week or two of overlap in the two methods of transport; a canoe and a sled are used in conjunction, the canoe carrying the sled over water, and the sled carrying the canoe over the still frozen larger lakes. Many authorities have mentioned the difficulties and danger of travel during the break-up period (e.g. Knight 1968:6). The Nichicun also complain about this, and the whole group prepares for break-up by collecting a large stock of firewood so that women are not required to leave camp during the period of melting ice. But my diaries show little let-up in travelling activities by the men during either freeze-up or break-up, although the feet are constantly wet at break-up, as the ice on the lakes which are crossed becomes covered with water.

The second seasonal economic distinction concerns the fact that much fur becomes prime at roughly the same time as the lakes freeze over. By always commencing trapping at freeze-up, the Cree avoid catching unprime fur, even if the winter starts unusually late. Trapping ends in March or April, except for muskrat and the otter—

Table 3.   ECONOMIC AND SOCIAL CONTRASTS BETWEEN SUMMER AND WINTER

		Winter	*Summer*
Temperature		Below freezing	Above freezing
Travel means		Snow (snowshoe and toboggan)	Water (canoe)
Economy		Hunting and trapping	Wage work and fishing
Residence group:			
	Size	Small	Large
	Stability	Fixed	Changeable
Diet		Game meat	Store food and fish

for these species break-up marks the time when the last traps are lifted.

The presence or absence of ice on lakes and rivers also determines the methods used for catching fish. A gill net is used during both seasons, but when it must be set under the ice there are severe restrictions on how easily it may be moved to a new position. Set lines are also used summer and winter, also with a corresponding difference in the way they are used.

The two-season annual cycle is also seen by the Cree as being a major force in the lives of many of the animals on which they live; two important examples are bears, which hibernate from about the period of freeze-up to about a month before break-up, and migratory birds, the arrival of the earliest being determined by the presence of open water, and which fly south, in most cases, during the month before freeze-up. Both the hibernation of bears and the migration of birds have important economic consequences, as well as providing (among others) the basis for models of a seasonal symbiotic parallel between the social life of men and animals.

At the present time, the hunters of Mistassini and Nichicun undergo a major alteration in residence and economic pattern each year. In summer they reside at Mistassini Post, although the Nichicun at times spend this season at Nichicun Lake, in a group of semi-permanent dwellings adjacent to a weather station. From these locations some of them leave to get wage work, while others, mainly the older and monolingual men, and the women, set up fish camps at the larger lakes in the vicinity, and alternate between living in the camps and at the settlements. In winter the hunters form into hunting groups of from two to about five family units, and usually remain on their individual territories until the following summer. The dispersal out to the hunting locales takes place well before freeze-up (late August to early October), and in most cases the return to the settlement takes place immediately after break-up. In general we can say that the winter residence pattern consists of a small, fixed, closely knit group, and travel is limited to hunting trips and short moves. By contrast, residence in summer for most families is extremely fluid, varying between large settlements and single households, and travel in this period includes long journeys.

A final seasonal contrast which ought to be mentioned, as the Cree themselves often speak about it, is in the realm of diet. Although much fish is eaten during summer, the basic diet at that season now consists of store-bought food, and in families without a substantial summer cash income, this consists largely of bannock, with canned meat, beef and chicken when money is plentiful. The winter diet of hunters is mainly fresh meat, principally moose, caribou, beaver and fish, with waterfowl in the spring and fall. Winter is the period of *nuhcimiic miicim*, 'country food', while summer is the period of *wemistikuusuu miicim*, 'White man's food'.

In summary, there is a basic temperature regime which produces a series of seasonal oppositions in a range of material conditions. These, in turn, form the basis of two distinct economies, and two residence patterns. Cree hunting, trapping and fishing techniques are highly adapted to the two season climatic regime. Provided that the basic features of the two climatic regimes remain in force, such that in winter the temperature remains below freezing, while in summer it is above freezing (this latter condition is less important), then the smaller, day-to-day variations in weather — that is, the daily amounts of precipitation, wind or sunshine as distinct from the seasonal climatic regime — are taken by the Mistassini very much in their stride, and thus have little influence in altering the pattern of daily social life. This relative independence of their daily activities from variations in the weather is all the more surprising because of the degree to which the Mistassini spend their productive time in the open air.

The basis for this statement is the observation, albeit of only a handful of hunting groups first hand, of the high degree of planning, and the small degree to which planned activities are altered or upset by unforeseen weather conditions. This general statement will be examined with respect to four particular weather features: wind, solar radiation, extreme temperature and precipitation.

(*b*) *Wind.* Wind itself normally does little to interrupt the hunter's activities. Strong winds cause blowing snow which bury some traps, but they also help to carry away the hunter's scent, and drown his noise. Strong wind when combined with cold produces severe wind chill, but extremely low temperatures are most often accompanied by calm. Very few winter storms are severe enough to prevent travel, although visibility is reduced by blowing snow, and sticks sometimes have to be used to mark the trail. Some hunting, such as for ptarmigan, is adversely affected by winter storms. In summer, winds are a constant threat to canoe travel on large lakes, and also make hunting from a boat difficult.

In a later chapter, on the subject of orientation, the Cree concepts of the four winds will be introduced. Table 4 shows the percentage frequency of wind direction from each of the four quadrants, with the average wind speed. This is a yearly average; the only significant annual variation is in the percentage of calm winds. The average amount of calm for the four coldest months (December to March) is almost twice that of the rest of the year.

Table 4 indicates that both the prevailing and the strongest winds are from the west and south, and that the winds from the east tend to be less frequent and less strong than from other quadrants. Some of my informants stated that only an east wind could cause a delay or postponement of their hunting activities. The relative infrequency

Table 4.   AVERAGE WIND SPEED, AND PERCENTAGE FREQUENCY,
BY QUADRANTS (Nihicun, 1959-66)

	East	South	West	North	Calm	Total
Wind speed (m.p.h.)	8	11	12	9		
Percentage frequency	14	27	34	21	4	100

Source: Wernstedt 1972:57

of severe storms with east winds suggests that major interruptions in hunting activities due to storms are rare.

(c) *Solar radiation.* Although Nichicun is climatically within the sub-arctic, its latitude (53.14°N) is well south of the arctic circle, and similar to that of Edmonton. Mid-winter days are short, and most outdoor activity is limited to the few daylight hours. The winter sun, although low, does have a considerable effect on diurnal temperature variation. On very cold days the women's activities outside may be delayed until the sun has warmed the land. Several birds, mammals and plants position themselves to take advantage of winter solar radiation, and the argument will later be made that a similar cultural sensitivity exists, although not via a response to a 'material' need. In spring, on the other hand, solar radiation combines with snow and glare ice to cause sunburn and snow blindness, although sun glasses are usually worn at this time of the year. The sun at this time also can cause softening of the surface crust on the snow, so that travel may be restricted to night time.

(d) *Extreme temperature.* Extreme cold has some effect on hunting activities, particularly if it is accompanied by a storm. Below about minus 30°C hunting is hampered and animals tend not to move about. Just as important, mild weather in winter poses problems. A thaw impedes winter travel, by clogging snowshoes (a stick is carried to tap the snow free every few steps), by making toboggans hard to pull, and by causing the traveler to become overheated. In winter dozens of complaints are made about the weather being too warm for every comment made that it is too cold. Travel by snowshoe, especially when pulling a toboggan, generates sufficient body heat to remain comfortable, without heavy, hooded parkas, particularly when trees offer protection from the wind. Of the several magical techniques available for altering the weather, most are designed to lower the temperature during mild spells in winter.

(*e*) *Precipitation*. As we have indicated, winter snowfall does little to interrupt a hunter's activity, although snow must be cleared from around the camp, and from traps, and snow does cover the tracks of the animals. The Cree, however, are usually forced to remain inside in summer during heavy rain. A major concern is that annual precipitation should be neither too high nor too low. The latter case, in particular, causes hardship to trapping, by drying up marshes and ponds, and to travel, by lowering water levels in rivers.

The foregoing indicates that the Cree are predisposed to view the climate in terms of two seasons, each of which has special ideal features. The ideal winter weather is cold, sunny, with a steady wind. Only thawing weather or gale force storms produce serious discomfort. In summer, the major fear is of winds which come up suddenly while people are out on a lake, particularly those storms accompanied by lightning.

2. *The land*

(*a*) *General features*. The importance of waterways, lakes and marshes to boreal forest hunters cannot be overemphasized. In the Quebec-Labrador Peninsula a significant percentage of the land surface is covered by water (Todd 1963:6). In the Mistassini territory surface water is fairly evenly distributed, but with concentrations at the largest lakes (Mistassini, Albanel, Nichicun and Naococane), and comparatively little in the upland areas, such as the Otish Mountains. The major rivers (particularly the La Grande and the Rupert) include long stretches as chains of lakes connected by rapids. The general orientation of the areas of high ground and the elongated lakes tends to be northeast to southwest, while the main drainage pattern flows across this direction, towards the west. The result is that in most of the region canoe routes can be found in any direction, along the north-south axis, using the lakes and the secondary rivers, and also in the east and west directions, using chains of lakes or the major drainage systems. Across the direct route between Lake Mistassini and Lake Nichicun there is some high ground extending from the Otish Mountains west to Lac Baudeau; although there are routes across this high ground, the Nichicun group normally used an easier route via Lac Baudeau, Tichegami River and the Eastmain River to reach Lake Nichicun when loaded with supplies. Although most of the region is accessible by canoe, only those parts of the routes containing the largest lakes are free from frequent portages.

The present territory of the Mistassini band is an area with the shape of an inverted triangle, about 360 miles north to south, and about 200 miles from east to west at the northern end. It is bounded on the east by the height of land, oriented roughly from southwest to northeast, although Mistassini hunters are increasingly crossing onto land to the

Plate 3. Two men out hunting. The man on the left is dragging a beaver, using a *niimaapaan*.

east of the height of land, since the land is now seldom used by its former inhabitants, the Lac St. Jean and Sept Iles bands.

In general terms, it is possible to classify the land by the types of vegetation cover (Hare 1959; Hustich 1946). These classifications do not, however, reflect the actual situation of a complexity of small habitats, each of which is of different economic significance in hunting and trapping. The vegetation classes do indicate broad regional differentials, for instance that between the northern and southern parts of the territory. In this case the significant line of demarcation is the northern limit of closed forest as the dominant vegetation type. About forty miles north of Lake Mistassini there is a rapid change in the percentage of closed-crown forest, from 90 per cent dropping to between 50 and 70 per cent within twenty miles to the north (Hare and Taylor 1956; Feit 1969:40-2). North of this line the percentage of lichen woodland (open-crown forest with a ground cover of caribou moss) increases, until north of the Otish Mountains-Eastmain River, this vegetation type dominates.

For the Mistassini, the above distinction is given some sociological recognition. The Mistassini who have territories south of this boundary region occasionally speak of the people who hunt to the north as inferiors deserving of pity. I was told that the Nichicun did not eat well, and that they were cold all winter, because of the open, windy

Plate 4. Transportation. Hauling moose meat to camp, using toboggans.

country, and the shortage of firewood. All this, of course, proved to be untrue. On the more positive side, the Nichicun region is recognized as having more caribou than further south. While all the inhabitants of the northern sector suffer from this low evaluation by the other Mistassini, only the Nichicun who gather every spring and fall at Lake Nichicun make up a regional division with some self-consciousness and recognition within the larger Mistassini band. This northern group may be compared to the 'inlanders' of Fort George, who are somewhat looked down upon by the 'coasters' (Anderson, J.W. 1961: 126). In both cases the distinction is based on the folk recognition of an ecologically derived contrast.

(*b*) *Habitat*. A second significance that the broad classification of vegetation types has is that it draws attention to animal distribution patterns, given a knowledge of the plant and animal association patterns in the region (Harper 1964). The closed-crown forest contains over three times the vegetation biomass, many more animal species, and greater mammal population densities than does the open lichen woodland (Cook 1972:16; Coutts 1972:4, 31). However, most hunting and trapping takes place, not within the closed-crown forest, but at the interface between the two ecological zones. The shores of rivers and lakes, usually with a thin strip of dense vegetation, are habitats for many of the smaller game animals (Coutts 1972:4). These relatively small areas of dense vegetation are often bypassed by forest fires, because of the moist conditions, as are small wooded islands in lakes and rivers.

Another way of classifying Mistassini and Nichicun habitats, apart from the classification of dominant vegetation, is in terms of a model of the development of the forest through a series of successional ecological stages. Feit has suggested that the whole area has been subject to long term growth cycles which begin with the destruction of the mature forest by fire, and continue by stages, at each of which different species become dominant. Each stage leads to a further stage which shows an overall biomass accumulation from the previous one (1969). Such a diachronic model may be seen reflected in synchronic data (e.g. as shown in a vegetation map made from aerial photographs), with the numerous contiguous habitats seen as being at various stages in the cycle. In the whole Mistassini territory there are some very large recent burn areas avoided by hunters; but for the rest of the region, in which most hunting and trapping takes place, the characteristic feature of the landscape is not large areas of uninterrupted, single stage forest, but a patchwork of habitats.

Only part of the patchwork pattern is directly due to the forest fire cycle. Other major factors are differential exposure to cold winds, and variations in soil depth and ground moisture (Cook 1972:3-5). The patchwork feature means that each hunting territory (an area of several hundred square miles) contains a variety of habitats. Also, the difference between the northern landscape around Nichicun and that of Mistassini proper, in terms of its available resources, is a matter of the balance — and not the composition — of the mix. For instance, large stands of birch are common around Lake Mistassini. In the Nichicun area the number of birch trees is very small, as they are restricted to fairly predictable locations, in valleys on the south-east slopes of hills. The use of birch is thus restricted at Nichicun to the manufacture of snowshoe frames, and several other wooden manufactures. There are few natural resources available to the southern Mistassini which the Nichicun group cannot find in their land but in many cases they are more thinly distributed.

(c) _Camp sites_. The criteria for suitable camp sites differ according to the group size, the season and the duration of habitation. In all seasons the site will be near a supply of fresh water, and near a travel route. A travel route implies not just any lake or river, but a river with a length without rapids which will freeze over quickly, or which will permit canoe travel in the open water season. Recently, with the use of aircraft, major winter camps must be selected to have a waterbody nearby suitable for both float planes and ski planes. The necessity for a travel route also means that the lake where a camp is located cannot be enclosed by hills or thick forest, and must have access routes to connect it with the network of travel routes that cover the whole territory. Whilst most summer and winter travel routes follow water courses, and have portages around falls and rapids, some summer portages cross between water routes, and winter travel routes may have overland stretches, providing the terrain is not steep or thickly wooded. In the Nichicun and other northern areas the open lichen woodland permits more frequent portages between water courses than is possible in the more densely wooded southern portion. The camp site must also have a supply of firewood, a significant proportion of which is deadwood — the recent remains of a forest fire is very suitable for this purpose — and a supply of spruce and balsam for floor boughs, tent frames, beaver stretchers etc., for which the immature tree is the most suitable. A fishing site and a source of moss should also be close at hand.

The specific requirements of a camp site depend on the hunting activity. Rogers divides the winter season into seven economic periods: fall travel, fall hunt, winter camp, early winter trap, late winter hunt, spring trap and spring travel (1973:3-5). Although no hard and fast schedule can be applied to all Mistassini hunters, Rogers' outline can be used to summarize many of my observations, including the different types of camp sites. Fall travel camps are normally found at carrying places, since the canoes must be unloaded there anyway; in one instance such a camp was made on an island of a large lake. The fall hunt calls for a camp which gives easy access by water to a large area, with as few portages as possible. Fishing by gill net for lake fish and gathering blueberries may be important at this time, so the camp may be located close to these resources. The winter camp site is chosen to provide a base camp for winter hunting and trapping. It is therefore in the centre of a suitable area to which it has good access by snowshoe. The amount of firewood, fresh boughs and moss which must be close at hand depends on the length of time for which it is intended, which depends on the richness of its resource hinterland. In the Nichicun area such a resource hinterland will recuperate faster than the immediate area of the camp site. I found several instances where a winter camp was built on the same or on a nearby lake to one used within six to ten years previously. However, in no such case did the new camp occupy a site close to the earlier one, even when the old tent frames were still intact (see Rogers 1963b:226). The reason given for not reusing the old site was the shortage of firewood and moss in the immediate area of the old camp. During Rogers' 'late winter hunt' period it appears that several different patterns of movement may occur. Most commonly (in terms of the data I have gathered, or found in the literature) the group stays together, and moves to a new location in January or February, which then becomes a new base to exploit a resource hinterland. The group may instead move camp continuously during this period, staying no more than a week at each camp, and

Table 5.   TYPES OF VEGETATION COVER AND ASSOCIATED ANIMALS

Dominant vegetation cover (in order of increasing biomass)	Animals					
	Small rodents and primary carnivores	Waterfowl[1,2]	Porcupine	Beaver[1]	Caribou	Moose
1. Burned areas	−	−	−	−	−	−
2. Bare rock, lichen	−	−	−	−	+	+
3. Bog and muskeg	−	−	−	−	+	−
4. Sedge and shrub tundra	+	++	−	−	++	−
5. Shrub woodland	+	++	−	+	+	+
6. Alder-willow thickets	++	++	++	++	+	++
7. Lichen woodland	++	++	++	++	++	+
8. Closed-crown forest	++	+	++	++	+	++

Key: − = absent; + = present, to limited extent; ++ = preferred habitat

Notes: [1] Located at or near water only
              [2] Present in summer only

Sources: Based on data in Cook 1972; Harper 1964; Rousseau 1948.

only exploiting the area immediately around it. Finally, the active hunters may go off for days at a time, leaving the others at the main camp. Each option makes somewhat different demands on a camp site. When travelling, tents are used, rather than a wood and moss lodge, and since this is the coldest part of the year, camps at this period are usually made among fairly heavy bush for protection. Spring trapping camps are located at rapids, which are the first areas of open water to appear, and therefore attract the first waterfowl. Otter are also trapped at such locations, so that the camp is located with access to as many such areas of open water as possible. Spring travel camps are again located mainly on portages.

(*d*) *Hunting territories*. When a map of the hunting territories is superimposed over a detailed map of vegetation cover, it can be seen that no territory contains a vegetation pattern of only one type, and it is likely that any territory contains a variety of habitats. No territory is without an extensive system of lakes and rivers which are used as travel routes, both summer and winter. It is significant in this regard to note that the boundaries between territories are generally found either along high ground or along very large rivers. They are seldom found to follow small rivers. The pattern of hunting territory boundaries is influenced by the travel routes, as well as by the natural barriers to travel which the country offers.

The four largest rivers in the Mistassini land are the La Grande, Eastmain, Rupert and Temiscamie (which is the main river flowing into Lake Albanel) (see Map 3); each is used as a canoe route by several groups travelling into and out of their territories, and each serves as a boundary between two territories. Smaller rivers, which are used only as routes to places within a territory, are used for travel in winter, since they freeze over and provide a hunter with access to the lakes within his territory. In winter the largest rivers often do not freeze over, or if they do, they remain dangerous to cross. For this reason territories tend not to straddle such rivers, giving an additional geographic reason for using them as territory boundaries. The water route which joins the Eastmain River with Lake Mistassini, via Lac Baudeau is also a territory boundary, since in this case it is a major access route from Mistassini for the hunters of the Nichicun and other northern territories.

The maps of Mistassini hunting territories not only indicate the well-known tendency for territories to become larger the further north they are (Hallowell 1949; Cooper 1942) but also north of the latitude of the Eastmain River the tendency for the rate of growth in size of territories increases dramatically. This question, like the previous question of the effect of travel routes, has an environmental and a socio-economic aspect. Those territories south of a line running east-west just below the southern end of Lake Albanel average 329 square miles; those

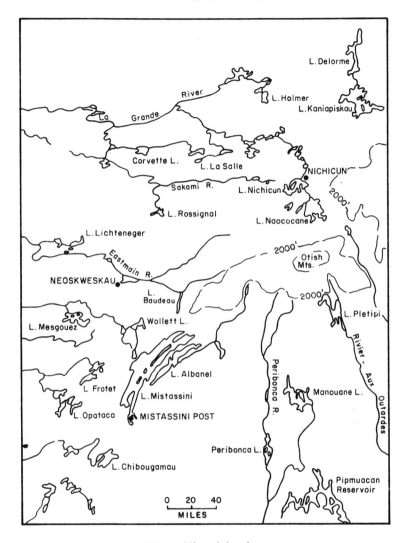

Map 3. Mistassini region

north of this line but south of the Eastmain River and Otish Mountains average 551 square miles. However, territories still further to the north, including those of the Nichicun local band, are on the average over twice this size, 1,302 square miles. The reason for the larger increase is that, apart from the general thinning of resources towards the north there is a quantum change in the nature of some of the key resources, and therefore in the way they are exploited. In a later section of this chapter we will show that the killing of large game plays a key role in the winter subsistence economy, and that the two critical periods for such large kills are in the fall, in which case bear, caribou or moose are most often involved, and in late winter, when caribou or moose may be involved. While moose and bear occur in fairly predictable areas at the time of year when they are hunted (that is, assuming that it is known that there are some animals to be found somewhere in the area in question), caribou travel over far wider areas. North of the Eastmain river the density of moose drops, and although they have only recently moved north of the La Grande, it is the caribou which play an increasingly important economic role as a resource which, if at all possible, must be obtained during these two limited periods of the year. Secondly, as we will later show, the single dominant economic species in this whole region is beaver because of its role not only as the most important source for market production but also as the dominant staple food in the sense that, unlike other meat, beaver is served regularly throughout the winter. Again, north of the Eastmain River beaver not only continue to decrease in density, but there is a quantum shift in the nature of the beaver's relationship to the environment. Beaver populations to the south consist for the most part of lodge groups of various ages who control a territory by driving off outsiders. A few bachelors live in holes in the shore outside these territories, but they make up only a small part of the total population. It has recently been shown that in the region of the La Grande River a different pattern obtains. The proportion of single beavers living in holes increases and the lodge populations themselves are smaller and more mobile, as they tend to exhaust much more quickly the territory they are able to defend of food resources. The diet of these northern beavers also changes, owing to the shortage of the deciduous flora preferred by more southerly populations. The result is that both the lodge populations and those that dwell in holes in the shore follow a pattern of temporary sedentariness, moving more often than southern populations as their food supply is exhausted (Clough 1972).

The above two factors which are characteristic of the most northerly territories — the economic predominance of a wandering species, caribou, rather than the more sedentary moose or bear, at certain times during the season, and the less sedentary nature of northern beavers, a species which is hunted throughout the rest of the winter — have the combined effect of making hunting in this region more nomadic, both seasonally and from year to year, than for the more southerly groups, even allowing for the reduced resource density. Consequently, territories are far larger. The major differences in the land use pattern between the northern and southern area are not, however, merely a direct reflection of differences in the ecology. The more nomadic pattern exhibited by the Nichicun hunting groups is founded in the system of social relations — the avoidance of each other's land by territory owners, the changing composition of the hunting groups, and the pattern of hospitality between hunting territory owners. By means of this system of social relations, hunters tend to make use of the land after the same fashion used by their major prey species, that is, following a more sedentary pattern towards the south, and a more nomadic one towards the north.

3. *Material constraints*

To recapitulate in a different form the main points made earlier about the material conditions within which the winter hunting group operates, a number of constraints may be mentioned, and the effects of these constraints on the organization of the group identified. Rather than linking these effects directly to unconscious functional mechanisms, however, I propose both here, and throughout the rest of this work, to see first of all the way these constraints are understood by the Mistassini through their cultural concepts, and the way these concepts are elaborated through symbolic expression. Secondly, I wish to show that the fundamental complex of social relations, which I have called the mode of production, is not simply a direct function of material conditions, but is a construct through which ideas and symbols about the material environment are put into action.

(*a*) *Climate*. The climate is interpreted primarily in terms of the winter-summer opposition. Furthermore, this two season model is used to divide the population (into summer-born and winter-born) (see Chapter 5), and is further reflected in two distinctive modes of production, that of the winter hunting group and that of the summer settlement. Within each primary season sub-divisions are recognized, and these conform to the general pattern of activities within each season. In mid-winter, for example, the hunting group usually adopts a communal residence. At the same time, long term changes in the climate in the past may have brought about transformations in the whole ecosystem, which in turn brings about a transformation in the material adaptation (Fitzhugh 1972:179).

(*b*) *Weather*. The above model of seasons specifies idealized weather conditions for each season. Variations towards extreme conditions are understood differently in each season. In winter, the occurrence of weather events controls the timing of economic activities through the season, but, apart from the occurrence of very extreme conditions, weather received minimal recognition for its effect on economic life. Explanations of weather are linked principally to the operations of the winds, and particularly the dominant effect of the prevailing winds from the west quadrant. The same system of explanation operates also to explain the non-appearance of some winter game animals. Warm weather in winter hampers progress, as does extreme wind, but activities continue; if production is affected hunger may result, and so magical means are used to control the situation. More normally, winter presents a sequence of environmental conditions which, in terms of the religious ideology, make it possible for first this species and then that species to 'give' itself to the hunter. In summer, extreme weather conditions are taken far more seriously, and explained not in terms of basic cosmological patterns, as is winter weather, but in terms of personified, localized natural forces.

(c) *Animal populations*. Every Mistassini hunter learns by observation and teaching the natural habits of the animal species he encounters. Sights and sounds when in the bush are constantly interpreted in terms of information about plant and animal populations. Population changes, including those which are short term, cyclical, and long term, as well as those due to major ecological collapse, are understood in terms of multiple causes, which include environmental factors such as the activities of hunters, availability of the species' food supply, surface water, weather, and forest fires, but which also include notions of animal masters and other beings who control the movement of particular species, and the ease with which animals may be killed. As a result, an area which appears short of an adequate game population is accepted as such, and avoided for several years until the adverse conditions (either natural or religious) are resolved through time. The effect of this on the group is of a constant change in the conception of what the group's territory is, change in the composition of the group as it adjusts its size, and the tactic of a temporary use of other land through a generalized exchange of hunting privileges (see Chapter 9), most often with neighbouring groups. Where the animal population of a territory is adequate, various survey methods are used in order to plan the winter's activities in conformity with the observed balance between the various available species.

(d) *Quotas*. As can be seen from the preceding paragraph, the idea of quotas, as applied by the Provincial Game Department to the beaver population of each territory, has some parallel with prevailing Cree concepts. However, there is less unanimity over Government control of moose and caribou. In some parts of the southern Mistassini area, mainly that used by the Chibougamau local band, attempts by the provincial government to apply highly restrictive game laws to Indians have been met with a mixture of incomprehension and resentment. This restriction acts as a material constraint on the activities of hunters using these areas. As a consequence the areas close to White towns and roads tend to be avoided by serious full-time hunters and trappers, and are instead used mainly by the elderly and part-time trappers, who are no longer dependent on hunting, but who instead rely on various kinds of transfer payments for their subsistence.

(*e*) *Land: the pattern of habitats.* The overwhelming pattern of vegetation cover is of a patchwork pattern of various habitat types, each of which favours a particular balance of animal populations. The Cree make extensive use of the vegetation pattern in the planning and execution of hunting and trapping. In a similar way, there is a complex system of classification of water bodies according to the type of lake or river bottom, as well as the type of banks, currents and surrounding vegetation found there. All these factors relate directly to their significance as habitats for a large number of important animals and fish. Main campsites are selected with reference to the availability of a suitable variety of land and water habitats, and of connecting travel routes.

(*f*) *Land: the northern/southern contrast.* Generally, the further north one travels in the Mistassini territory the smaller the trees become, and the more scattered is the occurrence of deciduous species. A dominant closed-crown forest gives way to a dominant open lichen woodland, with a consequent drop in total biomass. The caribou becomes increasingly more important as a big game species, and beavers become less sedentary, have a different diet, and are more thinly spread over the land. The Mistassini tend to conceive of these contrasts as fairly abrupt. Because they must travel so far between their territories and the summer settlement, and because they require far larger territories, those who hunt north of the Eastmain River and the Otish Mountains are thought of as more nomadic, and have the reputation of having less material goods and being less sophisticated in terms of the standards of life in the village. These and other beliefs about northern people stem from an ecological contrast. This contrast also affects changes in the pattern of production used by the hunting groups. Northern groups are smaller, move more each year, move more from year to year, and undergo more movement between territories by using a generalized exchange of hunting privileges.

(*g*) *Hunting group size.* Rogers has discussed this question in terms of upper and lower limits on group size (1963:77-82). Within the limits imposed by constraints like scattered resources and the need for assistance in emergencies it is possible to compare the activities of groups which are towards the upper limits with those which are towards the lower limits. Many informants spoke of a large hunting group, meaning one with four or five commensal families, as a preferred form, but one which could only rarely be used, because of the resources needed. In some cases two groups will share a main camp for part of the winter, and separate for the rest of the year. This happened a few years prior to my visit to Nichicun, and a few years before that there was a winter-long group of five families. Members of those groups recall those winters with particular pleasure; during the early winter period of residence in the communal lodge there was a convivial atmosphere each evening, and feasts became very grand affairs. In order to support such a group, the younger men are required to hunt and trap at such distances from the main camp that they are often away for days. Two men would set up a secondary camp together, and each set out his own traps by himself. Meat from big game animals must often be transported to the main camp, rather than moving camp to the meat. Small hunting groups, on the other hand, can be more mobile without breaking up, and without men staying away from their wives in the main camp for several days at a time.

(*h*) *Hunting group composition.* One may also conceive of the demographic composition of the hunting group as bounded within limits. The two most important aspects of this question are: (1) the ratio of infants, and no longer active older people to active producers, and (2) the ratio of men to women. Groups with one or more old people, who are not able to walk all day in snowshoes, are less mobile than those with none. On the other hand, such individuals usually operate snare lines for rabbits, and put out fish nets under the ice, which significantly contributes to production, and changes the nature of the subsistence pattern. Children similarly limit the group's mobility. Groups made up exclusively of younger families with few children are often more mobile, trap more intensively, but have a far narrower subsistence diet than others. The ratio of men to women is of major significance in trapping. One active trapper, given a reasonably rich territory, provides enough work for more than one woman preparing skins. This is particularly the case when there is a high proportion of beaver pelts, which require approximately four or five (depending on skill) women-hours of labour per pelt, not including the making of the stretcher, which is usually undertaken by a man. Moreover, the preparation of furs usually is handled within each commensal group, although I did observe women from different groups helping each other with these tasks during the period immediately prior to the visit to the camp by the H.B.C. manager, when the group was hurrying to have all the skins ready. Men were also called in to help, but only in unusual circumstances. However, if the proportion of women is low, men will tend to skin their furs themselves during those evenings when they are away trapping, rather than bringing back the animal with the skin still on, as is normally the case when a trapper returns to the main camp each day. Men will also at times assist women in gathering firewood.

The foregoing factors thus do not merely set limits within which the group's size and composition is restricted, but also allow variations within those limits, which result in hunting groups with different patterns of production. In terms of the movements undertaken by a group through the winter, we may identify three broad ideal types: (1) women and children remain in one main camp, men spend most nights at the main camp, and the camp is moved as the area within a day's travel of the camp becomes exhausted of resources; (2) the main camp with the women and children remains for the whole winter in one place, while the men spend most nights away in secondary camps; (3) the main camp remains in one place, but it is only occupied for part of the year. During the time of intensive trapping each commensal family sets up its own secondary camp some distance away from the main camp. Actual hunting groups in practice employ a mixture of the above tactics.

(*i*) *Relations with the Hudson's Bay Company manager.* Hunting groups differ as to the amount of capital goods, such as traps, canoes, outboard motors, guns, and most recently, snowmobiles, which they have. Each trapper requires a basic outfit of equipment, and the credit system is used to acquire these items. Thus the credit relationship with the H.B.C., even though it may include the use of welfare, family allowance or pension sources as a backing for the credit, determines the extent to which a trapper is adequately outfitted. Heavy equipment such as traps are normally stored between seasons in the bush, on cache platforms. However, if a trapper decides to hunt with a group with another territory some distance from that area he used the previous year it may be difficult to pick up his equipment, and he must then secure more. Many older trappers have such durable goods cached in several different parts of the country, but younger men have not had the opportunity to accumulate these items, and moreover, have less access to transfer payments as sources of cash or of credit. Changing fur prices to some extent alter the kind of animals that a trapper tries to catch, providing that the highest priced species are available to him. Finally, the amount of credit which a man can obtain affects the amount of store food he will take with him, or can purchase during the course of the winter. This in turn must affect the pattern of production, by placing slightly more or less emphasis on subsistence needs, depending on the commercial food he can afford.

The above material constraints do not exhaust the list of those which could be mentioned. But these cases demonstrate, within certain ultimate limits, that the constraints cannot account for the Mistassini hunter's adaptation as long as they are treated merely as an abstract 'condition'. Instead, each factor is to be seen in terms of the variations which it allows, and the way the difference between the permitted extremes imposed by the material constraints can be handled, and how this alters the basic pattern of the process of production. In this manner it is possible to avoid relying purely on an abstract conception of material conditions, one which is impossible to relate to the cultural cognitive processes, and the cultural actions which derive from them.

3
The Process of Production

1. *The annual cycle*

Those members of the Mistassini band who are full-time hunters and trappers have a pattern of productive activities which is sharply divided between two seasons, summer and winter. In winter the main productive activities involve killing animals, while in the summer, the main source of production is wages and welfare payments. Similarly, in winter, the main source of subsistence is from items produced by hunting and gathering, while in summer most of subsistence items are purchased. Hunting is a form of subsistence, as is, to some extent, trapping; that is, in both cases the unit of production, the commensal family, consumes what it produces. The winter is not entirely devoted to subsistence, just as the summer does not entirely involve market production, but there is a marked seasonal tendency in one direction or the other. In this chapter we are not concerned merely with the elements of the economy by themselves, but the way the parts fit together, and the resulting form which this integrated economy takes. Thus we are not only concerned with how the winter and the summer economy fit together, but also, within the winter economy, with the relationship between the subsistence part of the economy and the market-oriented part. In this chapter we will first of all outline separately the contributions made by each of these sectors, but towards the end of the chapter we will deal with the total process of production as a social form, and outline the conditions for its existence or its transformation.

The distinction between a hunting and gathering process of production in the winter, and a wage and welfare process of production for the summer is, I repeat, by no means absolute. The market economy is an integral part of all winter productive activities, including, for example, the provision of game, which requires guns, ammunition and a host of other purchased items. Trapping is the source both of subsistence, in the form of meat, and of furs which are sold; however, the meat of some fur-bearing animals is not eaten at all. Furthermore during the winter period some forms of transfer payments continue (e.g. pensions, family allowance), and are usually deposited in the account which an individual has with the Hudson's Bay Company, which is where most trade is conducted. Similarly, the summer period involves considerable subsistence fishing, and the hunting of water birds, as well as hunting some land animals, and the gathering of items like firewood and blueberries.

Plate 5. Setting a beaver trap underwater, through the ice.

The division between the summer and the winter pattern of production, then, is not identical to the distinction between two modes of production. Rather, within the hunting group mode of production, the seasonal division is accompanied by a change in residence patterns, and by a change in the kind of social organization employed by the group. The alternation in residence is a continuation of an historical pattern which probably reaches back to pre-contact times, when groups larger than the hunting group gathered for short periods at favourable sites where there were concentrations of resources (such as fish, water birds or material for stone tools). Trade and marriages probably took place at these summer gatherings (Rogers 1969:47). During the historical period the location of trading posts became places where people gathered in the summer.

We have mentioned that the winter season can be considered to last from freeze-up to break-up. However, in economic terms, the winter includes a longer period, from the time the hunters leave the settlement, until their return the following year. In the past hunters left Mistassini Post by canoe, taking up to several weeks to reach their destinations, depending on the distance. Recently there has been a trend towards using aircraft to travel at least part of the distance, particularly for those groups with distant territories. More recently still, aircraft have been used for the return trip in the spring. For example, the Nichicun local band all took aircraft from Mistassini Post to Nichicun Lake in September 1969; from here they travelled to individual territories by canoe, a journey of from 25 to 100 miles. The following spring there was considerable discussion among Nichicun hunters about returning by canoe to Mistassini Post (a journey of about 280 miles, but a relatively easy one because there was no freight to carry), but for the first time the decision was made to return by aircraft. While in the past the most outlying groups would leave the settlement in August, they now leave in mid-September; the last groups leave in mid-October. Groups wintering near Mistassini Post may return to the Post over Christmas, and may end their trapping in April, before freeze-up. Outlying groups in most cases remain away until after break-up, in the following May or June, unless a member becomes ill. The average winter season is thus about nine or ten months long.

After leaving the summer settlement at Mistassini the Nichicun local band assembled and remained together at Nichicun Lake from about mid-September to mid-October, 1969. This period of local band co-residence takes place every year, despite the advice of the Hudson's Bay Company manager, who believes the men would be better employed if they travelled directly to their territories and began preparing for winter trapping. Instead, the men spent the time on Lake Nichicun or its immediate vicinity, fishing, hunting water-fowl, beaver and small game, and looking for bears. None of the latter were killed in 1969, although I was told that in past years one usually was killed during this period. Several feasts were held during this period, each to mark the first beaver of the season killed by one of the hunters (see Chapter 8). Some interaction took place between the Indians and the men of a local weather station. The women made handicrafts to order, and received cash, and food, while the men got favours such as the loan of tools. Several evenings were spent in the recreation room of the weather station.

After leaving Nichicun Lake, the Jimiken group travelled to the location of its early winter camp, taking most of its winter supplies. On the way time was spent examining the countryside for signs of game, particularly for beaver. Freeze-up took place while this reconnaissance continued in the area around the early winter camp, and

Plate 6. The Hudson's Bay Company manager visits a camp in winter, to trade furs (background, centre) for supplies (foreground).

following freeze-up a journey was made to collect supplies, such as traps, snowshoes, a stove, sleds and blankets, which had been cached the previous year on another part of the territory. Such caches of equipment are normally made each spring on an island, to protect them from forest fires. Some time was spent looking for big game in October, but nothing was killed. In November a communal lodge was built and occupied by the whole group, followed by a feast to mark the beginning of winter. Following this, a routine was established, consisting of daily trips by the adult men usually individually, to check traps already set, or to find new beaver lodges. Beaver remained the focus of the trapping effort until April; traps were also set if signs of other fur-bearers were discovered while hunters were looking for beaver. At the same time, signs of moose or caribou were also noted and discussed at camp. If caribou or moose were discovered while a man was out trapping they would be shot at, but few animals were killed this way. Instead, the knowledge gathered from the observations of all hunters over a period of time was pooled, and finally a day was set aside from the regular individual trapping for a hunt involving several people. In this way one or more moose or caribou were killed every month from November to March, with a minimum of interruption to beaver trapping, and a minimum of hunting effort. Towards the end of January the winter lodge was abandoned, and the group spent about a month of almost continual moving. Camps were established and the area around trapped, but the group never stayed longer than a week. During March the group remained at one camp, and followed the earlier pattern of individual beaver trapping, with occasional group moose or caribou hunts. During April the pattern of frequent movements of camp was again used. Towards the end of this period the number of moose and caribou kills increased, and the group made its way to the location of its spring camp, close to a series of rapids. From this location activity centred around killing waterfowl, trapping otter, killing caribou and drying and powdering the surplus moose and caribou meat which had been killed previously. In June the last of the otter and muskrat traps were lifted, and the group headed for the local band gathering place at Nichicun Lake. Other groups arrived, and firewood was co-operatively gathered to last the group over the break-up period. Following break-up, the local band members returned to Mistassini Post.

One major change took place in the composition of the Jimiken group during the period just described. At the end of March one of the families left the group and returned to Mistassini Post, as the wife was about to deliver a baby. This family, consisting of husband and wife and three small children, did not return that winter. The other family, that of the hunting group leader, Willie Jimiken, consisted of the married couple, two unmarried adults, a son and a daughter, and a fifteen year old daughter. I lived as part of the Jimiken family, and in terms of productivity probably contributed the equivalent of a fourteen-year old boy.

2. Subsistence production

Table 6 gives a summary of the productive activities of the group. The conversions to pounds of edible meat are taken from figures supplied by Feit (personal communications) (cf. Salisbury 1972:21, 24) based on investigations in the nearby Waswanipi region. The edible meat is totalled together, although the meat of ermine and some fish were observed to be avoided at all times. However, this meat was fed to the dogs, which would otherwise have been fed with the same game meat that people would have eaten or with store food, such as oatmeal. As far as estimating the value of game meat is concerned, then, it does not appear critical to distinguish between that portion eaten by humans and that eaten by dogs.

The following table indicates that the leanest month for production of subsistence food was June, although there was no shortage at that time. Food was held in storage from the peak months of March and April. Following this, the next leanest months were September and

Table 6. JIMIKEN GROUP: MONTHLY MEAT PRODUCTION, 1969-70

		Sept.	Oct.	Nov.	Dec.	Jan.	Feb.	March	April	May	June	Grand Total:
Trapping and small game (number)	Beaver	3	3	17	11	13	20	27	14	1	0	
	Muskrat	0	2	2	0	1	1	1	1	0	16	
	Marten	0	0	0	0	0	0	1	0	0	0	
	Otter	1	2	3	0	0	0	0	0	3	6	
	Ermine	0	0	2	1	3	0	3	0	0	0	
	Mink	0	1	16	6	10	4	6	0	1	1	
	Squirrel	0	0	1	1	0	2	1	0	0	0	
	Hare	0	0	0	4	4	2	0	0	0	0	
	Porcupine	0	3	2	1	1	1	1	1	0	0	
	Ptarmigan	0	2	9	3	25	5	12	0	0	0	
	Spruce Grouse	1	6	0	3	6	22	0	4	2	1	
Edible meat (lb.)		47	58	258	146	175	259	352	178	39	69	
Big game (number)	Moose	0	0	0	0	2	1	2	6	0	0	
	Caribou	0	0	1	3	0	0	2	1	5	0	
	Bear	0	0	0	0	0	0	0	0	0	0	
Edible meat (lb.)		—	—	105	315	660	330	870	2,085	525	—	
Fish (lb.)		575	375	270	170	70	185	55	115	210	60	
Edible meat (lb.)		381	250	180	113	47	123	37	77	143	40	
Waterfowl (number)	Geese	3	0	0	0	0	0	0	0	18	3	
	Ducks	4	13	0	0	0	0	0	1	13	6	
	Loons	0	2	0	0	0	0	0	0	0	3	
Edible meat (lb.)		16	16	0	0	0	0	0	1	85	27	Grand Total:
Total meat (lb.)		444	324	543	574	882	712	1,259	2,341	792	136	8,007
Days		14	31	30	31	31	28	31	30	31	23	280
Average daily total (lb)		31.7	10.5	18.1	18.5	28.5	25.4	40.6	78.0	25.5	5.9	28.7

October; during these months fish made up a large part of the subsistence food production: 85.9 per cent in September, and 71.6 per cent in October. However, these figures may be somewhat unusual, due to the failure to kill any bear, moose or caribou during this period, the pattern reported by Rogers (1973) perhaps being more typical in this respect.

An alternative measure for the varying role of subsistence food is the percentage of the diet which comes from this source. Table 7 gives the percentages of subsistence food produced and eaten each month by the Jimiken group.

Table 7. SUBSISTENCE AND STORE FOOD BY WEIGHT CONSUMED
BY THE JIMIKEN GROUP, 1969-70

	Subsistence food (%)	Purchased food (%)	Total monthly subsistence production (lb.)
Sept.	66.6	33.4	443.62
Oct.	62.6	37.4	349.1
Nov.	68.9	31.1	572.82
Dec.	71.0	29.0	573.23
Jan.	81.7	18.3	882.44
Feb.	75.0	25.0	712.28
March	75.2	24.8	1,258.49
April	77.1	22.9	2,341.26
May	76.3	23.7	801.28
June	73.9	26.1	136.16
Mean	72.8%	27.2%	

Table 7 indicates that store food consumption rises in those months when subsistence production is low and no subsistence food is held in storage; i.e. in September, October, and to some extent in November and December. Thus one of the functions of store food is to fill the gap when subsistence production is low. Later in the year, store food consumption did not fall much below 25 per cent, despite the availability of a stored surplus of game meat. The monthly variations observed from January to June depended not on the availability of game, which was plentiful, but on the degree of group movement. While the group is travelling, food such as bannock and oatmeal porridge are eaten more frequently than when the group is more sedentary, because they can be prepared quickly. There is a preference for a small amount of store food consumption at all times.

From the data presented it can be seen that from November to February trapping and hunting together provided a steady and generally increasing portion of the subsistence requirements of the group. The contribution of trapping continued at a steady rate until April, while during the same period hunting productivity increased markedly to produce a surplus of food, which was consumed from May onwards when the productivity of all subsistence activities except fishing and waterfowl fell. When these data are compared with the weekly productivity of edible meat of another Mistassini hunting group in 1953-4 (Rogers 1973: facing page 78) a similar pattern emerges, with the exception that in the latter case there is an additional period of high productivity, from a successful big game hunt in the fall (see Fig. 2).

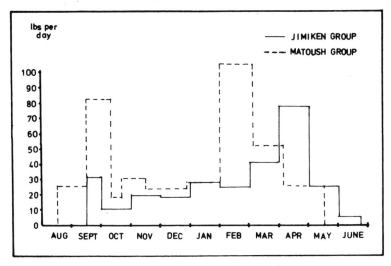

Fig. 2. Variations in subsistence production for the Jimiken group (1969-70) and the Matoush group (1953-4)

In Fig. 2 the two bar graphs show subsistence food production in pounds per day. The figures for the Jimiken group were averaged for each calendar month, while for Rogers' data averages were computed for each of the seasonal divisions used by Rogers, providing they were less than five weeks long; in the case of the two longer divisions (i.e. 'early winter trap' and 'late winter hunt'), these were divided up into four or five week segments, and the average daily productivity of each computed.

This pattern of production depends ideally on the existence of an adequate resource base and this is not always available. One group I observed undertook a series of moose hunts, where not only did the hunters know ahead of time where to find the animals (in another case I was told the sex and age of the animal and where it would be found two days before the hunt took place), but two of the moose were driven several miles before they were killed, in order that the carcasses would be in the most convenient location for the later transportation of the meat. Clearly, such a planned approach to hunting and trapping depends on an adequate environmental base, and the availability of a store of food, so that it is not absolutely necessary to kill on sight, nor always to follow whatever tracks are seen. Let me stress that I am not arguing here for the view that sub-arctic hunting is highly productive for a minimum input of labour time; on the contrary, all adults are involved in long hours of often back-breaking labour to achieve a level of subsistence which the Mistassini themselves find seldom much more than adequate. Neither am I suggesting that the planned approach to hunting and trapping could continue during conditions caused by a seriously impoverished environment. We have evidence of starvation at Mistassini, with deaths for example in 1834-5 and 1837-8 (Lips 1947:463, 467); other deaths appear in our genealogies during the period 1915-25. There was also the decline of the beaver population in the 1940s, although not as serious as that experienced by the Rupert House Indians some years earlier. Recollections of these latter two periods by the Mistassini suggest that at such times the group became dependent on small mammals, small birds and fish, which was usually the woman's productive speciality; the men scoured the countryside with a gun, living off small game, searching further and further afield, at first for big game, and sometime later seeking help. Hunting groups and even families were thus broken apart temporarily by starvation.

One difference between the Jimiken group's graph and that for the Matoush group (Fig. 2), apart from the latter's higher fall productivity, is that the peak month of the Jimiken's late winter hunt is almost two months later than was the case with Rogers' group. Rogers states that beaver trapping became less intensive in January, when attention shifted towards big game (1973:4).

The Jimiken group continued intensive trapping, with the focus on beaver, until April. The difference between this pattern and Rogers' observations could be due to different ecological conditions; after January the Matoush group moved into an area with fewer beaver, but this was not the case with the Jimiken group. It might also be an effect of beaver quotas, since by January the Jimiken group had still caught only half of its quota. Other Mistassini groups I have visited during the winter made large big game kills in February (in the case of another Nichicun group in 1969-70), or in January (see also Anderson, J.W. 1961:93). My impression remains that for the central part of the winter trapping is the normal focus of attention, but this changes if and when it becomes known that big game are easily available.[1] To what extent, then, is this subsistence pattern a standard one?

In a later chapter I will deal with the Cree notion of the hunting territory, and point out that its use is not identical with the concept of the beaver territory, as used by the government for quota purposes. However, the introduction of quotas, coupled with the availability of transfer payments, both of which were introduced after World War II, does appear to have had the effect that, at least in the Nichicun area, no group finds it absolutely necessary to hunt in an area lacking in adequate subsistence resources, particularly without an adequate supply of beaver. In the past, sharp decreases in beaver and big game populations, and subsequent starvations, took place throughout the East Cree area, and the most recent instance, during the 1920s and 1930s, led to the creation of the beaver quota system (Denmark 1948; Knight 1968; and Anderson, W.A. 1961). But, for Mistassini at least, the present quota system has had the effect of compelling an individual to remain away from a territory while the beaver population is low, and furthermore, the availability of welfare now makes it possible for him to remain at the settlement of Mistassini Post, in the unlikely event that he is unable to become the guest of another territory owner. The apparent existence of a relatively stable subsistence base today may also be seen within the context of the present integration between the cash and subsistence sectors of the economy, a matter which will be introduced in the last section of this chapter.

At the moment it is not possible to present statistical evidence of wider generality to show how standardized this winter subsistence pattern is. This is because government statistics refer only to the annual kill, rather than on a month-to-month basis. Government statistics also tend to underestimate the kill, since they are based either on the number of furs traded, overlooking the skins that are not prime or are damaged and used by the hunters themselves, or on voluntary returns submitted by hunters, which I have found to be somewhat less than the total kill, when this is measured independently. Table 8 is my own estimate of the Nichicun local band kill for 1969-70, using both government figures, observations and interviews.

Table 8.   ANNUAL SUBSISTENCE FOOD PRODUCTION, BY SOURCE, FOR NICHICUN LOCAL BAND, 1969-70

	Weight (lb.)	Per cent
Moose	11,550	33.84
Beaver	8,574	25.12
Caribou	6,294	18.44
Fish	5,150	15.09
Otter	588	1.72
Porcupine	420	1.23
Geese	320	.94
Ducks	250	.73
Blueberries	250	.73
Muskrat	228	.67
Ptarmigan	154	.45
Spruce Grouse	140	.41
Hares	127	.37
Loons	90	.26

Note: The band consisted of 25 adults and 17 children in 5 hunting groups.

Table 9.   REPORTED HARVEST BY HUNTERS, 1957-1970

Year	Trapping Population	Caribou	Moose	Beaver	Canada Geese	Ducks	Grouse
1957-8	325	46	162	6,710	194	1,202	842
1958-9	533	58	344	6,284	No data	3,729	3,291
1959-60	644	150	470	7,649	454	4,891	8,666
1960-1	672	102	301	6,797	461	4,735	12,854
1961-2	719	108	383	7,035	616	4,603	12,367
1962-3	664	114	257	8,019	734	5,465	12,290
1963-4	787	81	247	6,415	432	5,378	15,025
1964-5	648	218	344	7,404	956	7,725	14,925
1965-6	523	208	219	6,154	704	2,677	2,187
1966-7	562	116	206	5,209	1,026	4,413	5,870
1967-8	No data			5,980			
1968-9	768	79	274	7,691	778	5,229	6,657
1969-70	570	142	241	6,520	819	4,052	5,721

The figures thus far presented do not take into account variations in productivity which may occur from year to year. Table 9, based entirely on government figures, may not be fully accurate as to the numbers of animals killed each year (for the reasons just given), but it does give an idea of the range of year-to-year variation. The table shows the kill of beaver and moose to be relatively stable. One may guess that fish catches are also relatively stable. Caribou is a less important subsistence item for the Mistassini band as a whole than for the Nichicun group alone, so that the overwhelming bulk of the subsistence food requirement has been acquired in fairly stable amounts over this period. My conclusion is that the moose and beaver catches indicate an adequate animal population for the hunting pressure.

What is particularly notable in Table 9 is the variation in hunter's population size over this period (the figure, refers to the total men, women and children). During this period the Mistassini band population was increasing steadily. However, after 1963-4 the number of people going trapping fluctuates, probably due to attempts to find winter wage employment. As the price of furs rose generally, the number of trappers stabilized at a fairly high level: in 1970 approximately 185 (64 per cent) of the 289 adult men were full-time trappers, while an additional 50 (17 per cent) were part-time trappers. 14 per cent did no trapping, and the remaining 5 per cent were retired or crippled. An additional 32 boys below the age of eighteen were trappers.

We have seen that the basic production pattern is a mixture of hunting and trapping. Despite the different techniques involved, the two activities are, in important ways, very similar, as practised by the Cree. The productivity of each, and the amount of effort put into each, is dependent mainly on the availability of the animals concerned. Each animal is trapped or hunted at the time when it can be acquired with the least effort. Success thus depends on preliminary knowledge of the location of sedentary animals, such as beaver or bear, and on the location of special habitats likely to be attractive to nomadic animals, such as moose, caribou or waterfowl. Even when there is an assured beaver and big game population, such a basic pattern leaves two critical periods of uncertainty. First, in the fall, before trapping begins to be productive, and second, in June, after the flocks of waterfowl break up. A mixture of various contingencies may be employed according to circumstances to deal with these periods. First, and most important, stored foods are used: frozen or dried game meat, frozen or smoked fish, or purchased foods. Second, fishing efforts may be intensified during these periods. Third, big game is often hunted in the fall. Moose, which is easily killed during the rut, and bear, which may be trapped or shot in open areas of recent burn, where berries are found, are the major species involved. We may thus distinguish between two major kinds of staple food consumed during the winter season; fresh game food of any kind, whether trapped, shot or snared, which can be located and killed with the least possible effort (or, as the Cree ideology states, game which 'gives itself to the hunter'); and second, stored food, which consists of commercial food and preserved game food.[2]

Apart from the production of subsistence food, the Cree are involved in a number of other subsistence production activities. Each household burns about 30 cu.ft. of firewood a day, which takes about four to five man hours a day to collect and prepare by hand methods using an axe and a saw. During the period when men are engaged in intensive trapping and hunting, this labour is contributed mainly by women. Women also collect boughs for flooring, and moss for various purposes. Men collect materials and manufacture snowshoe frames (each adult owns one or more pairs, which are replaced or overhauled annually), toboggans (the Jimiken group manufactured three in the 1969-70 season), snow shovels (the group produced two), and a variety of other products used in hunting, trapping and around the camp. Women assist the men in netting snowshoes, and manufacture tents, moccasins (several pairs per person per year), mitts, hats, hunting bags, ammunition pouches and gun cases. Both sexes spend a considerable time in repairing equipment. Some of these activities are performed during the summer, but the critical importance of many of the items that the Cree manufacture themselves is not that it saves them money, or that no commercial equivalent is available, but that it can be manufactured quickly, on the spot, when it is needed. This attitude is necessary, not only because hunting groups remain out of touch with commercial outlets for most of the year, but in the case of the heavier items it means that they need not be transported everywhere the group moves. It is more efficient to manufacture them on the spot out of materials acquired as part of the hunting and trapping activities. Such items may then be cached at a camp site when it is abandoned, and recovered later, possibly years later, when the group is again in the area.

3. *Market production and consumption*

The focal point of the Mistassini Cree hunter's cash economy is the account which each individual maintains with the Hudson's Bay Company. Although the major source of earned cash income is from beaver fur, which cannot by law be sold to the H.B.C., in fact in almost all cases the fur is handled by this trading company which acts as agent for the official purchaser, the Province of Quebec. Furthermore, cheques in payment for beaver fur usually pass into the trapper's H.B.C. account. Other furs are purchased directly by the H.B.C., in competition with other fur buyers. However, there has been no independent fur buyer resident in Mistassini since 1964, and the independent trader before then was a former H.B.C. employee, who did business on very much the same terms as the H.B.C., including extending credit for the purchase of supplies at the beginning of the season. This trader was connected through marriage to several Mistassini families, and would spend a part of the winter visiting hunting groups on their territories. Since the founding of the mining town of Chibougamau, fifty miles south of Mistassini Post, there has been some activity among part-time fur buyers, one of whom formed a partnership with a bush pilot in order to fly into the camps. As far as could be determined the enterprise has not done any business among the Mistassini since 1968. However, in the minds of some trappers it remains a theoretical alternative market to the H.B.C., to be discussed when they feel dissatisfied with treatment they receive. Similarly, there is an awareness of markets in the Lac St. Jean region, or in Montreal. But in practical terms at the time of field work the H.B.C. was without competition as the market for fur.

Table 10.   CASH INCOME, BY SOURCE, 1 SEPTEMBER 1969
TO 31 AUGUST 1970

Jimiken hunting groups (6 adults)			Nichicun local band (25 adults)		
Fur	$2,474.70	47.85%	Fur	$12,491	42.28%
Wages	800.00	15.47	Wages	4,000	13.54
Family			Family		
Allowance	432.00	8.35	Allowance	2,736	9.26
Pensions	—	8.35	Pensions	3,240	10.97
Welfare	1,465.00	28.33	Welfare	7,075	23.95
Total	5,171.70		Total	29,542	

Table 10 refers to the income of individuals who spend the whole winter trapping, so that any wages received are limited to those earned during the summer period of part of June, July, August and part of September. Wage rate for such short term work, such as guiding, mineral exploration work and construction labour, tends to be low, and the duration uncertain. Sometimes steady wage employment becomes available, particularly recently since Mistassini Post acquired road communication in 1970. Such jobs are in the mines and sawmills in the towns south of Mistassini, or in Mistassini Post itself. Some men, particularly those of the Chibougamau local band of the Mistassini, who have residences on the outskirts of an industrial town, may become involved in such work for varying lengths of time, but by many employment is used as part of an economic cycle which includes either part-time or an occasional full-time season of hunting and trapping (Tanner 1968; La Rusic 1970). The subject of the present study is a different group; the majority of trappers who are limited to summer employment; and in most cases little or none is available to them.

Welfare plays an important part in the cash income of trappers. Not only are they dependent on it for most of their livelihood during the summer, on the frequent occasions when wage work is unavailable, but welfare has also become an integral part of the fur trade system of debt exchange. The day has long passed when the H.B.C. would advance a trapper the full extent of his expected annual earnings from trapping. Such a system worked under full monopoly conditions when the post was isolated even from the short-term fluctuations of the world price of fur. Now the H.B.C. manager is able to advance no more than a half of the expected return, often less. Moreover, market fluctuations make it difficult to calculate expected earnings. However, in recent years any trapper in need who has received full welfare allowance during the previous summer is also able to receive three months of welfare payments during the eight months of the following winter, while trapping. The H.B.C. will increase his allowable credit limit by this amount in the fall. The system works to the benefit of both the trapper and the trader, and, in addition, by ensuring that a welfare recipient goes trapping, the Indians Affairs Branch saves approximately five months in welfare payments per year, per recipient.

A second way in which the Mistassini H.B.C. manager is able to maintain the debt system with limited credit is by camp visits made twice each winter by aircraft. By collecting fur in January the manager is able to place credits in the trapper's account more quickly, in the form of furs purchased (except for beaver), and to speed the process by which the payment for the beaver fur can be credited to the man's account. Thus more credit, mainly in the form of food purchases, can be extended in January, to be repaid with furs collected on the second visit in March, and so on.

The bulk of credit for trapping is required for outfitting in the fall, when the purchases of durable goods, such as traps, stoves, and tent canvas, are made. For many groups this credit includes the cost of an airplane charter each fall, which may cost up to a thousand dollars. Again, it is the H.B.C. manager who, in effect, has taken over the function of controlling this credit, even though it is the airline which carries the debt. The airline company will fly only those trappers who carry a letter of authorization signed by the H.B.C. manager, stating the trapper's destination. In effect, the manager guarantees the airline that the charter will be paid by the following summer out of the trapper's H.B.C. account.

4. *Integration of the economy*

The tendency, in most recent attempts to characterize the economy of

Canadian Indian hunting and trapping communities, has been to point to new factors which have changed conditions from an earlier situation. Thus, the influence of the fur trade has commonly been characterized as a replacement of the mode of production, from 'production for use' to 'production for exchange', a factor which has produced a new form of social organization (Hickerson 1967; Leacock 1954; Van Stone 1963). Other studies have pointed to the more recent influence of transfer payments, which have lessened dependence on hunting and trapping, and permitted larger residential groups (Dunning 1959).

Furthermore, in dealing with a community like Mistassini, it has become popular to make use of a 'gradual acculturation' model, such as that enunciated as a general theory by Murphy and Stewart (1956), or as applied to Mistassini by Leacock (1954:36) and by Pothier (1967). These approaches are used to explain a supposed tendency for fur trade communities to become progressively more involved in production for trade, and to finally adopt an individualistic pattern of trapping, in which women and children remain at the post, and men make quick tours of a trapline, carrying a minimum of supplies, staying overnight in cabins, and engaging in little or no subsistence activities, i.e. what Leacock calls 'the white trapper's system' (ibid.: 26).

A more accurate picture of the process may be obtained with the use of a 'transformational' model, by introducing a separate intermediary structure, into which the 'traditional' system has to be transformed before the capitalist mode of production is able to interact successfully with it.

The intermediary structure to which I refer has often been used, in the course of history, by market-oriented, colonizing societies to organize production by an indigenous group, not only of fur. In the Canadian fur trade, this intermediary structure, historically prior to capitalism, was a pre-capitalist enterprise of a type called 'putting out', in which a merchant periodically advanced supplies required by the producer, who later turned back a product to the same merchant. In Europe such systems were replaced by wage employment, but in the Canadian fur trade the 'putting out' method of organizing production, being less capital-intensive, and requiring no national government, was able to survive, given conditions of geographic isolation, and a reasonably stable resource base (Tanner 1966). The post-colonial organization, into which the production of fur has been incorporated, is that of the capitalist state, in which there is a national infrastructure of communication networks, schools, markets and social services such as welfare payments coordinated by a national government.

In Canada, with the expansion of this infrastructure into the hinterland, the government has attempted to treat trapping somewhat on the model of forestry, as joint enterprises of provincial governments and private individual harvesters. Ownership of both the resource and the land is claimed by the government, which licenses individual entrepreneurs to harvest them, and collects taxes on the production. Under such a system there is an open market for the product. In practice, however, the transformation from the first to the second form of organization has been piecemeal, and in many cases the introduction of the open market institutions of the national infrastructure has brought about the collapse of the earlier merchant-dominated system without providing the means for the trapping economy to continue. In other cases the resource base collapsed, effectively ending the fur trade, even prior to the direct incursion of the dominant society. In several cases it was the opening up of communication links which broke the trader's monopoly, putting an end to the debt system, thereby limiting trappers to short trips, and making trapping as a full-time occupation uneconomic. Finally, in a very few places, considerable wage employment opportunities opened for Indians with the opening of, for instance, a mine, and there was a rapid replacement of the economic base. Given all the effects of the full-scale expansion of the national infrastructure, only in special circumstances is trapping by communal Indian groups in a modern capitalist state possible; it continues only in those few areas where the 'putting out' system has managed to survive.

Mistassini has for some time experienced the effects of the ongoing transformation, due to changes in the conditions necessary for the 'putting out' system of trapping to continue. For many of the younger trappers the essential conditions of the 'putting out' system have already passed. These conditions include a limited need for items that must be purchased with cash, where such a need is known well in advance of the use of the items. 'Putting out' assumes that all fur buyers are at the same time suppliers of all the items that a trapper might wish to purchase. It also assumes a lack of economic alternatives. On the part of the trapper it assumes a complex series of bush skills learned during the formative years, and access to a number of basic capital items, the rights to which may be inherited. Two recent factors, the availability of communications facilities in general which make possible interaction with the dominant society, and formal education in particular, have altered many of the above conditions for some young Cree people. Access to alternative markets for both labour and for supplies have made the maintenance of the credit relationship with the H.B.C. impossible. The attendance at school during most of the formative years has resulted in a lack in the essentials of a trapper's education. However, since not all young Mistassini people have abandoned the 'putting out' system of trapping, it is clear that the primary cause for the shift in young people away from this economy depends on ideological and not material conditions. Education and communications have given rise to possibilities for the development of other goals and other needs, needs which cannot be satisfied within the 'putting out' system.

The social and economic formation of trapping is not a question of the needs of individuals, but of the operation of a mode of production, one with its own ideology, which is articulated within a specific social structure. The Mistassini social institution which is of key significance in its merchant-dominated system of production of fur is the hunting group. The leadership of these hunting groups remains in the hands of the monolingual older individuals, for whom the only economic alternative to full-time trapping is full-time welfare. Although, as Pothier reports, there is an expressed preference for paid employment over trapping (1967:118), the hard reality of the situation is that for older people there are no employment opportunities, and for the younger educated people the few jobs are largely limited to the summer, and are often located far from the community.

There are other special conditions which have favoured the continuity and strength of the monopoly fur trade system at Mistassini. Historically, its position near the height of land between James Bay and the St. Lawrence, and thus on the margins of the spheres of influence of two trade empires, meant that it remained isolated, and even after a permanent post was established no missionaries or other contact agents were sent there until well into the present century. Since the Second World War, in a period when trapping has generally received little encouragement from the Hudson's Bay Company, and with declining fur prices and the introduction of welfare payments, the production of fur at Mistassini has nevertheless thrived, to a large extent due to the maintenance or modernization of specialized services for trappers within the Hudson's Bay Company 'putting out' system, and to the sensitive introduction and administration of provincial animal conservation regulations by a former freetrader, now employed by the provincial government's fur service, and by the H.B.C. manager. Both are long-term residents, well integrated into the community, fluent speakers of the native language, and with considerable experience of hunting group life. A further factor, additional to those mentioned by Pothier (1967:117-19), has been the lessening of trapping activities by neighbouring bands, particularly to the east, which has meant that the increasing trapping pressure which has accompanied the demographic increase since 1920 has been handled by territorial expansion, and has not brought about a collapse of the resource base. No serious shortage of resources has been experienced in those years since welfare has been made a viable economic alternative to trapping.

The isolated hunting group, as the unit of production of a raw commodity for the world market, fur, remains dependent on the 'putting out' system of organization of production, even while at the same time at the summer settlement and in the White communities beyond there are all the institutional structures for modern industrial organization of production. The 'putting out' system can in fact be understood as a transformation of the traditional system of Indian gift exchange, and it is therefore easy to understand why in the early days of the fur trade transactions with Indians frequently followed an established ceremonial pattern. The trader made a gift in goods; the Indian repaid it in furs, and the transition to capitalism is evident only in the final disposal of the furs, as well as in the production of the goods given to the Indians.

Transformation from the 'putting out' system to the full capitalist system tends, for reasons already stated, to follow the development of communication networks, competitive markets, schools, missions and social services.

A 'transformational' model of social change can be used to explain what happens following contact between an aboriginal population and a more powerful group of newcomers, and such a model is to be contrasted to a conventional 'acculturation' approach to the same situation. In the acculturation approach aboriginal traits and cultural patterns are seen as being gradually replaced by new ones introduced from the dominant society over an extended period of time. The transformational approach analyses the post-contact stage or stages as distinct from either that of the aboriginal society or of the dominant group. The post-contact society has a mode of production distinct from the aboriginal society due to technological innovations and trade acquisitions, but it is a mode of production that is also distinct from that of the dominant society. The Mistassini band has such a non-aboriginal, non-capitalist mode of production based on the organization of production by hunting groups linked through a 'putting out' trade relationship with the dominant society. The mode of production of the dominant society can be used to represent the final stage of a transformational model. The model does not predict that change from the aboriginal to the post-contact stage, or change from the post-contact to the dominant group stage must always occur. We can, however, specify, as we did above, under what conditions such transformations are likely. In Mistassini at the time of research, some 25 per cent of the Indian population had clearly made the transition from the second to the third stage, but the other 75 per cent were hunters and trappers whose mode of production and cognitive system conformed to the second stage. It is their cognitive system with which we are concerned in this study.

This continuation of a pre-capitalist system of production explains why, after nearly 400 years of involvement in the fur trade, the Mistassini hunting groups have yet to reach the situation which would be expected, using Murphy and Steward's model of acculturation due to the fur trade. In this regard, let us compare some of the points made in Leacock's well-known study of the Mistassini situation. She states that the shift from game food to store food made the individual family economically self-sufficient (Leacock 1954:7). This is a theoretical possibility but a rare occurrence today among the Mistassini. In 1969-70 the only Nichicun hunting group with less than two commensal units consisted of a married man without his wife (who was ill) who had a single man as his only companion. Perhaps significantly, the married man was pointed out to me with approval by the H.B.C. manager as an unusual type of trapper, meaning that he was extremely industrious. Most of the other small groups consisted of families living close to Mistassini Post, who had a camp near the road, and who could easily return to Mistassini Post in an emergency. Many of these single family camps were not seriously engaged in hunting or trapping, but were living to a large extent from cash income of various kinds. A typical example would be an elderly couple, both with pensions, and in some such cases they were also looking after several children, and receiving Family Allowance cheques. For those seriously involved in hunting and trapping almost no Mistassini family would care to go into the bush without at least one other family. Joining a hunting group carries with it the obligation to share game, and also to share equipment and supplies, with those other members in need. In point of fact then, economic self-sufficiency of the individual is not the observed pattern among Mistassini hunter/trappers.

At the same time, Leacock contends, as ties within the hunting group based on sharing are weakened and replaced by ties of exchange with the trader, 'the individual's objective relation to other band [i.e. hunting group] members changed from the co-operative to the competitive' (ibid.). Such competitiveness over fur is not now in evidence at Mistassini, and would depend, if it did appear, on a situation of a shortage of land, or of fur-bearers. We cannot rule out the possibility of the existence of competition prior to the introduction of beaver quotas, but we must also take into account such current counter evidence as (*a*) the extending of trapping rights to guests, even to non-kin, (*b*) the giving of gifts of parts of quotas from one hunter to another, and (*c*) the giving of gifts of furs, which are made primarily along kinship lines, but also to non-kin persons such as to the hunting group leader, to the band chief, and to the Church.[3] At the same time as we may note a lack of competitiveness in fur trapping, it is evident from the Mistassini material that competitiveness is far from being non-existent in the subsistence sector of the economy. A hunter is expected not to brag about the amount of game killed, or about what he considers his high contribution to the group food supply, although some young hunters are unable to conceal their pride, and may insist on the privilege of being allowed to make a kill during a group hunt. For others there are many unspoken, but eloquent, forms of social recognition for the hunter to compete for. Not the least of these is leadership.[4]

Underlying Leacock's characterization of the economy of fur trade
communities is, as we have said, the notion that they are based on
production for exchange, rather than production for use. It is clear
that Leacock considers the significant change to production for
'exchange-value' to have occurred for Indian trappers: 'The more furs
one collects, the more material comforts one can obtain. In contrast to
the aboriginal situation, material needs become theoretically limitless'
(1954:7). While this may correctly characterize the kind of economy
which the H.B.C. would like to encourage, it is not the observed
pattern. Rather, under the debt system, production is geared towards
only filling specific needs known in advance. The goods have in fact
for the most part been already received before the productive process
begins. An ex-H.B.C. fur trader, J.W. Anderson, has described the
use by the Mistassini of a technique designed specifically to gear
production of furs to predetermined needs.

Writing of Mistassini in the period 1913-18, Anderson recalls that
each trapper, before he left the post in the fall, received a statement of
account, consisting of rows of crosses and strokes, representing tens
and units of dollars of credit. He also received a firm quotation of the
value of each kind of fur to be brought in the following summer. As
the Indians trapped during the winter they marked off their remaining debt. Due to this system, in some successful years the Indians
would stop trapping long before the winter was over (Anderson J.W.
1961:105-8). While it must be recognized that in the form described such a practice is no longer possible, because of fur price
fluctuations during the course of the winter, the purpose of the
practice accords with some of my own observations. I did observe the
consultation of H.B.C. receipts during the winter, particularly the one
with the most recent data, which contains not only the amount of a
purchase, but also the overall state of the account. Accounts are also
brought up to date each time the trader makes his winter visits,
although he can only give an estimate of the value of the beaver fur
which he collects. Furthermore, living in the bush by choice for most
of the year is incompatible with an orientation towards exchange
value, since the ability to spend is severely limited.

How, then, do we best characterize the modes of production of the
Mistassini? First of all we must take into account that the *economy of
the settlement* is for the majority of the community only viable for
part of the year. This settlement economy consists, for the small
minority, in full-time employment as wage-earners. At the time of
most of my field work, there were also two small independent Indian
entrepreneurs. For the remainder of the population, production while
in the settlement consists of a cycle of mixed casual employment and
welfare. The other option, viable only for those with skills, and with a
satisfactory credit relationship with the Hudson's Bay Company, is
outside the settlement: the *economy of hunting and trapping*. Of the

two latter activities, hunting generally makes a larger contribution, even though less time may be involved. For example, Salisbury has shown that by assigning to subsistence food a value, based on Montreal prices, of $1.50 a pound, the whole East Cree area has a $3,864,300 per annum meat industry, supplemented by $300,000 per annum worth of fur production (1972a:3-9g). What, then, are the social relations central to the hunting compared to those of trapping? Is it correct to contrast these as two modes of production?

The early history of the fur trade is full of references to the struggle between the demands of the trader for the Indians to spend more time trapping, and their need for hunting (for a Nichicun example, see Davies 1963:68). These struggles were not within the Indian groups, but outside attempts to alter economic behaviour. However, soon after the introduction of the fur trade the procuring of subsistence and the procuring of furs began to be organized by the Mistassini within a single set of social relations, and for the most part this situation has continued until the present. Some meat production, such as for large game and waterfowl, requires coordinated group action, but in the same way that such group action is also required for moving camp, which must be accomplished when the supply of beaver available within reasonable distance of the camp for trapping purposes is exhausted. While the group is sometimes actively engaged in communal production and at other times in commensal family production, the organization of these differing requirements is handled by setting aside different times in the season for communal group and individual family activities. If we seek to apply to this situation the notion of two modes of production it would introduce an overemphasized and distorted distinction between a domestic and a group economy. In my view, it is more fruitful to conceive of one system of production, with all production organized within the hunting group.

Within this single system a balance has to be found between many conflicting forces, of which the conflict between the demands of hunting and trapping (in as far as such a conflict can be seen to occur) is but one. Two more of these conflicts involve the relationship between Indian hunters and the Hudson's Bay Company, represented by the manager (*ucimaaw*, 'boss'), and between the Indians and the Provincial Game Department, represented by its administrator (*amiskw ucimaaw*, 'beaver boss'). Furthermore, the hunting group, through its leader (also called *ucimaaw*), is engaged in indirect exchange of hunting privileges with other groups, particularly neighbouring ones, and the families within the group engage in generalized exchange, using subsistence products, with relatives residing at Mistassini Post. In each case these relationships can be a source of conflict, when one side wishes to have its opinion prevail over the other. Thus the fact that conflict may at times exist between the requirements of hunting and those of trapping need not lead us to the conclusion that these constitute separate modes of production. It is more significant to note that these two processes of production are organized within the same social framework by means of established social relations (1) between the hunting group members, (2) between the hunting group leaders, and (3) between the hunting group and the outside through the 'putting out' relationship with the Hudson's Bay Company. Hunting and trapping are thus best seen as constituting a single mode of production.

Furthermore, hunting and trapping ought not to be seen as constituting two distinct modes of production on the basis that the latter involves individual labour, whilst the former involves communal labour. While this distinction between hunting and trapping does apply to some extent, in my view it is more appropriate to recognize that both activities involve both individual and communal forms of action. Communal work, like communal sharing, does not result in undifferentiated roles; the tasks performed by each man reflects his function and his role in the group, just as do the activities which make up a solitary task. For example, in a communal hunt each man butchers first the animals he has killed, unless he is given the whole carcass of a newly-killed animal. After finishing these he will assist others; but where several men butcher a carcass together certain tasks, like the severing of the head of a large animal with an axe blow, must be performed by the man who owns the animal. At the same time, tasks performed by solitary individuals also involve participation in similar social relations. We will see in Chapter 6 that for a trapper working alone there is a quasi-ritual procedure by which he informs the hunting group leader that he has found a new beaver house. The rite symbolizes that the leader gives his formal permission for the lodge to be trapped, and this gives recognition to one of the underlying social relations involved in trapping.

Furthermore, by no means all trapping involves individual tasks, nor is all hunting communal. Two men will sometimes trap together, particularly when they must travel some distance from the main camp when they share a trapping camp for several nights. The initial survey which is made of a new area soon after the group first moves there, made for the purpose of assessing the trapping potential, is often undertaken by a group of men together. As this group comes across a place suitable for setting a trap, the men may take turns consecutively to set their own traps. At the same time some subsistence hunting, particularly of small game, is done by individuals. Most female productive tasks are done in the company of other women, but with little cooperative labour. Most cooperative labour involves women of the same commensal family, for subsistence activities like collecting firewood, or for market production, like the preparation of pelts and handicrafts made for sale. Preparation of large hides involves some tasks in which several women as well as men work together. Women also work with men in the tasks involved in moving the camp. In summary, then, it would be inaccurate to label either hunting or trapping entirely individualistic or entirely communal activities.

There is, however, a distinction in the patterns of production through the winter. Beaver and other fur trapping is the basic day-to-day activity, one which involves a temporarily fixed group location, usually by means of one main camp with men leaving the camp singly or in pairs. Opposed to this are all other activities, not only hunting, in which the whole group takes part together in the one activity. Among such communal activities, the moving of camp by the group is probably of equal importance to group hunting.

I have, furthermore, been unable to confirm that the Cree themselves cognitively lay any stress on the hunting/trapping distinction. Cree speech tends to avoid mention of the particular species which a hunter or trapper is after, so that both hunting and trapping are covered by the same general terms: either *natwaawhuw* or *maaciiw*. The first term may be directly translated as 'he sets out to ... [understood] do something', and is the most common way of referring to anything contained in the English category 'hunting and trapping'. However, it does not connote the idea of searching. The term *maaciiw* also means 'he goes away', but implies some purpose, so that context will indicate when hunting or trapping is inferred. Both the above terms suggest that the central explicit notion in hunting and trapping productivity is a journey which begins at the camp and goes away somewhere, where the game is obtained. The notion of hunting and trapping as a journey 'outside' the camp will be seen in the Chapter 5 and elsewhere to have basic symbolic significance.

In addition to the above terms that cover the whole semantic range covered by the two English terms 'hunting' and 'trapping', the other most commonly used terms employed by the Cree to refer to these activities are *naante maat* 'he looks for animal tracks', and *naaci wanhiicew* 'he checks his traps'. In neither of these cases is it implied by the speaker whether the animals being tracked or being trapped are to be killed for meat or for fur. Of course, no such distinction is implied by the equivalent English phrases by which we translate these terms. However, if it is held that Cree harvesting activities are of two radically separate and distinct types and that one kind of activity conflicts with the other, then one might expect that the Cree would pay some attention to this distinction in the terms used when discussing these activities. This, however, does not happen. For example, while *naaci wanhiicew* does connote that the animal is being trapped for its fur, the term used is formed by combining the word for 'trap' with the pre-verb *naahci*, 'to go and fetch from'. This same pre-verb is, in combination with various other terms, commonly used to refer to various subsistence activities, such as checking snares for hares, checking nets for fish or fetching firewood. In other words, hunting and trapping are not sufficiently distinguished by the Cree to have an exclusive vocabulary associated with each of them.

A similar lack of the hunting-trapping distinction is found in the context of the semantic classification of animals. Although there are several overlapping systems of categorization (see Bouchard and Mailhot 1973), these systems do not include the distinction between those animals hunted for subsistence purposes and those killed for their fur. Such a negative demonstration, of course, proves very little. However, when we look at the most common term used to refer to an animal pelt we find no distinction is made between hides that are for trade purposes and those that are for subsistence use. There are several terms which denote only fur intended for trade, but these terms are less commonly encountered, and have ironical connotations when used to refer to fur; their use is thus restricted to joking situations. One such term is *suuliiyaaw*, which has the principal meaning of 'money' (from 'shilling'), while the other is *upiiwii*, normally meaning 'his body hair'. The second term also often connotes female pubic hair, and its use for animal fur is usually restricted to joking occasions, when a number of humorous parallels between sexual conquest and hunting are used in verbal play. This humorous relationship between sexual activity and hunting applies to *both* trapping and subsistence hunting activities.

In summary, we may say that among the Mistassini who hunt and trap using the multi-family, winter-long hunting group, no clear separation is made between trapping production and hunting production, or between 'production for use' and 'production for exchange'. The Mistassini commensal unit is subordinate in its productive activities to the limitations imposed on it by the Hudson's Bay Company, and by the Provincial Game Department. It is also subject to the limitations imposed on it by membership in a particular hunting group. Both the Hudson's Bay Company and the Provincial Game Department are limited in the extent of the control they can exercise over an individual family, where this control conflicts with the interests of the group; in fact, both these agencies use the hunting group as a social institution for their own purposes. The Hudson's Bay Company accepts that hunting groups are necessary for winter-long residence in the bush; for the Game Department, the land associated with the hunting group is a convenient resource management area, and the group leader (sometimes referred to by them as the 'tally-man') is a convenient agent for use in this management scheme. Thus the hunting group is basic to both the individual fur producers interests and to those of the external agencies who control certain key aspects of the group's external economic relations.

4
The Organization of Social Space

1. *Nomadism and the standardization of camp space*

The hunting and trapping system of production of the Mistassini Indians depends on a pattern of frequent residential change, a limited form of nomadism. Quite early in my fieldwork I got the strong impression that despite frequent changes of dwellings and of localities, the Cree foster the illusion that their place of residence never changes. Whether it was a small oblong wall tent, a large dome tent, a wooden framed, canvas-covered tent or a log cabin, the standardized internal arrangement is such that the dwelling seems to always occupy the same space. It was much later, when I was told the following myth, that I discovered that the Cree are also aware of this. This myth is one of a cycle, all involving a character called Pukat Skwes, a woman who performs various marvels around the camp.

Pukat Skwes was with a group that was hunting; each time they moved camp she told the others to set out first. They were later surprised to find that she always reached the new campsite first, and already had the tent erected. A boy noticed that the poles of the tent were always the same ones [fresh tent poles are normally cut at each new camp location]. The group decided to try and find out how Pukat Skwes managed to overtake them; next time they moved camp, they pretended to start out, but doubled back and hid. They saw Pukat Skwes start to sing, and the tent began to fly through the air to the new camp. Because they were watching, however, she was unable to complete the magic, which she was never able to do again. Because of this, children are now forbidden to count the poles in a tent, and people say that no matter where they move their camp to, they are always really staying in the same place. [Told by Bally Husky.]

The frequent movements which the Mistassini pattern of hunting requires result from the fact that after some time many of the resources within one or two days travel of the camp are exhausted. This applies particularly to the relatively sedentary game animals inhabiting the area, such as beaver, moose, bear, muskrat, porcupine, hare and some species of fish. Although the Mistassini do also depend on a number of more migratory animals, these species are not normally a dependable resource, except for cases such as waterfowl, which are limited to short seasons. With each movement new dwellings are constructed for the entire group. Only the canvas covering is carried from one camp to the next; the frame is newly constructed each time.

It often happens that after a number of years a group will make camp in an area occupied previously, and the possibility arises that the old tent frames could be reused. The reuse of old camp sites seems, however, to occur most often during the summer months, at the summer settlement and at camps on portage trails. The Nichicun local band have several permanent tent frames at the locality where they gather each spring and fall, on Lake Nichicun. But between freeze-up and break-up there is some avoidance of old campsites, an avoidance which can at least partially be attributed to material factors.

The system of production used by Mistassini hunters and trappers involves dealing with their land as a number of regions, each of which can be exploited from a camp located somewhere near its centre. This I will call the residence-centred harvest zone. By the time a main camp is moved to a new zone, not only have the animal resources of the whole of the previously-used zone been reduced, but there has often been a severe reduction of those resources close to the camp, i.e. the resources which are exploited by women, children and old people. This makes it necessary for these people who exploit the resources near the camp to search further and further afield. These close-in resources include primarily dead trees, used for firewood, and green boughs suitable for flooring material. They also include moss, which is used for diaper material and dwelling insulation, and small game animals such as hares, ptarmigan and spruce grouse. Under normal circumstances the larger harvest zone will regain its animal population level and its potential for hunting and trapping within several years; for example, at Nichicun, where recovery is slower than further south, it is common for a harvest zone to be left for from five to ten years before a group makes use of it again. But the effects of the group's habitation on the immediate area around the campsite may last longer, particularly in the case of a large group which remains in the same camp for several months. After many years, when the area around an old winter campsite is well on its way to returning to the same condition as the rest of the forest, there may be some reluctance to reoccupy the site. The place will be visited, and material may be taken, but a new campsite, perhaps on the same lake, is usually chosen some distance from the old one.

In explaining this reluctance, the feeling is expressed by some Mistassini that when the group is hunting it is proper for them to establish each time a fresh campsite on new ground, ground which is clean (*peycuu*). This term signifies that the place is free from garbage, and clean in the sense that it is not offensive to the spirits of game animals and to entities who aid in hunting. When the group abandons a campsite they must spend some time cleaning up, in order to avoid offence to the spirits, but this mainly involves seeing that the bones of game animals are properly disposed of. If the campsite is not left in a proper condition it is thought that the animals will not return to the area. A Rupert House man explained the same idea to me in a different way. He said that a short time after a group leaves a place where they have camped the 'spirit' (*aataacaakw*) of the hunting group leader (*nucimaawinaan*) flies over the site. If he finds everything left as it should be he is pleased, and gives the group good luck in their future hunting. The hunting group leader's spirit cares about the condition of the land, and he can send the animals away if the land is not looked after. Along the same line of reasoning, the group may leave decorations behind at an old campsite. I have seen examples where the bones which were displayed in a tree were decorated with paint or ribbons, and antlers also displayed and decorated with ribbons. In the past a special tree at a major hunting campsite was decorated and known as a *mistikukaan*. The 'cleaning up' of an abandoned camp does not, therefore, consist in attempting to return the site to its original condition, but in counteracting the effects of human habitation, by treating the locality to some extent as a sacred place.

As a result of the winter nomadic pattern, with the avoidance of particular residence-centred harvest zones for a number of years, a particular family, or a group of families, is continually establishing new camps, in new locations, each of which is surrounded by a somewhat different set of landscape features from the others, and thus bears a different relationship to the various resources and travel routes of the region. But in contrast to this variety in the relations between the camp and these *external* features — a contrast which is to some extent elaborated in Cree culture, for example by the complex descriptive terms given to geographic features (see Denny and Mailhot 1976) — the relations between the *internal* features of the camp, and in particular the internal organization of the dwelling, is remarkably uniform.

In the following sections we will discuss the basic principles of this uniform organization of social space, and go on in Chapter 5 to show the symbolic aspect of spatial ideas. We will examine how this organization makes the camp, wherever it might be moved to, a standard central reference point within the hunter's concept of geographic space, as the myth I have just quoted suggests.

2. The organization of domestic space

The Cree family is the social unit which joins together with other such units to make up the hunting group. It is the unit which lives and eats together (thus often referred to as the commensal group), and is a nuclear family in form. Other boreal forest Algonkians have commensal groups larger than the nuclear family (e.g. Dunning 1959:63-4), but among the contemporary Mistassini this group, while it may include unmarried or widowed relatives who have attached themselves to the nuclear core, never contains more than one married couple.

During the winter hunting and trapping season each commensal family will, at times, occupy its own separate dwelling, usually some kind of a tent, alongside the tents of the other families, so as to form one camp. At other times of the year, most often during the period between freeze-up and mid- or late winter, the families of the hunting group occupy together a single dwelling, usually a communal lodge. Despite this switch to communal living, the commensal family organizes its domestic space in the same standardized form, as when it is occupying its own tent, although the form of each family's space is slightly transformed to adjust to the presence of the others. Also, the dwelling space of a commensal family may be round, oval or oblong in shape in different circumstances, depending on the type of physical structure used. Whatever is the case, there is a fire near the centre, a door opening on one side of the fire, and a living area on the opposite side of the fire to the door. In Fig. 3 a hatched line is used to indicate a division between the area around the stove, including the doorway, and the rest of the dwelling space which is at the rear. The basis of this

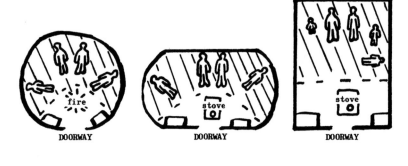

= sleeping area

Fig. 3. Basic layout of single-family dwellings

distinction is that the space at the rear is where people actually live; each person in the family has his or her own private place there. The area around the stove and the entrance is used by all the family. When any resident is inside the dwelling, whether he is working, eating, relaxing or sleeping, he always occupies roughly the same place at the rear portion of the dwelling. At night people sleep with their heads against the rear wall, and their feet towards the stove. During the day bedding is hung to air outside, or in a separate storage tent, or is rolled up at the rear of each sleeping place, and this leaves open the floor area, covered with spruce boughs, on which people sit. At meal times people move together slightly, in a semi-circle around the food, which is placed on a cloth laid out on the floor, but each retains his position relative to the others. Each adult keeps his or her own few items of personal property either hanging on the wall next to where his or her head rests at night, or in a container such as a box along the same portion of wall. If we refer to the area of the doorway and the stove as the 'front' of the dwelling space, we may state that there is a progression from front to rear in terms of a change from communally-used space to individually-used space.

In the single family tent, when people are occupying the living area, they normally face towards both the stove and the doorway. In the communal lodge each family has its own stove and these are placed in the centre of the building, and each family space is oriented to the stoves, but not to the doorway. However, the spatial distinction, which in the single-family dwelling exists between front and rear, is seen here as being between centre and periphery, and exists between the area used communally, and the private spaces used by each of the individual co-residents (see Fig. 4).

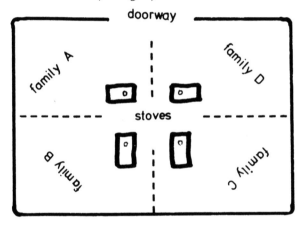

Fig. 4. Basic layout of the multi-family dwelling

Within the space occupied by the whole commensal family, both in the case of the single-family tent, and in the communal lodge, there is a second all-important division of space, that between area of the males and of the females. In this case we can speak of a sharp dividing line, which runs from the front to the rear of the dwelling space. All the males of the family, with the possible exception of small infants, remain on the male side, and women stay on the female side. In a demographically normal family this results in the division of space into two halves, or sides (see Fig. 5). The food supply, usually kept on shelves, is always located on the same side as the women, while those hunting and trapping supplies which are kept inside the tent (e.g. axes, fishing lines, and articles in the process of construction, like

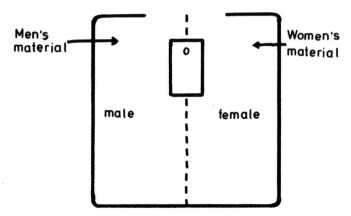

Fig. 5. Male and female sides

snowshoe frames, snow shovels and toboggans) are located on the same side as the men. The same division between male and female sides and materials also applies to the commensal families' living space, within the communal lodge.

This division between male and female sides not only results in men seldom entering the space of the women, and vice versa; it also provides a graphic demonstration that there exists a cognitive ordering of household articles in terms of the categories of male and female. We have seen the spatial division of the materials associated with the productive activities of each sex. One may also speak of game animals, or certain parts of animals, as being within the male or the female domain, according to where they are normally stored. For example, all meat of animals the size of a beaver and smaller are stored on the female section, but the meat of larger animals, i.e. moose, caribou and bear, are stored on the male side. After a meal has been eaten all bones are carefully sorted by the women, and most are stored on the women's side until they are taken outside for proper disposal. However, certain bones are stored by the men, for example, the skulls (only men are allowed to eat meat from the head). The scapulars of some animals, which are used for divination, may be stored by the women on their side prior to the divination performance, after which they are kept by the men. Women keep the castors (beaver scent glands, which are used as bait in trapping or sold to the H.B.C.) and the bones of embryo animals. In most groups the women also keep the group's calendar, on which they keep track of the days. The women are in charge of the food store, which is kept either on a cache rack outside, or on their side of the dwelling. Men both manufacture and store on their own side two special beverages which may be made from time to time: bone soup (*muuskamii*) and raisin beer (*suumins aapuu*). The bone soup is made in a large pot, and when it is drunk it is passed around the dwelling for everyone in turn, usually carried by a child. The men, starting with the most senior, must be offered a drink before a woman may have any. In general, with all important objects, one of the sexes has a clear priority over its use and storage, although all may have access to it. The item which is the exception to this principle is the fire. It is tended by both sexes; the women gather most of the wood, although the men also assist, while the men set the stove in place in the new camp, and usually prepare the kindling for lighting it each morning.

Each of the two sides of the commensal family dwelling space has a parallel and standardized spatial order (see Fig. 6), such that the male side is in exact reverse correspondence to the female side. The married persons' places are together in the centre of the space, and out from this central area, on either side of the couple, dependents of the same sex have their places, in order of increasing age. In most commensal families these dependents are the children of the married couple,

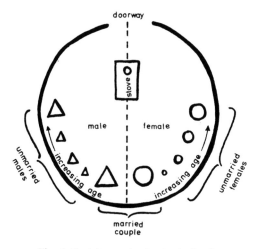

Fig. 6. Social space in the single-family
dwelling

although in many cases, particularly with old couples, there may be adopted children, or children who are being looked after on a temporary basis. In addition, the family may include single adult dependents, such as a widowed parent of either the husband or the wife. This person is located on the far end of the line of unmarried children of the same sex. As a result of this arrangement, the youngest children are often located between the same-sex parent and an older relative such as a same-sex sibling, or a senior generation relative of the same sex. Furthermore, it can be seen that when a senior generation person loses his or her spouse they can no longer have their own commensal group, and become (both spatially and sociologically) reintegrated into another family, in the position of the oldest unmarried person of their sex. The oldest unmarried female, if over the age of about twelve years, usually takes charge of the cooking, while the married woman of such a family is in charge of preparing the animal skins. Because of the possible addition of widows to the family, the senior unmarried woman may be a daughter or granddaughter of the married woman, or she may be a widowed mother or mother-in-law.

A similar situation also develops on the male side, so that young boys are 'sandwiched' between their father and the family's oldest unmarried male, who may be a brother or a grandfather. This oldest person, whether male or female, increasingly becomes independent of the same-sex parent, although earlier in life they would have been very close. In the case of the oldest daughter, she gains increasing control over one part of the household space, what we may call the 'kitchen', after her mother has taught her all other aspects of women's work. Increasingly, she takes charge of one end of a protective 'enclosure', the other end being the mother, for the younger sisters. On the male side, the oldest son, after about age 14, increasingly establishes himself as a hunter and trapper independently from his father, and begins to share with the father the care of his younger brothers. As the eldest son or daughter marries and leaves the commensal family group, the next oldest sibling of the same sex takes over this function.

The foregoing description of the spatial arrangements of the family is not just an abstract ideal, but is to a very great extent realized in day-to-day life. Because of the limited space inside the dwelling, it means that people do not move about while they are inside the dwelling, except when they enter or leave. Thus the existence of male and female 'sides' does not in effect act as a restriction upon movement, nor is it enunciated as an explicit rule of avoidance. I once observed a young man who, while teasing his sisters, moved over to the female side of the tent on the pretence of getting some water. Merely by remaining there, doing nothing, he managed to unnerve them completely. Ordinarily, each person remains in his or her own place, either squatting with their legs tucked under, or lying down, and if they require anything which is not in their immediate reach there is always somebody near who will pass it to them. Some work which takes up a lot of room is performed inside during bad weather, such as beaming moose or caribou hides to remove the hair, making toboggans or sleds, 'pulling' caribou or moose hides during the tanning process, or smoking hides. In these cases the other people present make room for the person doing the work, but each retains his or her position relative to the others.

As we have pointed out, the idea of the existence of an individual's own personal space becomes most marked at the rear wall of the

Plate 7. Interior of a communal lodge, looking at the female side of the living space of one family.

family space, as is illustrated by the articles of a personal nature which are stored there. These articles include the bibles, kept by most adults in a decorated moose hide or cloth bag, and normally hanging on the wall, a woman's sewing supplies, smoking supplies, and various personal sacred objects, such as the *niimaapaan* (ceremonial game-carrying string), divination bones and the sticks taken from beaver houses, showing the teeth marks.[1]

The spatial organization of the dwelling space used by the commensal family provides us with a model of the social organization of the family. For example, the spatial model shows a definite and complete separation between the sexes, a separation which increases with age, except at the point of a marriage bond. Moreover, this separation may be breached for small children, but becomes institutionalized with the approach of sexual maturity. Another example where the spatial order in the dwelling is replicated by a recognized social relationship is in the relations of relative age. On the spatial level, we notice within the dwelling the same-sex siblings are positioned relative to each other in an age hierarchy. It is also the case that relative age is a common feature signalled by many Cree kin terms, and in particular by separate terms which are used for older and younger siblings of the same sex as the speaker.

In summary, Fig. 7 indicates how space inside the dwelling is organized in terms of basic dimensions of nuclear family social relations.

COMMUNAL

SENIOR   SENIOR

MALE   SINGLE   MARRIED   SINGLE   FEMALE

JUNIOR   JUNIOR

PERSONAL

Fig. 7. Spatial contrasts which reflect social contrasts

3. *The organization of camp space*

We have just seen that the living space occupied by any commensal family while in a hunting camp is organized, in a more or less standardized way, so as to conform to some of the principal structural elements on which the family is organized. In a similar way, certain spatial relationships between the commensal families which make up the hunting group, with more or less standardization, also give an indication of the organization of social relations *between* the various families of the group. This is so even though there are two apparently quite different forms of spatial organization of camps, the first in which each commensal family occupies its own tent, the second when the whole group lives together in a communal lodge. In this section I wish to indicate the extent to which the change from individual tents to the communal lodge is a relatively simple structural transformation, which leaves the significant spatial relationships between the families unchanged, and the extent to which those relationships which do undergo a change can be seen as indicating concomitant changes in relationships between the component families which occur at the time of these shifts in living arrangements.

When the commensal groups which constitute a hunting group are each living in a separate tent it can be said that the camp structure is a topological transformation of the structure of the communal lodge camp, in the sense that the circle arrangement of the lodge is transformed into a straight line arrangement (see Fig. 8).

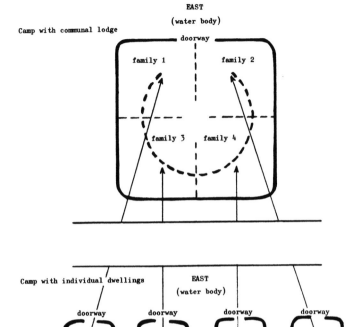

Fig. 8. Spatial transformation in the camp

If we take these two variations as ideal types, then it may be said that the second is typical of the summer camp, in which case orientation of the door is primarily determined by the water, which is usually nearby, while the other is typical of the winter camp, in which case the place where the sun rises is of more importance in the orientation of the door, if this conflicts with the direction of water. Thus when individual family dwellings are used in the winter the tents are often grouped together with their doorways very slightly turned inwards to each other, to form a slightly curved line arrangement, while in summer the line is either quite straight, or the tents follow the irregular line of the shore of the adjacent water body.

In Fig. 8, the numbers given to the four families are intended to indicate the typical order, in terms of increasing status of the families, with 1 marking the highest status position. This order is, however, a still tentative proposal, based on inadequate data, and was not confirmed by informants, who insisted that the order is up to individual choice. This, of course, does not rule out the possibility that the locations at either end of the line of tents, or on either side of the doorway of the communal lodge, still tend to be selected by preference by the hunting group leader, and by the family of the next most important man in the group, as my limited data suggest. During the fall, while the group is travelling to the location of the winter camp, there seems to be more variation in the order between the tents of the various families, whereas later the order of the first winter camp establishes the order which will be adhered to for all subsequent camps established by that group for the rest of the winter.

When considering the spatial arrangements of different family units within the communal lodge two connected points must be considered. The first of these, a subject already mentioned, is the position taken by each family within the communal lodge. This question is affected not only by the relative status of families, but also by an explicit rule that adjacent families must not have members of the opposite sex immediately next to one another. Furthermore, the predominant pattern is for those family units located on either side of the doorway to have their female sides on the same side as the door. The combination of these latter two rules produces, at least for groups with an even number of family units, a spatial organization as illustrated in Fig. 9. The family unit to the left of the door (as one enters) has its female side to its left, and its male side to its right, while with the family unit next to it this order is reversed, and so on around the perimeter of the dwelling.

The above rules governing the organization of communal dwelling space have their effect on the position which a particular family will take within the communal lodge. Informants differed as to the principles they used in deciding where any particular family would be

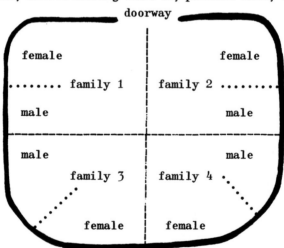

Fig. 9. Organization of sexes within the multi-family
dwelling (even numbers)

Plate 8. Winter hunting camp. Note the large supply of firewood, and the beaver pelt on a stretcher.

located. Some informants spoke of the idea that the group leader first established his preferred place, and the other families then arranged themselves in a circle around the central fires to the right of the leader's family in descending order of status (which would often mean in the descending order of age of the married men of the family). The example was given to me of a leader who lived with his married sons. The sons would be arranged to the father's right in decreasing order of age. This model was also used by a Fort George informant, although he spoke of the leader's family as always occupying the position to the immediate right as one enters the dwelling. Another Fort George man said that the leader's family took the position to the immediate right as one enters the doorway and the other families located themselves to the leader's right in the order in which they joined the group. Another consideration for a family in selecting its position within the communal lodge is whether a particular position requires that the family retains or has to change its accustomed order of which side of its living space is male and which is female (following the principles of separation of the sexes just mentioned). The apparent practice in this matter is for the more senior families to retain the same organization of family space (i.e. male right, female left, or vice versa) after joining a communal lodge as they would normally employ when using an individual dwelling. Thus the tendency would be for a senior family to have its choice of locations within the communal lodge, and the junior families to occupy the remaining places such that the above rules regarding females next to the door, and the alternation of sexes for adjacent families are followed.

Fig. 9 shows the basic order within a two-family and a four-family communal lodge. This diagram may be extended to cover any even number of families living in one dwelling, by adding or subtracting family spaces from the rear of the dwelling furthest from the door, and following the rule that only same-sex members of different families can be located next to each other. However, an odd number of families creates a problem in following both the latter rule and the rule that females must be immediately adjacent to both sides of the door. From the cases I have gathered it appears that it is the rule prohibiting members of different families of the opposite sex from being located next to one another which is fudged in such a case. The usual solution is for the odd family to be located in the middle of the rear area opposite the door. This means that opposite sexes will be adjacent between this odd family and *one* of the families next to it. In order to make the separation from the families on either side, an alcove or recessed area is built in the rear wall (see Fig. 10). I have observed the abandoned frames of two such lodges in the Nichicun region.[2]

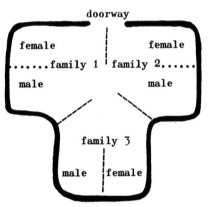

Fig. 10. Organization of sexes within the
multi-family dwelling (odd numbers)

A second solution to the problem of spatial organization posed by a communal lodge with an odd number of families is for all the unmarried men (who are, in a sense, the cause of the problem) to be located together at the rear of the lodge, away from any unmarried females. This solution is similar to a summertime living arrangement which is sometimes encountered when unmarried men of several families will share a tent, although each of them continues to eat with his own family.

What these comparative data on communal dwelling camps and single family dwelling camps show is that the move to a communal dwelling brings about a minimum alteration in the use of domestic space by the individual commensal group, and the relative autonomy of each group is preserved. In individual family tents virtually no accommodation is offered to visitors, who must cluster around the door, while the communal lodge does allow relaxed conversation between families within the hunting group. Men can compare observations and plan group hunts more easily. However, the light canvas which the tents are made of ensures that there is little or no privacy between families, even when they are living separately, and conversations can be carried on between tents, except on windy days when the canvas makes a continual noise.

The change to the communal lodge means a change in the orientation of the commensal group. Each commensal family remains oriented towards its own fire, and the dwelling doorway remains oriented towards the rising sun. As we will see, the principles of geographic and cosmic spatial organization do not, for the most part, pervade the internal organization of the dwelling in any obvious way. The doorway, then, is the most important feature which connects the systems of internal and external space. On the other hand, as we will shortly see, the use of domestic space in the context of ritual, and the use of specially-constructed tents for ritual purposes transforms internal space in the direction of the external model.

5
The Ritualization of Space

1. *The hunting journey*

In the last chapter the organization of space within the hunting camp was examined as a reflection of the social organization of the hunting group. In this chapter this subject of the organization of space will be pursued further, by considering a number of rites which, it will be argued, express symbolically ideas about spatial organization. This will bring us to the central issue being posed in this study, that of the significance of the religious ideas of the Cree hunters, as these relate to the hunting mode of production.

In this and the following three chapters I will show that there are a number of activities engaged in by Cree hunters that have what I refer to as a ritual quality and which must be interpreted as deriving from ideas and motivations of the actors even though such ideas and motivations are not entirely explicit. All behaviour has an ideational component, but ritual behaviour, like the stories told in myths, involves underlying ideas and connections that the ritualist or myth-teller would find inappropriate to explain. But if an outside observer remains unaware of the existence of the ideas from which this behaviour stems he cannot attach significance to it, or judge its relationship to the conditions in the real world. Some ritual actions are predicated on the belief in, for example, entities which the observer can only know about from the descriptions given him by the participants. Even when these beliefs are taken into account the relationship between the actions in question and conditions in the external world is not always self-evident. Because of these difficulties in understanding it is assumed that there exist ideational components which underlie observed behaviour. In what follows I will be looking at ritual mainly as a form of 'symbolic action', so that the hypothetical ideational components of this behaviour will be seen as symbols which the participants manipulate in the ritual in order to achieve some goal.

Let me give an example. Later in this chapter I will describe various activities which are undertaken by Cree hunters in order to bring about changes in weather conditions. Even when the explicit ideas of the Cree about the entities which they believe to be responsible for particular weather conditions are spelled out, the significance of the actions involved in these weather control rites is not self-evident. If we then compare the various kinds of weather control rites that are practised, including both the variety of techniques employed by a single group, and the variations observed between the equivalent techniques practised by neighbouring groups, I believe it can be demonstrated that there exists a systematic relationship among all the variants. Moreover, when a specific activity is treated as part of the overall matrix of weather control behaviour, signification can be deduced by the relationships among the elements in the matrix itself. This matrix, or symbol system, can well be unconscious to most actors, since their interest is in the goal of the ritual action, not in how that particular formula arose.

Symbolism is part of the mode of production, since it is an aspect of the process of production of cultural knowledge. Symbolic knowledge is exemplified in but not restricted to myth and religion, where it is capable of expressing concepts and relations that would be impossible or too complex by means of explicit, or 'denotative' knowledge. Yet symbolic knowledge is related to both explicit knowledge and practical action. In what follows these connections will be emphasized. First, the selection of data on symbolism gives priority to symbolic action over symbolic expression, and to cases of symbolic action where it is a part of behaviour having a practical outcome. For this reason more attention will be paid, as primary material, to rites, where symbolic action has some goal, as distinct from myths, which will be used more as background explanatory material. Secondly, rites will be presented in the context of their association with social organization and economic production. The present chapter, for example, concerns those rites which are linked to life cycle changes and changes in the natural environment which are relevant to the processes of economic production. In later chapters rites will be presented in the contexts of each of the three phases of hunting production.

Cree cultural knowledge has a well developed conceptualization of geographic space, but there is little in the way of an explicit conception of cosmography outside of a religious or mythic context. In many rites and in myths the predominant conception given of the space in which events take place is a concentric model with the camp space at the centre, surrounded by geographic space, that is the forest and lakes, inhabited by the animals, at the farthest reaches of which, as well as above and below, are located various spiritual entities associated with natural forces. In those rites that use this implicit cosmography two themes stand out: first, the distinction is drawn and emphasized between the domestic and the geographic or the spiritual domains of cosmological space; second, the gap between the two domains is mediated in order for the ritualist to control, or to know something about, events in the natural world. In several rites this relationship between the domestic and the surrounding domains is established by the use of the symbol of the hunter's journey, which moves outwards from the camp to the prey and back again. The conception of space which the hunting journey makes use of informs, in my opinion, other Cree ritual symbolism where no direct reference is made to the hunting journey idea. The implicit cosmography which underlies those rites that use this hunting journey idea is helpful for the understanding of Cree ritual in general, and it is the elements of this conception of space that this chapter is intended to outline.

The Mistassini treat hunting and trapping as a journey, a round trip from the camp to the bush and return, ideally followed by a communal distribution of food. This way of looking at the process of production in the hunting group recurs repeatedly in symbolic form in both myths and rites. For example, Lefebvre, in analysing the structure of seven episodes of the *cikaapes* myth cycle, gives the following common referential model for all the episodes: (1) An initial enquiry and receipt of information by the hero from his sister. (2) The hero sets out. (3) The hero encounters strangers. (4) The hero acquires a goal. (5) The hero has a concluding interchange with his sister (1971:15). If we look at the hunting and trapping process of production as the prototype for a simplified version of this model, we may say that, at the symbolic level, (*a*) the gathering of information is, for hunting, marked by divination rites, (*b*) the encounter with strangers (which in hunting are represented by the game animals) is marked by hunting magic, and (*c*) the return to the domestic group is marked by the code of respectful behaviour towards the victims. This division of hunting rites into three phases of a cycle will be used when this material is described in the next three chapters.

In this chapter I will discuss rites not part of this cycle, but which demonstrate much of the implicit ideas involved in ritual action. The first two cases are of rites in which the hunting journey is used, and where the relationship between the camp (*nipisikahiikan*) and the bush (*nuhcimiihc*) is underscored. Another set of terms which are commonly used to refer to this distinction between the domestic space and the space away from human settlement is the 'inside' (*piihtak-amihc*) and the 'outside' (*wiiwiitimihc*). In the 'Walking Out' ceremony and the pre-Christian wedding rite the distinction between these two spatial spheres is stressed, and hunting is seen as a model for the successful establishment of relations between the two aspects of the world represented by these spheres. The second two sets of rites described in this chapter, concerned with weather control and dwelling orientation, carry the idea further. The distinction between inside and outside is used to stress the initial disjunction between man and the personified forces of nature which are identified with locations on the farthest limits of the 'outside'. Some of the rites end, however, with a closing of this gap and its mediation by means of ritualized acts of exchange.

2. *'Walking Out'* (ewiiwiithaawsunaanuuhc, *'they make him go outside'*)

A ceremony is held soon after a child can walk, which formally marks the change from when he must always stay inside to when he may begin to spend time outside the dwelling. I have observed the ceremony during the spring and summer, both at the camp and at the summer settlement, but I have been told it may also be conducted in winter, on a very sunny day. The child is led by his parents along a path leading straight out from the doorway to where a small decorated spruce tree has been erected. The path is normally made of spruce boughs laid on the ground. A boy child carries a toy rifle (or in some cases a bow and arrow), and a girl child a toy axe. With these toys the child is made to mimic adult activities symbolic of their sex; the boy 'shoots' an animal, usually a beaver or a goose, whose carcass has been placed under the tree, and the girl 'chops' a pile of firewood, or gathers spruce boughs. The child is then made to circle the tree clockwise, and to carry or drag back what has been gathered, often in a miniature *niimuutaan* (decorated hunting bag). The child is led inside the tent where he makes a clockwise circuit of the dwelling, is greeted by members of the residential group, and presents the pack to the same-sex parent or grandparent. A small feast (see Chapter 8) follows, using in part the material brought in by the child, who is complimented by the family members for 'providing such a magnificent meal'.

Variations in the ceremony include several elements found more often among the bands of the east coast of James Bay, where the ceremony is held communally in the summer settlement for several children at one time, and the gifts are presented by the children to the hunting group leader, the settlement chief, or to the oldest man. This individual presides over a large feast attended by all the families of the children. The decorated tree is lacking, and the path may consist of a strip of white cloth laid on the ground. The path made of cloth placed on the ground was known to some of my Mistassini informants, not for use in the 'Walking Out' ceremony, but for use when the 'ceremonial hides' were displayed outside the dwelling (see Chapter 8).

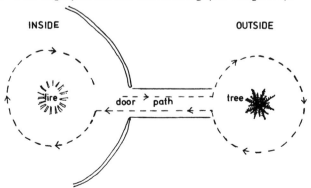

Fig. 11. Plan showing the inside and the outside

The doorway marks the dividing line between the inside and the outside phases of the ceremony. These two phases can be seen as homologous to each other, since each of them involves a clockwise circuit around a central object. Clockwise movements in general often appear in Cree religious symbolism, always in the context of contacts between men and spirits.[1] The tree standing alone is, in both myths and rites, a potential means of communication between man and the spirit world. Mention will be made in Chapter 6 of the lone tree, which is where the hunter makes his initial encounter with the spirit *Mistaapew*. Another such tree is the *mistikukaan*, meaning a 'made tree'. It is usually described as a tree from which all the branches have been removed, and which is then decorated, sometimes by cutting away bands of bark and sometimes by painted designs. It was, in the past, made at a hunting camp, and the bones of various animals were hung from it as offerings. Informants at Mistassini remember these trees in use, but they have now been replaced by a structure which looks more like a conventional European flagpole, although those encountered outside the settlement of Mistassini, at hunting camps, are not used for flying flags. I have observed two of them in the Nichicun region. Both were surmounted by a weathervane structure, both had animal bones hanging from them, both were colourfully painted (blue, in both cases), and both were located between a dwelling site and a water body which the dwelling overlooked. I was told that such flagpoles (also called *mistikukaan*) were erected by a group leader outside his own dwelling. In Mistassini Post the band chief and the immediately previous chief each have flagpoles of the European type outside their houses; no other houses in the village have flagpoles apart from those of White institutions. The significance of trees in spiritual communication is found, for example, in the 'Shaking Tent' ceremony, where great emphasis is placed on the selection of trees for the structure. These poles are sometimes reported as having a tuft of branches left at the top of each (e.g. Preston 1975). In myths the tree is often employed by the hero to travel from the earth to a world above (see Lefebvre 1971). At the same time, the fire in the centre of the dwelling, which in the rite has an homologous position to that of the tree in that a second clockwise movement takes place around it, is also a means of spirit communication. As will be shown later, at feasts there are rules imposing a clockwise movement around the fire. The host also always employs the fire to make offerings to the spirits. Like the tree, it is the vertical dimension of the fire, in the form of the column of rising smoke, that provides the connection between men and the spirit world above.

The ceremony also shows the significance attached by the Cree to walking, and to the feet. Cree ideology states that all inanimate things, including body parts, as well as all animate beings, contain a spirit. Of the body parts, the feet are treated with a special importance.

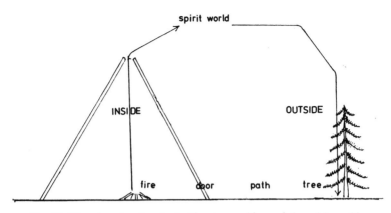

Fig. 12. Elevation showing the inside, the outside, and the spirit world

This is shown by the fact that moccasins are often decorated, particularly the first pair worn by children; snowshoes are always decorated. One can say generally that decoration of objects among the Cree always indicates that they have a sacred significance (see Speck 1924:271). It is said, for example, that it is the spirit of the moccasins and of the snowshoes that leads the hunter to his prey, and prevents his legs getting tired, and thus these items are decorated to please these spirits. The 'Walking Out' rite is another way by which the Mistassini people emphasize the spiritual importance of the feet, and of walking.

3. *Pre-Christian marriage*

The following account of a pre-Christian marriage was told to me by a man of the Nichicun local band who was seventy-five in 1970. According to him, no missionary visited Nichicun in the era of his parents, and only a few people travelled to the posts on James Bay. However, many of those who did were converted by missionaries there, and those who married coastal women were married in church. The following account is used here as a cognitive model, not as fully detailed ethnographic fact; for, whatever it may lack in detail, it stands as the informant's conception of a rite. It shows a number of significant contrasts with the present form of that rite, and it is these particular contrasts which the informant wished to stress, and which I also wish to draw attention to:

Before the church came there was no wedding ceremony. A man who was about to get married would go and kill something. It had to be 'big game', like a caribou, or a bear, or a beaver. While he was away a curtain of caribou hide was used to partition off a part of the bride's parents' tent. The groom would return with his kill and take it to this tent. He would give it to his bride, behind the curtain. She would prepare the meat, and a feast would be given with this food. After this, the couple would continue to live together, but they usually moved into a tent of their own.

There are two points to note about this very brief description. First, it is contrasted explicitly by the informant with present day marriage,[2] and this contrast has many similarities to the winter/summer residence group opposition. Present day marriages take place at the settlement in summer, and often several couples are married at the same time. The emphasis of the occasion is on the relation between the couple and the whole community; everyone first greets the couples with a formal handshake as they leave the church. They are then greeted by them as the couples visit every house in the community, and the community provides a feast and a dance after the marriage. On many of these points, according to the description above, the pre-Christian ceremony was opposite to this. It apparently takes place in winter, or if not, the only group specifically involved is the bride's family. The creation of a commensal unit is symbolized by the sexual division of labour, and by a spatial separation within the communal dwelling which, as we have noted, are both features of winter hunting group social life. Secondly, the account states, in the simplest terms possible, the outline of what I have earlier referred to as the hunt journey, followed by a return, and an expression of communal identity, in this case, by commensality.

4. *Weather control*

Among the Mistassini Cree there are two basic systems of weather magic. In one of them, which is generally used only in the winter season, the main ritual action must be performed by a person born in winter or by a person born in summer, according to the kind of weather that is needed. In the other system actions are directed by anyone to spiritual entities associated with specific localities, such as a lake or a mountain, and their purpose is mainly to prevent storms during the summer season. This distinction is a convenient way of looking at the principles of operation of weather control rites. However, the distinction is artificial, in the sense that the Cree do make use of the principles from both systems in at least one of their weather control rites. This rite, which involves a summer-born or a winter-born person pointing at a particular mountain in order to bring either warm weather or a snow storm, will be discussed later in this section.

Before examining these, I will first enumerate some of the basic religious concepts which the Cree use to discuss weather. Winter weather is primarily attributed to the action of one of the winds. There are essentially four winds, one blowing from each of the cardinal directions. However, the notion of cardinal directions is not exactly similar to European concepts, since in addition to the reference system of four winds there is a second system of four directional terms which are used for orientation with reference to the position of the sun. The first set of terms, from which the names of the winds derive, refer essentially to locations beyond the horizon. The term for 'the east wind is blowing' is *waapiniiwew*, while the direction itself (which is also considered to be a person or what we might call a spirit) is called *waapinsuu*. The south wind is *saaweniiwew*, the south person is *saawensuu*. Most Mistassini informants use a single term for winds of both the north and the west quadrants, as winds from these directions are considered to be of one class, in terms of their effect on the weather. These winds are called *Ciiwetiniiwew*, which in other dialects of Cree refers to the north wind only; the spirit is called *Ciiwetinsuu*. Several informants also knew an alternate term for the west wind (*nakaapeniiwew*), and the west spirit (*nakaapenausuu*), but most persons normally distinguish between 'north' and 'west' wind by adding to the *ciiwetin* root the affix for 'old', in order to refer to 'north', and the affix for 'little', to refer to 'west'. Winter weather, associated with north and west winds, is cold and stable. South wind weather is much milder. East winds are associated with very unstable weather, such as sudden storms or changes in temperature. Because of this instability, east winds are the least favourable, since a hunter is never sure of what allowances he must make in planning a trip. From this it can be seen that some of the meteorological significance attached by the Mistassini to the winds concerns not so much the weather which *accompanies* particular winds as the weather which *follows* them. Phenomena which are believed to follow an east wind include sudden wind storms which cover animal tracks, and freezing rains which can render traps useless.

The above conception of the winds in terms of a circle of four spirits which surround the hunter is given explicit expression in myths, which refer to the winds as four brothers. As we have seen, siblings of the same sex are positioned in the dwelling alongside each other and, like the winds, along an arc of a circle with the oldest at one end and the youngest at the other. This same arrangement, this time in terms of a value scale, is implied by this reference to the four cardinal directions as brothers. In the myth they are ranked not by age, but according to their friendliness to man. The winds do not carry the same values in all versions of the myth, collected over a wide area, but in a Mistassini version the east wind is by far the meanest, followed in order by the north, the west and the south (Speck 1935:63).

Apart from the winds, the more abstract orientation system which we mentioned earlier is used when describing locations within sight, or when recalling journeys and giving directions. The Cree terms refer to the position of the sun; thus, *piisimwataahc* is 'towards the south' (*piisimw* means 'sun'); *aatimaapiisimw* is 'towards the north'; *waapinutaahc* is 'towards the east' (cognate with the terms for both the east wind and the dawn); and *acistuu* is 'towards the west'.

Along with the winds, the two major seasons are important weather factors. Just as each wind is associated with a spiritual person, with its own personality characteristics, so the two seasons have spirits, which alternate in their influence.

The third set of factors influencing weather are the spirits that are believed to cause sudden and dangerous phenomena, such as thunder storms and squalls. These are attributed to particular local spirits, such as underwater people, or mountain beings. Two unusual meteorological phenomena occurred during 1969-70. There was a partial eclipse of the sun, for which I could obtain no folk explanation, and a small but violent tornado which cut a swath through the forest and completely uprooted several large trees. The latter was attributed to an *atuus*, a human-eating monster about which there are many beliefs and myths. The event took place about 20 miles from Mistassini Post, and I was told that one shaman had foreknowledge that the *atuus* was about to descend on the settlement, and was able with the help of other shamans to divert his path from the village.

Magical techniques to make the weather in winter colder involve some action by a person born in the winter. I was told that it is preferable to use someone born in the mid-season, but that the category 'winter person' (*pipuniinuu*) applies to anyone born between freeze-up and break-up, and if necessary a person not born in mid-season would be asked to perform the action. One of the more common techniques is for this person to make a model of a hare out of snow, and face it to the west. Another technique involves the use of a tight bundle of bushy branches of black spruce, called 'witches'-broom' in English and 'North man's head' (*ciiwetinustikwaan*) in Cree. This bundle grows on an otherwise normal spruce tree, and is caused by a parasitic dwarf mistletoe, *Arceutholium pusillum* (Baldwin 1958:44). The bundle may be tied by a long string to a dog's tail, set on fire, and the dog set free to run around on the ice. In another version, the bundle has ptarmigan feathers and birch bark stuck into it, and is suspended from a pole which is stuck into the ice at an angle before the bundle is lit. Other Mistassini people merely set the witches'-broom on the ice, or a winter person sets it on fire and kicks it around on the ice. Another method is for a winter person to go outside the tent and strip to the waist. Finally, to make it snow, a person throws snow at a dog, or puts the fur of a hare in the fire. These latter methods are at other times tabooed behaviour, two of several to the general effect that men must respect animals.

Methods to make the weather warmer in winter are less numerous and less frequently used than those to make it colder. They would only be used during extremely cold weather when the movement of animals

Plate 9. 'Witch's Broom' growing on black spruce (right centre).

becomes inhibited by conditions, thus making hunting and trapping difficult. The principal one mentioned by informants involves the use of the heartwood, which is the inner core of a tree, and which sometimes separates easily from the rest when dry. A piece of firewood is split so that the heartwood breaks away separately and remains in one piece. The Cree speak of the heartwood as a separate smaller tree inside the larger tree, like a baby inside a pregnant woman; it is called *ukusimewaatikw* 'the tree son'. A person born in the summer (*niipiniinuu*) sets fire to the heartwood, and beats or wipes the snow with it, or simply places it on the ice.[3]

In the literature on the East Cree region references to magical techniques to make the weather warmer are also rare. Skinner, writing on the Cree of the east coast of James Bay, describes a method used to turn the wind away from the north, which might well imply an intention to make the weather warmer. A stone was wet with saliva, a piece of charcoal stuck to it, and the charcoal was then hit with another stone (1911:59). I was told of the same technique by a Rupert House informant, who spoke, however, of using burning embers taken from the fire rather than charcoal.

This informant, an unusually thoughtful man on religious topics, also gave me an outline of all winter weather control techniques in terms of a scheme which was somewhat different from the one I had put together on the basis of my Mistassini data. The Mistassini material indicated that techniques to make the weather warmer differed from those to make it colder in two ways. First, the ritual action had to be performed by a summer-born, as opposed to a winter-born, person, and second, the materials and actions involved in the weather-warming techniques were quite different from those used in the weather-cooling magic. But according to the Rupert House informant each of the weather-cooling techniques used at Mistassini could be employed, with some small alteration, to make the weather warmer, providing that the action was performed by a summer-born instead of a winter-born person. For example, he said that the model hare made of snow was faced *north* (not west) by a winter-born person to make the weather colder, and faced *south* by a summer-born person to make the weather warmer. Similarly, the ember taken from the fire must be hit by a summer-born person to make the weather warmer, and by a winter-born person to make the weather colder. I did not have the opportunity to observe the extent to which Rupert House hunters make use of similar techniques for both weather-cooling and weather-warming purposes, but at Mistassini the only technique I came across which has this characteristic of being used for either purpose was the mountain-pointing case. Apart from this, the technique of a summer-born using burning heartwood was the only weather-warming rite encountered among the Mistassini hunters.

The case of the mountain which, when pointed at, brings about a change in the weather was told to me because a storm had recently been caused by a young winter-born child pointing at it. The mountain, located northwest of Nichicun, is called *kwaanawesikaaw*. It is noteworthy in that it rises in the form of a regular cone from otherwise fairly level surroundings. Other hunters who were away from camp at the time stated that the storm was restricted to the local area of the mountain, since they did not encounter it. I was then told that the same mountain could be used to alter the weather intentionally. If a winter-born person pointed at it storms and cold weather would result, but if a summer-born person did so it would bring mild, sunny and calm weather.

As was mentioned earlier, weather control rites used in the summer involve relations with entities associated with specific localities. In spring, to hasten the break up of ice in rivers and lakes some tobacco is placed on the ice in a container. In summer tobacco is used in various ways to prevent, or to drive away, storms. When travelling on a lake by canoe tobacco is smoked just before or while people are setting out. Tobacco is also put in the water if a storm threatens.[4] These practices are all directed at entities associated with the water. Other practices relate to beliefs about mountains, which are considered to be the dwelling places of spiritual entities, and places where shamans go to practise magic. A number of mountains in the Mistassini territory have taboos connected with them. There are common beliefs that certain mountains will cause storms if they are pointed at, or even looked at, especially while crossing a lake by canoe. In one case a mountain is said to be impossible for anyone but a shaman (*mitew*) to climb. If a man tries a fog descends on him and a storm drives him back.

All the weather control rites can be seen as kinds of 'offerings' made to various spiritual entities believed to control particular weather phenomena. With summer weather control rites the entities are associated with local features of the terrain, all located at a different horizontal plane from man. Some are located *below* (underwater entities, which usually fall into the category of creatures called *ntaampekiinuu*) others *above* (including entities associated with mountains and the *atuus* monster, which is said to be taller than the trees). The entities below are controlled by means of *positive* prestations (gifts of tobacco) designed to placate them, while the entities above are controlled through negative relations (actions designed to drive them away, or taboos designed to leave the entities undisturbed).

The winter weather control rites are of a different order. Concepts of winds and seasons are combined to produce a binary structure of idealized 'winter' weather (cold, snow, north and west winds), which is the domain of winter-born people, and 'summer' weather (warmth, sunshine, rain, south wind), which is the responsibility of 'summer' people. As far as could be determined, these 'Season of birth' groups have no other role except in weather control, and this magic is only employed in winter. In performing these rites, two systems of natural objects are employed: (1) representatives of particular 'winter' animal species, and (2) parts of certain trees. The animals are, primarily, the dog and the hare, with some ptarmigan feathers, while the tree parts are the witches'-broom and the dry heartwood, with some burnt wood and birch bark.

What distinguishes the animal species used in the rites from the other 'winter' animals is their association with a habitat similar to that chosen by man. They are not animals of the water, or the hills, at a great distance from man, and furthermore, they are found around the immediate area of a camp. The dog is, of course, domesticated, and the other two animals can be considered closer to man than others in the category of winter animals. In terms of production, the hare and the ptarmigan are more domestic because they are killed by women in the vicinity of the camp.[5] The species chosen in weather control rites are associated with the cold; at the same time, they can also mediate between the camp and the bush.

In the case of the objects made of wood, these are first of all connected with man-made fires. The black spruce is the most common species used for domestic firewood, and most of the trees selected for this purpose are those that are dead. The heartwood of the tree is believed to carry the life, in the sense that a tree is said to die because the heartwood dries out. In winter, the moisture in a tree retreats to the inner part, and only comes out again the following summer, when the sap flows.[6] On the other hand, the witches'-broom is of no significance for domestic fires; like the rest of the branches, if found it is discarded normally and only the trunk is used. However, it has the same general form as the ground dwelling dwarf varieties of evergreen trees which are found in sheltered dry places in the barrens where there are no trees, and which are particularly useful for making outside fires in such areas. The smallest branches of spruce trees lose much of their moisture during winter and can be collected from a green tree and used to start a fire outside. The witches'-broom is composed of such twigs, and for this reason can be set afire easily in the winter. The fact that in the rite birch bark is occasionally added to the witches'-broom seems to support the interpretation that the action symbolizes the making of an open fire such as is used while on a hunting trip, since birch bark is often used to start such fires.

The association between heartwood and domestic firewood is of a more complex order than that of witches'-broom. Firewood is of two kinds; that which comes from dead trees and is dry (*paahkatikw*), and that which is cut while the tree is still living, and is to some extent moist (*cikskaatikw*). The latter fuel is used to produce a slow-burning fire, used, for example, the last thing at night, or on mild days. Firewood with a heartwood section which can be separated easily from the rest may be caused by the tree having been cut while it was alive, and later allowed to dry. Thus the heartwood is, in one sense, both moist and dry. Separable heartwood appears mainly in the firewood of a group which has camped in one place for a long time, because not only must the group have been stationary long enough for green wood to dry out, but they may have used up all the dead wood in the area, and have cut green wood as a principal fuel. Another source of separable heartwood is live trees killed by a forest fire. Both heartwood and witches'-broom thus share the somewhat contradictory idea of being a living part of the tree which nevertheless burns easily.

The symbolic significance of heartwood and witches'-broom, from among the burnable parts of the tree, is of additional significance; each of them has the form of a miniature of a whole tree. In the case of witches'-broom, the miniature tree grows out of a full-sized one, so that it is like a tree suspended in mid-air; the heartwood is inside the larger one, a tree within the tree. In both cases, the key object in each rite falls between being a tree and something other than a tree; in each case there is a part tree which is nevertheless a complete tree. Beyond this fundamental similarity between the heartwood and the witches'-broom, the two objects are also opposed to each other. Each is a quasi-tree, but the former is *inside* a real tree, tall and straight, while the latter is *outside* the real tree, stunted and twisted.

The two rites of making the weather colder and making the weather warmer can be treated as having parallel structures. The action of the rites in both cases is the same, even though the outcome between the two is opposite. In both cases a very special quasi-tree is used to symbolize a generalized tree, which in Cree religious ideology is a symbolic mediator between man and the spirit world. Given this communication link, the ritual object is then burned. The effect of this burning depends on the nature of the symbolic tree which is burnt. The opposition between heartwood and witches'-broom is used to represent the opposition between summer and winter. Thus the witches'-broom must be identified with cold, and the heartwood becomes symbolic of warmth.

The following equations summarize the ritual facts involved in the weather control rites which use witches'-broom and heartwood:

Witches'-Broom + Winter Person ———→ Cold
Heartwood + Summer Person ———→ Warm

where witches'-broom is an *outside* metonymic tree, and heartwood is an *inside* metonymic tree.

5. Orientation to the rising sun

The point has already been made that the winter dwelling faces the rising sun, and it also faces a water body. Rogers states, 'Because of the prevailing direction of the coldest winds, the western shores of lakes were most often chosen. If the campsite was established on an eastern shore, it was usually placed farther back from the lake than on a western shore' (Rogers 1967:9-11; see also 1963b:226). I have observed only one campsite which was not located on a western shore. This was a site that appeared to have been a portage camp, and in this case the door faced east, but not towards the lake. While it is the case that the location of the winter camp is to a large extent an adaptation, the orientation of the door is a more aesthetic judgement. It must be remembered that the door is the only part of the dwelling used for looking out, and the water body provides the camp with its access route, so that, given a camp location on a western shore, the orientation of the door towards the water (and, therefore, towards the rising sun) makes most ecological sense in terms of access to the dwelling, and for the view of the outside which this orientation affords. Given this adaptive basis for the camp location and for the orientation of the door, and the fact that the Cree are fully aware of these factors, it is significant that there should exist two additional explanations which are offered to account for the orientation of the door.

In the first place, there are the explanations which state why the Cree like the door of the dwelling to face the rising sun. Some say they like to sit inside the tent and watch the sun rise, while others say it is auspicious for the hunter to be going outside through the doorway in the morning into the direct sunlight. This action is supposed to ensure hunting success. Another informant mentioned that the rear of the tent was the favoured seating place, because the person in this position can look outside the door to the direction of the rising sun. This calls to mind the concept of the 'Seat of Honour' found all over North America (Paulson 1952), as is the preference for the eastward facing doorway. These facts themselves suggest that the full explanation of dwelling and door orientation lies beyond the narrow ecological conditions of the region east of James Bay, although the prevalence of westerly winds over the whole continent including James Bay is no doubt a significant factor.

For the Mistassini Indians the direction of the rising sun is positively valued, even though a negative evaluation is placed by them on the east wind. Speck quotes a Mistassini myth which seems to imply an explanation of the practice of facing towards the east in terms of the hunters' fear, rather than their admiration, of the east. The hero of the myth kills a cannibal creature, *wiihtikuu*, after which the people gather around, 'some on the north side, some on the west and some on the south but none on the east side', with the *wiihtikuu* corpse facing east, to await the arrival of the most feared spirit, the east wind, to collect his share (Speck 1935:63). However, my own informants never suggested that the door faced east out of negative feelings for the east wind, but rather always instead made positive comments about the rising sun.

The Mistassini terms for both the east wind and the dawn, or rising sun, come from the same root, which is also related to the term for 'light'.[7] Although their names are linguistically cognate, the spirits of the east wind (*waapinsuu*) and of the rising sun (*waapinuu*) are not the same. The term for the latter (*waapinuu*) is, according to Rousseau, used at Lac St. Jean refer to the shaking tent, in which a shaman communicates with a variety of helpful spirits (1953:143). The shaman enters the tent after sunset, from the side facing the place where the sun rises (cf. Vincent, 1973:72).[8] Among the Mistassini the shaman inside the shaking tent normally faces east, but in several of the regional variations of this rite, including the Mistassini, the idea is maintained that the orientation of the shaman determines the kind of spirits with which he is able to communicate. Thus a shaman would face west in the shaking tent only after the death of an old man, so that he could see the spirits which sometimes accompany the dead person on his westward journey.

The most specific data I obtained among the Mistassini concerning the spirit of the dawn was related to the decorated articles which are displayed outside, around the camp,[9] and which are sometimes called *intucikan*. These include the inedible remains of animals hung in trees or placed above the ground on cache platforms. In the case of the mounted skulls and antlers of 'big game' which I have observed at abandoned campsites, these are permanently mounted to face east. Some of them are decorated with paint or ribbons. Moreover, when 'big game' animals were cached, or when animals were temporarily stored or displayed inside the dwelling, care was taken to orient the heads to the east. The 'ceremonial hide', although no longer used for this purpose, was in the past hung outside on a fine day facing southeast as a display to *waapinuu*. One informant stated that the ceremonial hides were hung on either side of the doorway. Another person said that the ceremonial hide was displayed for both the 'daylight' and the 'outside'. The door flap itself, which is used for both tents and log-walled lodges, is the only part of the exterior of the dwelling that is always decorated. The part of these decorations are explained as offerings to spirits. In all these various practices involving displays made facing towards the east we see the notion expressed that there is a dawn spirit to which positive offerings, in the form of displays and decorations, are made.

In the literature there has been some confusion between the two concepts of the dawn spirit, *waapinuu*, and of the spirit of the east wind, *waapinsuu*. For instance, Lips, who worked at Lac St. Jean (1947:388), refers to the term *'wuapannishu'*, which he translates as 'the daylight man' and 'the man of the east'. He states that animals as well as men are thought to pray to *'wuapannishu'* in order to stop the snowfall. This information conforms far more closely to the Mistassini attitude to the day (*waapinuu*), rather than to the east wind, which Lips' term appears to indicate.

The second religious explanation which some Mistassini informants give for the standard east or southest orientation of the dwelling door is to avoid the spiritual entity, *Ciiwetinsuu*, who is associated with the north and the northwest, and is in charge of cold weather, snow, and 'winter' animals (i.e. animals that do not hibernate or migrate in winter). By this account, dwellings are oriented so that people inside have their backs turned to the northwest. This is part of a general pattern of avoidance of *Ciiwetinsuu*, although there is also some evidence of positive attitudes being shown towards him. For instance *Ciiwetinsuu* is credited with providing hunters with winter game animals, and when spoken of the honorific phrase 'your grandfather' is used. Offerings of fat are made to *Ciiwetinsuu* at the winter feast. However, the myth which gives the origin of these gifts concerns a man who insults *Ciiwetinsuu*; the latter retaliates the following winter with massive attacks of cold and snow. The man only just manages to save himself by throwing the fat he has stored into the fire. Thus even the gift made to *Ciiwetinsuu*, which is placed in the fire, expresses a negative, or at best an ambivalent relationship.

At the beginning of this section on the orientation of the dwelling and its door, the notion was expressed of a consciously-perceived ecological determinancy, based on the prevailing cold winds, onto which has been grafted an additional structure of ideas and ritual attitudes. The result is that the dwelling provides, in addition to a

Plate 10. Tents at Nichicun. Note the typical decorated door flap.

spatial display of the social structure of the commensal family and the hunting group through its standardized internal arrangements, an outward projection onto the geographic environment of a set of abstract models for thinking about problems in the conception of reality. This abstract spiritual thought can reach conclusions about ecological conditions which are more sophisticated than the non-spiritual concepts about the individual ecological determinants on which we have said that they are grafted. The initial material condition leading to the orientation of the dwelling doorway is the need to avoid the prevailing cold winds, but this idea of a *turning away* on material grounds has been added to with the idea of the positive orientation *towards* the southeast, and *towards* the rising sun on spiritual grounds. Thus the Cree spiritual model of dwelling orientation is more elaborate than their own material explanation; while the material explanation deals only with cold winds, the spiritual explanation is based, in the final analysis, on both cold winds and solar radiation.

It happens that a large number of northern life forms do actually position themselves in order to both maximize solar radiation and minimize the effects of cold winds. In the Nichicun region, there are several such life forms which are resources used by Cree hunters. The Cree, in hunting, make use of this characteristic in order to locate such resources quickly. Trees which in the Nichicun region are close to the northern limit of their distribution, such as birch and some other deciduous species, are found exclusively on the southeast-facing slopes of hills, and on the southeast side of islands (Baldwin 1958:38). Associated with these hillside stands are the places where moose 'yard' in the late winter, when the snow is too deep for them to travel. This is the time of the year when most moose are killed, because both finding the animals and killing them requires a minimum effort. On cold days porcupines are said to position themselves on a tree towards the sun. On open ground, on the sides of hills, bush willows tend to grow more abundantly on the southeast-facing slopes, and associated with them are flocks of ptarmigan who, according to informants, like to sun themselves on calm, bright days. Closely analogous to the location chosen by the Cree for winter camps are the locations of beaver lodges, at the edge of a lake. A high proportion of the lodges I observed were on the west or northwest shores of the lake, the same observation as that made by the naturalist Rue, who states that beavers tend to locate their lodges in order to catch the maximum amount of sunshine (1964:100).

For the Cree, then, it may be said that orientation towards the rising sun, as is the case of the animals and plants noted above, represents a double orientation; in the first place, orientation towards solar radiation, which by itself would mean any southerly orientation; and secondly, orientation away from the northwest quadrant, or in other words, by placing themselves so that high ground and trees give protection from winds on this side. Thus, when we say that spiritual ideas are grafted onto an understanding of material conditions, this is not to say that these spiritual ideas necessarily move away from the questions of the comprehension of material conditions. On the contrary, the result, in the case of spiritual ideas about spatial orientation, could be said to offer a more complete understanding of material factors in that it links the traditions of spatial orientation, which have their origins in practical, material considerations, to the Cree cosmology as a whole. The example by itself is perhaps trivial, but it does illustrate a mode of integration of religious thought and material conditions which has some relevance for the study of ritual.

6. The sociology of ritual relations

The rites which we have examined in this chapter are techniques to mobilize non-human powers, based on some kind of model of human interaction. The first such model is that of social exchange, or what was referred to earlier in this chapter as positive relations. In this case men make offerings, in the form of gifts of food or tobacco or with displays, and these are followed by gifts in the form of game animals which are sent for the men to kill, or calm waters for men to navigate.

The second model on which the weather-control and dwelling-orientation rites are organized is that of a negative relationship, i.e. avoidance or taboo. A situation exists such that man is permanently subject to rules imposed by a spiritual power. An interaction then begins with a failure by man to observe a rule of avoidance, and this is followed by a retaliation which is harmful to men generally. A situation of permanent subordination is suggested. When taboos are broken, it is spoken of as an 'insult', or a failure to 'respect' a particular spiritual power.

The basic ongoing relationship between man and *Ciiwetinsuu* is an avoidance relationship, shown, for example, by orienting the dwelling away from *Ciiwetinsuu*, and also in hunting and feasting rites to be discussed later (see Chapters 7 and 8). However, it is possible for other modes of interaction to be employed. *Ciiwetinsuu* does not appear in the shaking tent, and none of the 'ritual hangings' displayed around the camp are directed at him.

The third model used in the foregoing rites is where men 'trick' *Ciiwetinsuu* by intentionally breaking a taboo and turning the punishments into rewards by selecting the appropriate time when they are needed. Thus when cold is needed he performs a ritual which insults an animal associated with *Ciiwetinsuu* for example by making a model of a hare from snow, facing towards *Ciiwetinsuu*. This provokes *Ciiwetinsuu* to send a storm as punishment, even though this is just what the hunters need at that time.

It should also be noted that in this case the rites do not merely consist of behaviour which in other circumstances constitutes a taboo. For instance, there are taboos against leaving blood on the snow while hunting, and the result of a failure to observe the taboo is a snow storm sent by *Ciiwetinsuu*, which covers the tracks of animals and makes it difficult to hunt. As it happens, blood is not, however, deliberately left on the snow to cause snow.

The rites constitute especially contrived deliberate inversions of the attitudes which are supposed to be in force always, and which the taboos merely symbolize. The neglect of the taboo as such is insufficient. We have already noted that the rites for the control of summer weather phenomena follow different principles from the winter weather control rites. In the case of phenomena affecting the condition of water bodies, the rites express a relationship similar to that between a hunter and the spirit powers that aid him in hunting. I do not know of any cases in which the spirits involved, the *ntaampekiinuu*, appear in the shaking tent, but as with the shaking tent spirits, offerings are made to them with the expectation of a reward. This, however, can be regarded as a negative exchange, in the sense that, unlike exchanges embodied in hunting rites, offerings to the *ntaampekiinuu* are made in order to avoid a punishment, not in order to obtain a reward.

Finally, there are the cases of summer weather control involving localized spirits above the earth. In these cases rites are prompted by threatening signs of adverse meteorological phenomena (thunderstorms, winds, the approach of an *atuus*), and consist of magic designed to drive off the disturbance. In the case of mountains which are believed to cause weather disturbances, an avoidance relationship exists.

Although particular rites can be classified as expressing one of several specific modes of social interaction (positive exchange, avoidance, trickery or resistance), the spiritual beings towards whom these actions are addressed cannot, as we have seen in the case of *Ciiwetin-suu*, be classified so clearly, or permanently. In ideological statements about spirit powers, the Mistassini prefer to speak of a generalized respect which is due to all spirits and all animals.

6
Rites of Hunting Divination

1. *Religion and divination*

Although this study deals at length with the use of religion only in the context of hunting, it is useful to first provide a brief overview of the scope of Mistassini religion. Let us take as a working definition of religion that institutionalized complex of symbols which, through their use in rites, myths and beliefs, refer to the existence of a level of reality which is normally hidden; contact with this hidden reality may be made by the use of techniques of symbolic action. Such a definition subsumes under a single category the 'classical' anthropological concepts of 'magic' and 'religion', where the latter is, by definition, separate from magic. Cree religion, from this perspective, includes inputs from two historical traditions: the aboriginal religious tradition, and Christian missionary teachings. Some degree of syncretism between these two traditions has taken place, particularly in the belief system; for example, the Christian pantheon has been given a position in the world of supernatural beings. A division of religious activities into the major types might include (1) hunting magic, (2) sorcery, (3) rites of passage, (4) weather control and (5) communication with distant persons. Christian ideas and practice, and the reference to Christian standards of morality, are most clearly represented in certain passage rites (baptism, confirmation, marriage and funerals), and by implication in sorcery, since the practice is opposed by reference to Christian morality, and the Christian concept of the devil is often spoken of as being associated with such practices. Both of these religious activities with which Christianity is directly identified are mainly confined to the village of Mistassini Post, and are in the hands of a few specialists. Some village religious activities, such as the 'Shaking Tent', and certain feasts, are developments of the traditional religion, although some Christian elements have been absorbed. Unlike Christianity, the aboriginal Cree religious tradition places particular emphasis on the development of religious competence by the individual. Thus most techniques of hunting magic (within which I here include divination, magic used during the hunt, and the code of respect towards the animal victims), weather control and sorcery (about which I was able to learn very little) are constitutionally suited for use in the context of the two or three family hunting group. Most Christian elements which have been introduced into religious practice at this hunting group level do not refer to the specialized institution which the Christian church has now become within Cree society.

The relationship between these two sources of religious tradition can be seen, also, as associated with one or the other of the two modes of production which are realized within Mistassini society. That is, traditional Cree religious sources predominate in the context of the hunting group, while Christian sources are most apparent among the Indians in the context of the cash economy and at the level of the village of Mistassini Post. Since we have earlier in this book recognized the dominant position of the capitalist mode of production, some explanation is required if we now make the assumption that the religious ideology appropriate to capitalism, i.e. Christianity, is not the dominant religious ideology among the Mistassini. This is only in part explained by the fact that the Mistassini avoid placing the two traditions in single contexts such that it becomes necessary to choose between the two. More importantly, if we recognize within the Mistassini band as a whole the existence of two social groups, the hunters and the village residents, then although it is the case that the village residents participate most directly in the capitalist mode, and that their participation in the domestic mode is minimal, it is also the case that their position within the capitalist mode is that of a weak, peripheral group within the total capitalist social formation. Thus for the villagers the hunters function as a positive reference group, and the religious ideology appropriate to the hunting mode acts for both villagers and hunters as an important ideological source.

In the last chapter it was suggested that the Mistassini Cree hunters treat the central productive process, the killing of wild animals, as a sequence of activities, divided into three major phases, information gathering, killing and distribution. Furthermore, they have developed an understanding that this process is a cycle, and that each animal killed is subject to this process. Hunting production in the abstract involves the repetition, in sequence, of these phases. Empirically, one of the phases might be missing (such as when a hunter comes on game unexpectedly, and there is thus no prior information gathering), and the sequence for one instance of killing may not have ended when another one has begun (for instance, when the location of an animal is known months before it is killed). It is in a cognitive sense that the phases form a cycle.

In the three chapters that follow we will deal with rites concerning animals in terms of the above cycle, with a chapter devoted to each of the three phases of ritual, divination, killing rites and treatment of the slain animal. In addition to separating the material into these three phases, and thus following the sequence of the cycle of interaction between men and animals, each chapter will focus on a particular paradigm which is developed in the entire ritual symbolism, as a whole, but which is best elaborated in one or another of the phases of the cycle.

The divination paradigm refers to a process of gathering information about the hidden state of affairs existing between men and game animals, a state of affairs which becomes fully revealed, and may be controlled, during the actual hunt. If the hunting rites can be said to provide, at an ideological level, a fantasy of hunting, then divination provides man with the information required to construct this fantasy. While, from the religious viewpoint, killing need involve only a single hunter and an animal, through divination it either comes to involve the whole group, or it concerns one individual who receives divinatory information, and another who performs the actual killing. In this way divination spreads out the responsibility for the killing from an individual to the group, and the active hunters obtain their power from the old men, so that as an ideology divination is particularly significant in the context of the micro-politics of hunting groups.

Mistassini religion, in the sense of an interrelated complex of symbolic thought and activities, involves the actions of certain individuals who are credited with having particular powers. A major distinction which is recognized within the general realm of religious power is between that of a *mitew* and that of an *emitewaaciiyt*; the former is a person who has the ability to change events in the world by magical means, while the latter's power is more limited, in that he is only able to know what is happening, or is going to happen, both in the spirit world and in places which are physically distant from him.

Despite this clear-cut distinction, the role of either of these practitioners is often somewhat ambiguous, in that one or the other may also be said to have the power to harm others. We will not undertake a full examination of the use of religious ideas to manipulate social relations, by means of such actions as fights between shamans, the cure of sickness, communication with distant persons, the prediction of the arrival of strangers, the practice of sorcery and the finding of lost objects, but my impression is (1) that such activities are most frequent during the summer period, (2) that such activities are the exclusive prerogative of recognised specialists, and (3) that the general frequency and importance of such activities is far lower than has been reported among Cree and Ojibway groups in the boreal forest further west (see Rogers 1969). By contrast, the role of religious beliefs and rites in hunting is (1) confined mainly to the winter period, (2) is to some extent practised by all hunters, and (3) has a relatively high frequency of usage, compared to other contemporary northern Algonkians.

Confining ourselves to the use of religion in hunting, we may recognise in the above distinction a contrast between attempts to control events by magical means, and attempts to obtain knowledge of what is hidden, i.e. the use of divination. But in hunting magic there is no sharp division between specialists and others; the important factors which characterize the most active users of magic and divination are age, past hunting ability, and leadership in a hunting group. These kinds of prestigious individuals are the ones who have some control over the sacred material. One might speculate on whether in the past, as some informants suggest, divination was controlled by an élite, and whether techniques such as the shaking tent, the steam tent, scapulimancy and drumming dominated the practice of hunting divination, and were controlled exclusively by specialists. I find such suggestions perfectly feasible, except that each small hunting group would have been required to have one, and in any case it would be difficult to prove whether this was the case using historical data. The present situation is that, rather than a sharp division between specialists, who employ hunting magic and divination, and non-specialists, who do not, there is a range both in the level of activity between individuals, and in the amount of skill or power which an individual is recognized as having.

Divination among the Mistassini, then, is part of a general intellectual approach to hunting, and includes a variety of techniques, some of which are used only by skilled specialists. But even where a specialist is involved there is very little that is held in secret from the clients, and in fact very little indication that specialists use their skill for personal gain. However, skill in magic or divination is feared at the same time as it is admired, because there is always the implied understanding that such a skilled person might use his power to harm others if he is provoked.

2. *The 'Shaking Tent'* (kusaapicikan)

In Speck's book on the religion of the Montagnais-Naskapi of the Quebec-Labrador peninsula, in which frequent references are made to the Mistassini, a special emphasis is placed on divination. Its importance according to Speck stems not only from its frequent use, but because 'it embodies the innermost spirit of the religion' (1935:127). Further on in the book he makes more explicit his concept ·of the relationship between divination and the religious system.

Divination is the sequel in action to dream revelations and promptings coming from the soul or Great Man of the individual. Dreaming, wishing, intention, and exercise of will form the theory of religion, the consultation of animal oracles form the practice. (ibid.:138).

Speck devotes a separate chapter to divination, although neither in it, nor anywhere else in the book, does he include information on the 'Shaking Tent' ceremony. The reason is that he divides divination into 'unprofessional, or individual conjuring — the minor individual rites — and professional conjuring' (ibid.:48). The latter Speck reserved for a separate work, which was apparently never published.

The 'Shaking Tent' is a public performance which takes place at dusk and may last well into the night. The shaman goes inside the tent, and the onlookers, who may include anyone present at the time, sit on the ground around the tent. The arrival of spirits into the tent is signalled both by the swaying of the whole structure, and by various sounds which are heard. The voices of the spirits are heard, many of them incomprehensible to the onlookers, although their identity may be known. Conversations are heard between the spirits and the shaman, and the onlookers may themselves shout questions. The performance itself has no set form, but depends on the individual shaman, the particular spirits which are heard, the particular purposes for which the ceremony was undertaken and the endurance of the shaman, among other things. In short, it is a shamanistic séance for the purpose of mediating messages between men and the spirits, which are actually brought to and displayed for the people.

It is doubtful if Speck's criterion of professionalism, if it in fact applies at all, would be sufficient to separate the 'Shaking Tent' from other kinds of divination. The 'Shaking Tent' is not merely a part of the preparatory rites for hunting. For one thing, it is now seldom performed by the Mistassini, and when it is, it usually takes the form of an entertainment at the summer settlement. Summer use of the 'Shaking Tent' for the assembled band was reported in early contact times (e.g. Speck 1935:21); it was performed as recently as the summer of 1972 at Mistassini Post.[1] The person who performed it was requested by several Mistassini people to do so as part of a 'pow wow', a newly-instituted summer event in which band members compete with each other in 'Indian' skills, such as canoeing and backpacking, and during which a social dance and a feast are held. This was the first time the 'Shaking Tent' had been used at such an event, although it appears that many of the performances done in the settlement, as distinct from those performed in the winter camps, over the previous twenty years had been those requested and paid for by Whites. The general reaction to the 1972 performance was of only mild interest by young people, and dissatisfaction by most older people, who thought it did not measure up to those of the past. 'Shaking Tent' performances held in summer are not primarily for the purpose of divining future hunting. This is confirmed from the published accounts of such performances (Rousseau 1953a; Preston 1975), in which most attention is concentrated on discovering information about distant band members, finding lost objects, and generally amusing the onlookers. The purpose of amusement is often stressed by informants wishing to emphasize its harmlessness, because of the fact that the 'Shaking Tent' is known sometimes to be used to harm others, although at such times it would be done in secret. In summary, the 'Shaking Tent' has several purposes: as a general community amusement, as a form of 'social' divination, as hunting divination, and, most importantly, to educate and give substance to religious concepts and entities, belief in which underlie the everyday rites.[2]

The shaking tent itself is constructed by one, or more usually several assistants, according to the exact instructions of the *mitew*. It consists of a circle of upright poles of specified tree species driven well into the ground and lashed together with two hoops one half way up and the other near the top. The round top is left open, and the sides are covered with canvas. The performance takes place after dark. The *mitew* approaches the eastward-facing side of the tent, walks around it once clockwise, and enters by crawling under the canvas. The tent shakes violently during the performance, not, it is believed, due to the exertions of the shaman, but because of the presence of spirits.

At the 'Shaking Tent' held at Mistassini in 1972 four senior men acted as assistants. They sat around the tent, one at each of the cardinal directions. At first the tent would not begin to shake, so a small child was made to walk around the tent clockwise. In most descriptions of the rite, the first spirit to enter the shaking tent is said to be *Mistaapew*, who is the host of the ceremony. According to some informants, *Mistaapew* is the only spirit who speaks in human language, and he translates what other spirits say. The other spirits make noises, sounding like whistling or singing, which can be heard but cannot be understood by the onlookers. However, in the 1972 case I was told that the *mitew* was unable to contact *Mistaapew*. The reason given for this failure was that someone among the onlookers had a tape recorder hidden under his coat. The first spirit who was eventually contacted was named *wesiiyuu*, and was identified as having come from Sept Iles, a large Montagnais community several hundred miles to the southeast, one which has few social contacts with Mistassini. Each different account of the 'Shaking Tent' in the Mistassini region mentions the same two or three central spirits which appear, but each account may include other spirits, about which little information can be elicited, and which do not appear in other accounts. According to one informant, the first spirit to be heard after the shaman enters the tent is called *paamhaawiiynuu*, 'the flying man'. It is he who then leaves the tent and returns with *Mistaapew*, who then acts as master of ceremonies. The same informant, whose deceased husband, and her husband's father, both performed the ceremony, said that *paamhaawiiynuu* appears again at the end of the performance to take *Mistaapew* back again.

Most informants describe *Mistaapew* as a great joker when he is in the shaking tent. He is said to be particularly fond of making women laugh. Another characteristic usually noted is his fondness for tobacco. During the performance a lighted pipe, or sometimes a pack of cigarettes, is placed underneath the tent wall for him. In most such accounts the pipe or the package is quickly returned empty, showing *Mistaapew's* extraordinary capacity in this regard. In some accounts, he asks for more tobacco throughout the performance. If we compare the present-day Mistassini information about *Mistaapew* with references to the spiritual being of the same name among the neighbouring groups, a problem of identification arises, one that has been commented on by several ethnographers (Cooper 1944; Flannery 1939; Preston 1975; Vincent 1973). Speck places great importance on this entity, which he describes as the individual 'soul spirit' of each person. Speck's interpretation of Montagnais-Naskapi religion depends to a large extent on this concept, since according to him almost all religious activities consist essentially in an individual catering to the requirements and the instructions of his own personal *Mistaapew*.

However, among my Mistassini informants Speck's concept of *Mistaapew* did not receive full confirmation. Each person is believed to have a 'spirit' (*aataacaakw*),[3] although it is not known by the name *Mistaapew*. I was told that everything in the world has an *aataacaakw*, animals, plants, rocks, clothes, tents, even doorways of tents. While it is affirmed that anything that can be named has a spirit, it is also the case that the spirits of certain things and objects are spoken about, and are treated as having more importance than have others (cf. Rousseau 1952:189). In addition to these individual spirits, certain categories of beings, in particular animal species, or classes of animal species, have an associated spiritual being, which is said to 'own', or to be the 'master' (*ucimaaw*) of, that group of beings. One of the most consistent general characteristics of the present-day Mistassini concept of *Mistaapew* is that the term refers to a spiritual being with the same essential relationship towards man as the 'masters' of the various species and groups of species have towards them.[4]

One question raised by the East Cree data regarding the identity of *Mistaapew* is whether there are one or several in the world, as there are some inconsistent data on this point. In answer to direct questioning, every Mistassini informant said that there was only one *Mistaapew* in the world, and that he was the boss of the shaking tent. Some added that at other times he lives in the forest, and he communicates with hunters, who hear him in the trees. It was claimed that only a *mitew* can communicate with him. Others say that anyone may establish contact with him, even a White person, as long as they believe in him. Both Flannery (1939:15) and Cooper (1944:80) say that among the East Cree *Mistaapew* is not the 'other self', or 'soul', reported by Speck, and Cooper specifically includes the Mistassini in this statement. Rousseau, describing a 'Shaking Tent' performed by a Nichicun man, proposes that the leading spirit in the performance is the soul spirit of the shaman (1953:146-7).

On the other hand, some references were made to multiple *Mistaapewac* (plural) by informants, sometimes with reference to any of the spiritual beings which appear in the shaking tent, sometimes to other spiritual beings which are met in the forest. In each of these cases, the term *Mistaapew* was used as a cover term for 'spiritual being', and more precise terms for the specific beings spoken about were also available. I also noted that among acculturated young people, who did not yet know much about traditional religious concepts, because they had been away at residential school for several years, the phrase 'to believe in *Mistaapew* and that sort of thing' was the most common way of expressing the idea of belief in traditional religious concepts. In other words, *Mistaapew* is sometimes used for the general notion of 'spirits' believed in by the Cree but not the Whites. Thus my own observations on this problem leads to the conclusion that at Mistassini the *Mistaapew* is a single particularly important spirit being, but that the·name is sometimes also used for a whole class of helpful spirit beings (cf. Savard 1971:12).

Recently there have been two other attempts to deal with this problem, one from the point of view of the data at Rupert House (Preston 1975) and the other for the data from Natashquan (Vincent 1973). Preston appears to follow Rousseau; he states that *Mistaapew* is both the soul concept as employed by Speck, and the Master of Ceremonies of the 'Shaking Tent', as proposed by Flannery (Preston 1975:105-6). In his extensive account of a 'Shaking Tent' performance, Preston speaks of the *Mistaapew* which is the central figure in the ceremony as 'the conjurer's *Mistaapew*'. He also recounts what is said to be a true story, during which it is stated that an old man had a *Mistaapew*, but now his son has it. Preston notes that this inheritance of a *Mistaapew* follows the pattern of inheritance of land (ibid.:143 and footnote 42). At the same time, the term *Mistaapew* is also used throughout his account of the 'Shaking Tent' to refer to all other beings which appear in the tent. According to Vincent's account, there is a separate world inhabited by *Mistaapewac* (pl.) some good, some bad, who live in a separate place to the east, connected to this world by an arm of land.[5] They have their own chief, and this is the being that is referred to when myths speak about a single *Mistaapew*. This being is the chief spirit of the 'Shaking Tent', but other *Mistaapewac* also enter during the ceremony, good ones from the south, bad ones from the north. Particular men have direct and permanent relations with a particular *Mistaapew*, relations which are established either by the *Mistaapew* contacting the men in a dream, following which the man performs·a 'Shaking Tent', or by the man seeking a *Mistaapew*, by such activities as sleeping for one night at the foot of a tree with an eagle's nest, or three nights at the foot of a tree with an osprey's nest (Vincent 1973:79-80). Among the Mistassini, both birds and trees are also involved in the initial contact between man and *Mistaapew*, since the cry of the owl or the flight of a raven indicates the direction which the man who is seeking *Mistaapew* is to take, and a particular species of tree (white spruce) standing alone marks the place for the encounter, which is made by circling the tree in a clockwise direction. Such symbolic parallels indicate that underlying the regional variations in the oral tradition respecting *Mistaapew* (variations which in the case of Mistassini exist even between different informants) there is a single symbolic structure. However, Speck's account of *Mistaapew* presents us with the most difficulty, particularly to this study, since Speck's account claims to include Mistassini data.[6]

However, while there appears to have been a crossing over of the two concepts of *aataacaakw* and *Mistaapew*, the confusion lies only at the level of exegesis, not at the level of the cognitive structure of the ritual. If divination consists of messages which are received, the implication is that these messages have a sender. In the 'Shaking Tent' a fairly clear conception is developed of who these senders are; they are personified natural forces. However, in other divination it may not be considered important to elaborate where the messages come from, and informants may feel satisfied simply with the message itself, and may thus tend to speculate to satisfy the questions of ethnographers.

3. *The 'Steam Tent'* (muutuuciiswaap)

We have pointed out that only one of the purposes of the 'Shaking Tent' was as a preparation for hunting. The 'Steam Tent' also served more than one purpose. Informants today emphasize its use as a cure for sickness, although earlier accounts tend to point to its use in the preparation for hunting. However, it must be remembered that cleanliness and health are not only ends in themselves which result from the use of the 'Steam Tent', they are also means to hunting success. Ill health is a serious threat to hunting ability, since at times great endurance is required; the 'Steam Tent' also removes body odour, which facilitates stalking game. At the symbolic level, the complete cleansing activity signifies that the hunter prepares himself to enter *nuhcimiihc*, 'the bush', which is the domain of the animals and the helpful spirits, and which in contrast to the camp is spoken of as being 'clean'. As a technique to prepare for the hunting activity, the 'Steam Tent' is not explicitly divinatory, although communication with spirits, occasionally of a divinatory nature, is sometimes reported. But like the specifically divinatory rites the 'Steam Tent' marks a forthcoming hunt as particularly important. There is a belief that wishes are themselves sources of power in bringing about the desired outcome. The 'Steam Tent' stands alongside the divinatory techniques as an expression of desire about a forthcoming hunt.

The 'Steam Tent' is no longer, as far as I know, used by any Mistassini hunters for hunting preparation, but it was in common use thirty years ago, and several middle-aged people are able to demonstrate the technique in detail. The performance I observed followed closely the published accounts for this region (e.g. Rousseau 1953a) and began with the construction of a framework dome, about 5 ft. 6 in. in diameter, which was then covered with several layers of canvas. It was oriented so that the bather when seated inside faces southeast, and towards the lake on whose shore it was located. As we have seen, this is the required orientation of the camp generally, and of the shaking tent. Inside the tent, on the side towards which the bather faces, a wooden support is built on the ground on which the hot stones will be placed. The rest of the floor is covered with spruce boughs. A number of large smooth rocks, of a type selected because they do not shatter when made red hot, are heated in a fire nearby, and carried to the tent. The canvas sides are lowered, and after some time the bather crawls in and sits with his legs under him. The beneficial effect is said to come from the rock itself, and the heat of the fire merely releases this potential power. The bather faces the rock, and when he becomes accustomed to the heat he may sprinkle water on the rocks to produce steam, allowing the rocks to increase their effectiveness. The bather remains inside as long as possible, and it is said that in the past he would sing special songs, or tell myths to those seated outside. According to informants, some men could remain inside for several hours, and this ability was considered to be evidence of the person's close relations with the spirits, and evidence of future success in hunting.

4. *Scapulimancy* (mitunsaawaakan)

Speck's chapter on divination devotes most of its space to an examination of scapulimancy, a technique of forecasting in which a flat bone, usually the shoulder blade of an animal or the breast bone of a bird, is heated by fire and the resulting chars and cracks interpreted. It is perhaps unfortunate that the two subsequent theories of divination which have made extensive reference to Speck's material, that is, the ecological theory of O.K. Moore (1957) and the sociological theory of G.K. Park (1963), refer only to this scapulimancy data, overlooking the fact that Speck includes in the chapter and elsewhere shorter notes on a variety of other divinatory techniques. However, it is probably true that scapulimancy was the single most common form of hunting divination, and the most elaborate, if we exclude the 'Shaking Tent'. I will deal with the specific technique first, and consider the general question of divination later in this chapter.

During my first winter in the field I observed four sets of scapulimancies. A set here refers to all scapulimancies performed consecutively as attempts to reveal a particular future event. In the first instance, the shoulder blade used was that of the first porcupine killed in the fall, by a man of the Nichicun local band. This took place in September, before the Nichicun group had broken up into individual hunting groups. The porcupine was not the subject of a feast, but it was given by the man who killed it to the man who was sharing his dwelling at the time. The latter person undertook the careful burning of the quills which is necessary before a porcupine is butchered, and his wife cooked it. Portions were then sent around to all of the houses, as is normal when only one hunter makes a kill. The recipient of the porcupine performed a scapulimancy the following day, and the bone was carried around to the other dwellings by a child so that it could be examined by all the others in the group. At that time I was unable to get any firm statement on its meaning, but was told that it related to the hunting fortunes of the whole Nichicun local band for the coming winter.

The second scapulimancy was also with a porcupine shoulder blade, and was also performed the day after the animal was eaten. It was performed in January, and like the first example, it took place during a period when a move in the campsite of the group was being planned. The camp had recently been visited by the H.B.C. manager by aeroplane, at which time he was informed of the planned location of the group's March camp, some distance to the north. During the 'reading' of the bone I again had difficulty in obtaining a clear statement of interpretation. A scapular is very roughly pear-shaped, and I was told that the narrow end represented the north. Along the length of one side of the bone is a raised part, called the lateral process. On either side of the lateral process there is a thin bone membrane, which is slightly thicker around the edges. The bone in question received a burn on only one side of the lateral process; this burn mark had a hairline crack in it. I was told that it possibly meant that there was a bear somewhere to the east. Two days later we began to move camp, which took two or three days of hauling by toboggan. Two further moves of the camp were made during the following two weeks, during which time only beaver, other fur-bearers, and small game were hunted. The third camp was about ten miles due north of the camp where the scapulimancy had been performed. As soon as this camp was established a moose hunt was undertaken, in a hilly region to the east, and two moose were killed the first day. I was then told that it was these moose which the scapulimancy had forecast over two weeks previously, and was reminded that they were indeed located to the east. Of particular interest in this scapulimancy was the fact that the bone was held over the fire by attaching it to a miniature snowshoe frame made at the same time. The frame was later given to the children for a toy, although it had previously been withheld from them. The divination was, by means of the snowshoe frame, made to refer to the journey about to be undertaken.

The third scapulimancy again involved porcupine scapulars, in this case two of them. At this time, in mid-February, the group was spending every day hauling their belongings, as an arrangement had been made previously for an aircraft to meet them at a particular lake, which was still some distance away. Thus there was great interest in the question of whether the aircraft would arrive on the date scheduled. For the Cree, bush planes are notorious for the apparently erratic timing of their operations, no matter what arrangements are made ahead of time, and in mid-winter there is some concern about such rendezvous, since anyone who wishes to meet the plane is forced to suspend hunting and to remain in camp until it arrives. In the case in question, the date arranged was about a week away from the time the scapulimancy was performed. The first scapulimancy indicated nothing about the aircraft, but did indicate that several caribou would be killed. In this case, I could get no opinion on how the bone should be oriented when reading it, and therefore no opinion on the direction of the caribou. However, the place for the camp at which it had been arranged for the aircraft to meet us was close to some hills, and, at around the same time of the scapulimancy, plans for hunting in this area were being discussed. Since the first bone had been unsuccessful in giving any information on the aircraft, the second scapular was burned. In this case an aircraft was indicated as arriving from the direction of Nichicun, which was the place from which the expected aircraft was to come. As it turned out, the aircraft arrived, but a week later than had been arranged, and I was reminded by the others of the augury. Following this, both moose and caribou were shot in the hills, and I was later told that this was the kill forecast by the first bone.

The last case took place with another hunting group during that same winter, but also concerned the arrival of an aircraft. Again a meeting place had been arranged, and the group had arrived there several days before the aircraft was due. Starting on the day the plane was due to arrive, and over the next four days, thirteen scapulimancies were performed, using the bones of hares caught over the previous few months and kept for this purpose. There was never less than two scapulimancies performed in one day, and there was a maximum of six. The same man did the burning each time, but immediately afterwards it was given to a child to carry around to the other tents to be examined by everyone. As in all scapulimancies observed, the children were excluded from the tent where the actual burning was conducted, or, if it was in the evening, were made to hide under a blanket. The actual activity of the burning was not a focus of interest for people from other commensal groups, although the divination was sometimes undertaken when adult visitors were present. In the interpretation of the message of the bone, the man who did the burning was not treated as having any kind of special ability. In fact, it was said that the wife of another hunter was best at the interpretation, based on past results. Most of the comments I heard were that the message was inconclusive, or that nothing was indicated one way or another about an aircraft. Particular interest was shown when two consecutive bones gave a similar char pattern, but it was said in such cases that nobody present was skilled enough to understand the meaning. As was the case with the earlier group, I was encouraged to state my own opinion of the meaning.

During a subsequent winter visit to a different hunting group, two scapulimancies were observed while on a week-long beaver trapping and moose hunting trip with three men, at which time the women stayed at the main camp. Again, one man did both scapulimancies, although the first was a failure, because while the bone was being held over the fire it was accidentally dropped, and when it was raked out of the fire it was too charred to be of any use. The second attempt, two days later, like the first, used a beaver scapular. Both of these scapulimancies were done at times when there was an expectation of seeing moose the following day. The first attempt had been made on the evening of arrival at an area which I had been told beforehand might be a good area for moose and wolf. In fact, on the following day two moose were seen, and tracks were also seen the day after, but none were killed. One wolf was killed. At this time the group moved into an area of high ground, which was full of lakes and small rivers and a suitable habitat for beavers. The trapping turned out to be unexpectedly poor, although it was known that many beavers had inhabited the region some years before. Fresh moose tracks were followed for several miles, but with the approach of night the trail had to be abandoned. The next day it was decided to leave the area, because of the poor trapping, and because there was no wish to haul any meat shot down from the difficult hilly and heavily wooded country. The group already had a good supply of stored meat, and was only willing to kill more under convenient circumstances. The second scapulimancy was performed at the camp at the foot of this hilly country and the interpretation of the bone by the man performing it was that he could see the trail of the moose which had been earlier followed descending from the hilly area. However, the moose or its tracks were not seen again, and the group returned to the main camp.

This last case illustrates what is a general feature of the scapulimancies I have observed, i.e. that the divination is not undertaken at a time when the hunters do not know where to go hunting. This point needs to be stressed, because the reverse of this seems to be the impression given by other accounts of scapulimancy. All Speck actually states on this point is that he was told by Sept Iles Indians that they consult the shoulder blade oracle frequently when there is a shortage of food (1935:151). Moore, apparently on the strength of this, concludes, 'when the Naskapi do have information about the location of game, they tend to act on it. Ordinarily, it is when they are uncertain and food supplies get low that they turn to their oracle for guidance' (Moore 1957:71). Similarly, Park includes Speck's data within a general theory of divination, a practice which is said to be used in circumstances when there is a decision which is both difficult

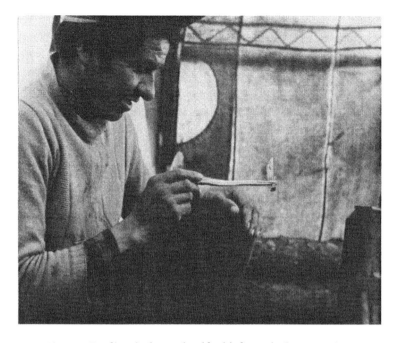

Plate 11. Reading the burnt shoulder blade oracle (hare scapular),
immediately after the bone was burnt in the stove.

to make, and of great concern to a social group (1963), suggesting that
Park also assumes a condition of food shortage. There is, at the same
time, some evidence that it is also the hunter's view that scapulimancy
is only performed in time of need. My own informants stressed that it
was wrong to use scapulimancy too often, since this would amount to
making fun of the practice. Henriksen, in a recent study of the
Naskapi of Davis Inlet, says that, although scapulimancy is no longer
used by them in hunting, it was in the past only used at times of
extreme uncertainty (1973:30). There are several possible reasons for
this discrepancy between Naskapi ideology and my recent observations
among the Mistassini. In the first place, we must distinguish between
a condition of shortage of a particular kind of animal and an absolute
shortage of food. In most cases of scapulimancy observed among the
Mistassini, the oracle was undertaken at a time when some change in
the pattern of hunting, or in the pattern of residence, was known to be
about to take place. Moose and caribou hunts, and the arrival of aircraft, represent major redirections in the pattern of production, a
change from daily trips by individual trappers to check old traps or to
set new ones, to some more communal activity. From this point of
view, there is evidence to support Park's emphasis on the relation

between divination and group action. The above examples all represent a change from individual to collective action, and often also to hunting a species not hunted for some time.

However, collective action does not always follow scapulimancy. In 1972-3 M. MacKenzie conducted linguistic field work with a Mistassini hunting group. She reports (personal communication) that two of the group's three hunters did scapulimancies, in one case every few days, using hare scapulars. Burned blades were sent by the man who performed the scapulimancy to the other families in the group for examination only at those times when the men planned to go moose hunting together. At other times the hunters' scapulimancies were done to predict their own individual beaver trapping, by foretelling if beaver houses would be found in a particular region, or if beaver would be caught in traps already set. The divinations were done either during the evening before, or in the early morning of the day to which they referred.

Neither the observations of MacKenzie nor those made by myself were in situations of any long-run hunting failures, or shortages of game food. Starvation and hunting failures are believed to be caused by the masters of the animals and other spiritual powers withholding the game from men, because of some offence such as the breaking of a taboo. Under such circumstances of hunting failure, it is easy to see how scapulimancy, which is an attempt to see into the hidden spiritual level of animal distribution, takes on a particular significance. However, our data do show that scapulimancy also has significant use when there are no critical shortages. When it is used under plentiful circumstances it is not as a decision-making device, as all previous commentators on the subject appear to suppose.

Scapulimancy, as a divinatory rite, occupies an intermediary position in a whole series of such rites, from the group to the individual. Each type of divination, of whatever kind, has its particular social context, a group to whom it is addressed. The 'Shaking Tent', when not used for the purpose of sorcery, is addressed to the largest possible audience — to the band, or to the residential hunting group. At the other extreme, some rites and games are private, for instance, dreaming, although the private aspect has been over-emphasized by Speck, since even dreams are discussed with others, and may refer to the future of the family or the hunting group. Scapulimancy may, according to circumstances, operate either at the level of the hunting group, or of the smallest productive unit, which is the commensal family.

Within scapulimancy, distinctions are made in terms of the kind of bones used. There is a relationship between the species of the animal whose bone is used and the interpretation of the oracle. At the same time, distinctions are made according to the appropriate occasion on which to use a particular animal's bone. The most important distinction between the various animal bones used is size. Scapulars of large animals (moose, caribou) are said to be difficult, (and with an implication of dangerous) to use, and few people today are able to read them. It is believed that they were more frequently used in the past, but that now there are fewer individuals with sufficient spiritual power (*mite*) to employ them. Among the smaller animals there are also individual preferences, as some individuals develop their skill with one species more than another. There is also a relation between the character of the animal and of the prediction which its bone gives. A porcupine is an extremely slow-moving animal, and its divination takes a long time to be realized. The hare, on the other hand, is fast, and so is its divination. The scapulimancies that were observed all fall into the category of small animals, and therefore of somewhat less importance than if they had been performed using moose or caribou scapulars. The large scapular bones themselves continue to have a special importance for the Mistassini, since I observed that they were in most cases hung separately in a tree (like the skulls of several animals) and not put on the bone platform, as were the rest of the moose and caribou bones.

The interpretation of scapulimancy offered here is in contrast to that of Moore, Park and Henriksen, in part because we begin with the observation that scapulimancy was not used only when hunters had no idea where they should go hunting, and that therefore the oracle ought not to be assumed to be a decision-making device. It is possible to conclude that there are two kinds of scapulimancy, one more serious, using the bones of the largest animals, and used only in times of great need; our data cannot confirm this, and we are restricted to the use of the rite in what we judge to be normal circumstances.

As it happens, Speck's data are also arranged to show two kinds of scapulimancy, but based instead on geographic distribution. He distinguishes between the scapulimancy of the bands to the south and west, and that of the bands to the north and east of the Quebec-Labrador peninsular. The contrast is not made systematically in his book, but Table 11 (see over) shows the major points of contrast.

The distribution pattern of the types shown in Table 11 roughly correspond to the distinction between those bands which have access to large herds of caribou (bands to the north and east), versus those where the big game is found individually or in small groups, and who are also dependent on beaver. The scapulimancy data from Nichicun and Mistassini places them clearly within the 'bands to the south and west', with whom they also belong on the above ecological grounds. However, for the Nichicun, at least, there is now no aversion to the use of moose and caribou scapulars, but rather the idea is held that in the past they were used commonly, although now people have lost the power to do so (cf. Rogers 1973:12). Speck's data make it clear that locating game is not the only result of Type A scapulimancy, but the

Table 11.   THE TWO TYPES OF SCAPULIMANCY (Speck 1935)

Type A *Bands of the South and West*	*Type B* *Bands of the North and East*
1. Oracle refers to various events, hunting, weather, health, arrivals, (pp. 140, 150).	Oracle refers exclusively to hunting (pp. 147-8, 150).
2. Oracle may indicate only success or failure of hunt, not always the direction of the game (p. 140, and examples 139-46).	Oracle indicates the location of game, but not hunter's success (p. 151); Oracle is 'more pictographic' (p. 147).
3. Only shamans can use 'large' (i.e. moose and caribou) scapulars (p. 146); others use small game.	Practically all hunters do the one kind of divination (p. 147).
4. Some people have personal preferences in using bones of particular species (p. 146).	Caribou scapulars used most often (p. 147).
5. A 'prompting' dream prior to the scapulimancy is not obligatory (p. 150).	A prior 'prompting' dream is obligatory (p. 150).

prediction of success, weather, health or the arrival of strangers may also be foretold. This tends to confirm our above proposition that Mistassini and Nichicun scapulimancy is not necessarily a decision-making device.

The distinction between the above two kinds of scapulimancy may also help us to understand how Park and Henriksen arrive at such opposite interpretations to our own in the analysis of the practice. Clearly, it is not scapulimancy by itself which we are investigating, but scapulimancy in a specific ecological and decision-making context. According to Park and Henriksen, Naskapi scapulimancy reduces social strain by externalizing the risk-laden choice of where to go hunting (Park 1963; Henriksen 1973:49). What our data indicate is that this cannot explain scapulimancy entirely, since a nearby related group, the Mistassini, continues to use the same technique, with a few variations, even when there is no requirement of making risky decisions. Scapulimancy consists of a form of expressive behaviour. It is not an isolated technique of divination, but as we can see, is one of a number of forms of divination which share a common symbolic ideology. Furthermore, divination as a preparatory rite is part of a linked set of rites concerning man's relationship with animals. For example, if we look through all the divinatory and preparatory rites we find again and again that it is bones which are in some way manipulated. Following the hunt we again find that it is bones which are offered or displayed to the spirits. Thus scapulimancy must be seen in the wider symbolic context.

5. *Divinatory signs* (weciiyaawham, '*something will come*')

Mistassini divination can be separated into those techniques which people initiate, by undertaking some action, and other divinations which are in the form of 'signs' that simply appear without the person making the first move. The two types of divination may be related, as when initiated by a person, like scapulimancy, for example, must sometimes be preceded by a prompting sign of some kind. However, we will distinguish between 'voluntary divinations' which men initiate and 'divinatory signs' which appear without prompting. The most commonly-reported divinatory sign, in this sense, is dreaming. The Mistassini, as might be expected, have developed a set of ideas related to the interpretation of dreams. Dreams which I heard being discussed among the hunting group (and most winter-time conversations are of a more or less public order) included one of an aircraft landing on the lake at which we were camped (an aircraft was expected, and did arrive that same day), and one of meeting a strange animal in the bush, which was later interpreted to refer to an unexpected meeting with another hunter which took place following the dream. Although these cases deal with the meeting of strangers, and not the outcome of hunting expeditions, I was often told that dreaming is the most common way for hunters to learn about their hunting success in advance.[7]

Most dreams which predict hunting results require interpretation; one of the common rules is that any appearance of members of the opposite sex, particularly strangers, is to be taken to refer to a game animal. Secondly, dreams which indicate a meeting with or the killing of small animals often in fact refer to different larger game animals which are going to be killed.

Some examples I was given include the account of a dream of a man in which he meets an Eskimo woman, who invites him to live with her. The man refused the invitation. Later he was hunting and sighted a caribou, which ran away. The hunter gave chase, shot at it, but missed, and it got away. In some cases the dream will be remembered, and months will pass before the event referred to in the dream takes place. A man had a dream about boy and girl twins. It was not until four months later, when he came across and killed two moose, one male and one female, that he knew what the dream was referring to. Women are also said to have dreams which refer to hunting success, in the same way that they may have wish power which brings success to their husbands. Just as females who appear in men's dreams usually refer to game animals, so too do the men who appear in the dreams of women. Dreaming of a baby indicates that a bear will be killed.

Later in this chapter we will note how sacred objects are used to promote dreams. A person who lives in a hunting camp is taught to pay attention to and remember his dreams. Some people say that the dreams they had as children included important premonitions about the success of the adult hunters of the group, even if this information was not used by the adults to allow them to make the kill. For instance, one person told of dreaming that the father killed game; the dream experience happened during a period of hunger, when no game had been killed for a long time. The next day the father made a major kill. Such dreams, although they have no practical use, are held to indicate that the person potentially has spiritual power. Dreams most commonly contain, in code, as it were, information which, while it may not allow hunters to make tactical decisions, marks the hunt, or whatever is the action referred to, and the dreamer as being of special importance. Power which remains with an individual is sometimes thought to arrive in dreams, in the form of formulae for songs, or shamanistic techniques, or ideas for the decoration of clothing or other objects. One woman said that the complicated technique of lacing snowshoes came to her first of all in a dream. Although it is clearly correct to treat dreaming as a form of divinatory sign about future productive activities, the significance of dreams is not limited to answering the questions of tactical importance in the productive undertaking. Dreams offer instead a partial interpretation of productive activities, an opportunity to uncover not merely what lies hidden in the future, but also something of the significance of everyday events at a level that is normally obscure. They can also be used to signify that particular individuals have spiritual power.

In addition to dreams, there are numerous divinatory signs, just as there are numerous minor oracles and divinatory games. Each authority who has investigated these questions has produced a different list (e.g. Speck 1930, 1935; Rogers 1973; Cooper 1930; Rousseau 1953; Skinner 1911; Flannery 1971), which suggests that the total list may be considerably larger; my experience was that a field worker must to some extent rely on coming across the less commonly used techniques more or less by accident. As we might expect, my list is most similar to that of Rogers (1973:11-15) who also worked with a Mistassini hunting group. In the present study I will only deal in detail with those I have observed in use spontaneously, since the timing of the oracle plays an important part in an understanding of it.

Several of them consist of unusually-shaped natural objects which fall into the hands of the hunter as part of his productive activities. He may find that a porcupine he has killed has an intestine with an unusual shape. The object is given to the hunter's wife or mother, who makes it into a miniature grease container, which is filled with the rendered fat from the intestines of the porcupine. The special feature of this sac is the shape of an appendage, and this shape tells the hunter what game he can expect to kill. If the shape has a sharp angle, like the foreleg of a caribou, a caribou kill is predicted. If the angle is rounded it is said to mean a bear or an otter. An intermediate angle indicates a moose. The object, which is kept by the women (who consume the fat) is called *uutuuskenhaaw*, 'his elbow'. While fishing a man may come across a rock or a stone with the shape of a game animal; I was shown an example of a rock found in a fish net, which was said to indicate a future kill.

The bone of a pike may have a lump on it, and this is said to indicate a future kill. The size of the lump is directly proportional to the importance of the animal to be killed, and the distance from the upper end of the bone to where the lump is located indicates the time that will pass before the predicted kill will take place. This is called *ciispuu*, 'he is full (of something solid)'. A similar divination is based on the lumps which are to be found on the lower jawbone of a beaver born the previous winter (called a *wecis*). The number of these lumps, which varies from two to about five, is said to indicate the total number of *wecis* in the same lodge from where the original animal came.

In addition to unusual shapes, unusual noises have divinatory significance. The Canada Jay occasionally makes a call which the Cree say sounds like a fleshing tool in use; to hear this call is an omen of hunting success. If the fire makes a special kind of cracking noise it is said to indicate a future kill; the fire may also throw sparks during a meal, and this is a good omen for the person whose plate they land on and has particular reference to bear hunting; I was told that hiccups indicated either bad weather or hunting success, and that when a gust of wind blows open the tent flap it is an invitation to a hunt which will be successful. Many of the above are never used as methods of determining the outcome of a hunt, but are events which set off a familiar round of jokes or comments. However, both serious and humorous divination often employ the same elements, and may thus be thought of as parts of the same system.

All of the objects which contain divinatory signs, and also the objects which are used in voluntary divinations including scapulars, are kept for a while next to the wall where the head of an individual lies when he sleeps. These objects are placed there to promote dreams about the events referred to in the divination. This part of the tent or lodge is called *taawpwaataakan*, 'that which brings dreams'. It is associated with the head, and therefore with knowledge. This is one of the places, along with the doorposts, which are smeared with fat during the feast held when the group first enters into its winter dwelling; fat is also rubbed into the hair to promote thoughts and dreams. One myth told to explain the significance of this part of the dwelling concerns a hunting group who were being attacked by a mythical animal, *mistatimw* ('giant dog'). The group succeeded in killing it, and wanted to burn the body, but the leader told them that first they must lay it inside the tent, with its head next to the place where his head lay at night. It was left there for one day, and then the body was burned. For this reason these monsters no longer bother men. The placing of the animal's head close to where the leader's was laid at night was sufficient for the latter to gain control over the animal's power.

6. *Minor oracles*

Although Speck and others have focused attention on the burnt shoulder blade divination, the point has been made that this technique is only the most complex of a whole series of oracles, many of which also employ the bones of game animals. Speck mentions the 'burnt beaver pelvic bone divination' (1935:141), and this was known by my informants, although I never saw it used spontaneously. In this method a crack made by placing the pelvic bone in the fire indicates the direction of game. The beaver pelvis also was frequently used in a game with divinatory significance. The bone is held in one hand and the index finger of the other is held out, and the two arms are raised in a semi-circle to meet above the head. If the index finger enters the hole in the bone, and particularly if it enters the socket of the thigh bone, these indicate future success in hunting. The sexual connotation of this action is not lost to the participants; this is a further variation of the endless play on the hunting/sexual parallel.

Another 'game' with divinatory overtones involves breaking a beaver tibia wrapped in cloth. This is said to require more than strength, and sometimes a weak person succeeds where a strong one fails. With this technique, and with the beaver pelvis oracles, there is often a competitive spirit, as the bone is passed around for everyone to try. However, the divinatory aspect was taken seriously by the group I observed; when someone succeeded in breaking the bone a careful count was made of the fragments of bone which broke away at the edge. The breaking itself was said to indicate the hunter would find an occupied beaver lodge, and the fragments, according to their size, indicated the mature and immature beaver that would be found there. The tail bone of a beaver was put in the fire at the beginning of the hunting season, and a count was made of the cracking noises emitted. Each of such noises was said to represent a major kill during the coming season.[8] Another divination using fire is the burning match, which when held upright indicates the direction of game by the direction towards which it bends.

Several divinatory games involve tossing an object, usually an animal bone. I observed the use of fish bones, one variation of which was the attempt to get the bone to stick into the tent canvas overhead. This game was not treated as a serious form of divination, although it was undertaken in mid-winter, at a time when fishing activities had just recommenced after a lull of several months. The tossing of a muskrat skull with a stick protruding from the nasal cavity was also observed; not only was this treated as a game, but also its divinatory character had an inverted form. The questions are generally playful and personal, as Speck also noted (1935:165), such as, 'Who has been bad?' or 'Who has a lover?'; however, it was said that the answers given to these questions, by the stick pointing at one of the circle of persons, was the contrary of the truth, because the muskrat is such a notorious liar.

In addition to the above, members of the group had in the past practised scrying which involves foretelling the future by staring into a bowl of water, a mirror or a decorated object, in this case while the diviner was seated and completely covered by a blanket. Like the 'Shaking Tent', this technique was also used in sorcery (cf. Bauer 1973:37-41). One man had seen an otter tail divination, in which an otter tail is skinned and placed outside the dwelling overnight; in the morning it is examined for hairs which indicate both the number and the species of forthcoming kills. The cedar bundle game, described by Speck (1935:198-9), was observed, and the cup and pin game was known; both involve tossing an object, or set of objects strung together, and attempting to catch it (or one of them) with a pointed stick. As with many such activities, both games and divinations, the activity passed around the dwelling for each to take a turn.

When comparing the size of the above list with the total of all divinatory techniques which have appeared in various ethnographic descriptions of the area, both those treated with great seriousness and those for which it is said that they are done only for fun, it seems that among those who continue to hunt actively divination has continued both in the variety of its technique, and the degree of its use, for at least sixty years without significantly diminishing. Unfortunately, the earliest accounts, by Skinner and Speck, do not give any indication of the degree to which they were used; but while I observed no technique being used to a very great extent, such as before every hunting expedition, I did see a fair range, and even observed a few which have not been reported before in published form, within the activities of a single group for a single year.

7. *The symbolism of divination*

The various individual techniques of divination which we have examined need not be left to stand each by itself. Each is a member of a set the whole of which exhibits a structure. The techniques differ, for example, in the seriousness with which the performance is treated, in whether the divination arrives spontaneously or is sought, in whether it produces a direct sign or a message requiring expert interpretation, and the degree to which a particular technique also acts as a form of magic. On the last point, Honigmann has pointed out that Cooper's fourfold division of Northern Algonkian magic into hunting magic, weather magic, cradle charms and the 'Shaking Tent' fails to separate clearly divination from magic (1964:323).

In some rites, particularly the use of the drum and the singing of hunting songs, divination and magic are both present. If we define magic as a rite in which man pretends to intervene in the operation of natural forces, divination is the associated technique of revealing the state of affairs behind this imaginary causal system. The same technique (a message from man to the spirits) may in some circumstances prompt a divinatory message, and in other cases control the outcome of a hunt. The 'Shaking Tent' is similarly open to this double usage. Both divination and magic are part of the same ideology, and are expressed within the same system of symbols.

Of the materials which are principally used in the rites, bone recurs most often, with some fur, skin and intestine from game animals. All of these materials are by-products of the hunt which, although they each have a productive use, present the Cree with a problem of over-abundance. A central attitude in the conduct of hunting is that game animals are persons and that they must be respected. The rules of respect after the killing involve essentially taking care of all elements of the carcass, and not allowing anything to be thoughtlessly discarded. Thus blood and intestines are consumed, buried in the snow or fed to the dogs, bones are made into tools, hung in the trees, put on bone platforms, or put in a lake, and all uneaten meat is fed to the dogs or put in the fire. Fur and skin no longer present a problem of surplus because of their use in trade, and in manufacture for trade, although prior to the fur trade (if we can presume that beaver formed a significant part of the prehistoric diet) it is possible that there was a problem of the disposal of fur — in the same way that porcupine quills present this problem, solved by burning. Bird feathers have a use in stuffing pillows, and wings are used as pipe cleaners and as brushes, but both arrive in camp in surplus quantities, and most must be carefully disposed of, the former usually by burning, the latter, together with the bird skulls, by hanging in a tree.

It is not a sufficient description to say that ritual materials are those which come from a 'sacred' source (i.e. game animals) and which appear from time to time as surplus by-products. Particular objects are selected for use from such an assemblage by the application of a logic of the Cree equivalent to Lévi-Strauss' *bricoleur* (1966:Chapter 1). One feature of such objects is a sheet-like or membrane quality. This feature is found in rites in which the actor uses the membrane to communicate with the spirit world, a world which is represented as being on the other side. Thus the covering of the shaking tent (originally made of hides) shakes and moves to reveal the action of the spirits which are on the other side, that is, inside the tent. A commonly-reported feature of the ceremony is the part in which *Mistaapew* has a fight with the spirit of the bears; *Mistaapew*'s victory indicates that men will be able to kill bears in the future. The presence of the bear inside the shaking tent is revealed by the impression of the shape of a claw that can be seen through the tent cover by the onlookers. Preston, who observed a 'Shaking Tent' ceremony at Rupert House, was told that the spirits who knocked on the tent at the people who sat around were just like someone who was knocking on the window of a house which all the people were inside, since the spirit can see everyone through the canvas (1975:49). The membranes of the drum and the rattle are made of caribou skin, or sometimes, in the case of the rattle, of fish skin, and are beaten or shaken by the person who operates them.

In addition there are buzzers or small stones which pick up and continue the sounds of the membrane. Spirits are said to 'speak' in the sounds made by these instruments.

The membrane is thus the element that both links and separates the performer and the spirit. In the chapter on feasting the argument is put forward that the feast tent in which all the openings are sealed, and the cloth used to wrap feast food taken out of the tent, are both boundary-maintaining and membranes, which both seal off food which is in a sacred condition and symbolically separate the inner cultural world of man's dwelling and food from the outer domain of the spirits. There are numerous beliefs and mythic references to a world of beings under the water, so that the surface of the water, or the ice covering it, can be seen as a membrane between two worlds. In scrying this membrane is used to see into another world. With the porcupine intestine sign, like the example of the bear claw seen inside the shaking tent, the outline of a characteristic part of the animal is seen in the shape of the membrane. In the case of scapulimancy this membrane feature is essential, as can be seen by the fact that the only bone which can be substituted is the breast bone of a ptarmigan or spruce grouse. In fact, the reading of the burnt bone is often made by holding the translucent membrane up to the light.

All the examples of divination using a membrane depend to some extent on the ability to read the sign. A person with power, either an *emitewaaciiyt* or a *mitew*, can interpret the message unfailingly. But these divinations are performed whether or not such a person is available. One reason for undertaking a divination for which there may be no person available with the skill required to read the oracle is that by doing so a sacred object is created which is put at the person's place at the rear of the tent, to give him dreams and increase his power. Since there are very few rules regarding the interpretation of the oracle, the way to become a powerful man is to learn the skill through practice, by comparing an attempted forecast with later observations.

The inedible parts of an animal are treated as containing part of the animal's power. For instance, during the performance of a scapulimancy the practitioner may address the bone, sometimes telling the animal to fly around the country and tell what is seen. At the same time, the normal method of disposal of the most sacred bones (i.e. the skull, the front limbs of the bear, beaver and some smaller animals, the scapulars of large animals, and many antlers) is by hanging them on display in a tree. These displayed bones may also be decorated, and are always oriented in an easterly or southerly direction. All other bones are either used to manufacture artifacts, which is sometimes spoken of as being pleasing to the animal concerned, or are stored out of reach, those of land animals and birds being placed above (on a bone platform) and those of water animals below (under the water). However, bones used in divination are treated quite differently from the ordinary bones of game animals when they are disposed of.

Some conclusions can be drawn from the foregoing, both on the way the Cree use symbolic interpretation to arrive at the content of divinatory messages, and on how this process relates to the general field of cultural symbolism within which Cree divination stands. It may be said that divination rites involve the reception of a message believed to come from the spirit world, a message that is received through the medium of any number of kinds of material that for the Cree are relatively 'sacred'. The material objects which contain these divinatory signs or oracles must, moreover, be treated with 'respect' after the reception of the message. Although the divinatory messages arrive 'in code', and are of conscious interest to the Cree, there are relatively few explicit or elaborate rules for 'decoding' them. There is a wide variation as to how transparent a message may be. In the 'Shaking Tent', for example, and in divinatory games, the message is fairly obvious to anyone. 'Decoding' what is often the obscure oraculary message given by scapulimancy is, by contrast, an example of a more complex divinatory technique, as is the interpretation of dreams. The interpretation of divinatory symbolism is complicated by the fact that in addition to the symbolism involved in the message itself, the ritual is also part of the more general level of symbolic interpretation that is shared by the general body of Cree religious ideas and ritual. For example, the 'Shaking Tent' must be understood in terms of the complex spatial symbolism of Cree cosmology (see Vincent 1973), and the several forms of divination using animal bones should be interpreted in terms that include consideration of the symbolism of the various parts of the animal in relation to each other, as revealed in rules for serving food, and in rules for the proper disposal of inedible remains (see Chapter 8).

Hunting divination is a rite which involves two levels of communication. First, its explicit purpose is to receive communication from animals and the entities that control them. But secondly it is like any other rite; it is a symbolic performance in which materials and actions, in the context of cultural knowledge, make statements of a more general nature, and of ideological significance. According to the folk conception of the process divination involves a prompting message from man to the animal, followed by a message from the animal to man. Another, more paradoxical way of looking at the divination rite is as the receipt of a message which has no sender (the oracle), the receipt of which is achieved by means of the participants composing another message, which has no particular receiver (the ritual symbolism).

8. *Conclusions: divination and hunting*

In the chapter on hunting group production at Mistassini it was suggested that hunting and trapping productivity is best treated as a single activity centred on a journey from the camp and returning with game. In practice, however, the process of killing animals must be preceded, usually by several days, and sometimes up to a year or more, by a process of gathering information about the presence and activities of game animals. This prior information gathering applies equally to hunting and to trapping. Such information is needed first of all to plan the general area to be visited during the year, and to plan the size of the group that can be supported. Knowledge of the lakes and rivers, and of the habitats, in terms of vegetation patterns, enable a hunter to plan where to look for signs of particular species. Many of the animals hunted by the Mistassini are either relatively sedentary, like the beaver, or tend to move back and forth along the same trails, like bears in summer and fall, otters in spring, and mink, marten and hares in the winter. Thus, when a man leaves the camp with the intention of hunting or trapping, he does not rely merely on the chance that he will meet an animal. He does not take all his guns, to be ready for every kind of animal he might shoot, or every size of trap for every kind of animal he might happen to come across. Each animal is shot or trapped so as to minimize time spent searching, and time spent checking the traps and hauling the carcass.

While it may be inviting to see Mistassini divination as a magical response to the threat of starvation, it must not be overlooked that starvation was by no means common. Divination does, however, have a close parallel with the gathering of information about game. The general observations of divination which I made in visits to three hunting groups were compatible with the view that it was conducted as an intellectual exercise which accompanied the collection of hunting data. When the oracle arrived, people were generally already aware that some new game was likely to be found, due to environmental signs or to a change in the seasons, just as scapulimancies to predict the arrival of aircraft were done only at a time the plane was expected. This is not to explain away divination as a trick, since this connection is not hidden. The kind of information divination gives is just that kind that cannot be known in advance from an examination of environmental signs. Divination fills in gaps in knowledge, which cannot be learned from the environment.

A common problem for the study of Mistassini religion is to take a general impression, such as the one just given (i.e. that divination is not a substitute for environmental data gathering, but a parallel process which is of a symbolic order) and to formulate from this impression a testable hypothesis. All that can be said at the moment is that our model accounts for the observations better than any previous ones of which I am aware. Furthermore, such a viewpoint allows us to see how divination symbolizes part of the process of production (environmental information gathering), although it works at other levels. It takes as its field of observation symbolic data outside the environmental level of significance, from the context of the complex of spiritual ideas. Thus the end point of divinatory ideology is not directly limited to the context of material production.

What are the social implications of the ideology of Mistassini divination? In the first place, it emphasizes the distinction between the man with special power, who can undertake specialist techniques like the 'Shaking Tent', from the man who has only acquired the ability to interpret oracles like dreams and scapulimancy. These men with different degrees of skill can be differentiated from others, who, even though they have no such skill, may have divinatory dreams, or engage in minor divinatory games. Seen as a set of social distinctions, these different levels of involvement in the divination process parallel the three basic categories of producers, and the relationships between them. The oldest men generally make use of their knowledge of animals and of the environment, a knowledge which is analogous to, and spoken of as, a spiritual power. Middle-aged men are far more active in the actual hunting and trapping, but their success is held to be in part dependent on the older individuals who have title to the land, or who at least give advice, and who have known the area for many years. The third group is that of the younger unmarried men, who after about the age of sixteen are generally as productive as older men, but who lack experience, and are subordinate to the married men. Thus, while divination tends to replicate the social relations between producers, it also tends to explain the inversion of the relationship between status and productivity. Single men, although they have less experience, tend to be at least as productive in the bush as married men, since they have less family responsibilities to keep them in camp. Older men remain productive as long as their legs remain strong, but tend to be a lot slower, and are usually restricted to hunting and trapping close to camp. Thus status is not a reflection of material productivity, but of the *cultural interpretation* of productivity, which places the real credit for success with the members of the group with long experience, with knowledge and with spiritual power. This success is demonstrated in divination.

It has also been shown that divination tends to mark, and to draw attention to, particularly significant occasions of productivity. We will see later how feasts do the same sort of thing. Emphasis in both cases is principally on first occasions; the first animal of a species killed in a season, the first animal of a species killed by a young man, and the first animal of a species to be killed after that kind of animal has not been killed for some time. In many cases, the marking of such events is virtually equivalent to the marking of a calendrical event (i.e. the progression of the seasonal cycle), or the marking of a life cycle crisis. What the divination material suggests is that not only is the ending of such hunts celebrated, but their importance is also foreshadowed by divination. In this way the arrival of natural events, which signal the arrival of the time when certain animals can be hunted with minimum effort and maximum chance of success, are treated, by divination rites, as social events.

7
Ritual Relations Between Hunters and Game Animals Killed

1. *Animal friendship*

In this chapter we continue the discussion of the religious aspect of Cree hunting production by looking at the religious symbolism contained in rites which take place during the actual process of killing. For the Cree, the activities and events which are involved in particular cases of the production of meat and furs by the hunting of wild animals have one obvious level of significance in the use of knowledge about particular species in providing for material needs, but at the same time the same events have a second, more obscure significance. This second level of the events of the hunt can only be appreciated if the animals and their actions are 'reinterpreted' in more or less anthropomorphic terms. The facts about particular animals are reinterpreted as if they had social relationships between themselves, and between them and anthropomorphized natural forces, and furthermore the animals are thought of as if they had personal relations with the hunters. The idealized form of these latter relations is often that the hunter pays respect to an animal; that is, he acknowledges the animal's superior position, and following this the animal 'gives itself' to the hunter, that is, it allows itself to assume a position of equality, or even inferiority, with respect to the hunter.

This notion that there is a double significance to the events of the hunt is strikingly made use of in a myth which was told to me by Matthew Rich, an Indian from Northwest River, Labrador. The myth, which need not concern us in all its details, is about a young man who marries a caribou girl. At the start of the myth the young man is hunting caribou with his family, and the story describes the hunting encounter between the hunters and the caribou from the normal human perspective. However, during the hunt the young man becomes able to see these same events from a different perspective, that is, from the perspective of the caribou. This caribou perspective consists of the transformation of the caribou reality into human terms. The story gives details of how a number of phenomena involving the caribou appear to the young man (caribou reality), and how these same phenomena appear, by contrast, to the young man's family (human reality). For example, the young man sees what to him appears to be a beautiful young woman, while to the hunters this appears as an ordinary female caribou. After the boy marries the caribou girl he joins the other caribou, who to him appear as Indians, living in small hunting groups. Later they all assemble together in a large house. The caribou leader is the father of the caribou girl. During a caribou hunt the hunters and the young man see the same events, but to each they appear quite different. The human beings see the caribou running from the hunters, and when one is shot the animal falls down and dies; but the young man, seeing the same event, sees a person wearing a white cape running away and then throwing off the cape, which the hunter then picks up as the carcass. At another time, what appears to the hunters as the rutting of the caribou in the fall is seen by the young man as a soccer game played by the male caribou.

This double perspective regarding the normal appearance of events to human eyes, as compared with a more obscure 'animal' reality, is to be found in many of the myths and religious ideas of the Mistassini. Another example is contained in a Mistassini myth, 'The Boy who was Kept by a Bear', the text of which is quoted in full later in this chapter. In this story a boy is being kept by a bear, and the boy's father sets out to find his son. The bear tries to lead the father astray, and the actions he uses to this end are described as taking place simultaneously at two levels, the level of human reality and the level of bear reality. At the level of bear reality, the bear is a hunter who gathers animals for food, like beavers, porcupines and partridges. But when the bear throws such an animal outside his den, this event is realized, at the human level of reality, as the father coming across an animal of this species living in its natural state. The myth gives details of the ritual treatment given to the forearms of bears, establishing one of the conditions by which some kind of communication can be established between these two levels of reality.

We have given examples of the explicit reference to the idea that game animals participate simultaneously in two levels of reality, one 'natural' and the other 'cultural', in the sense that it is modelled on conventional Cree patterns of social and cultural organization. These examples come, significantly, from mythology. We must therefore be careful in assuming that the modern Cree accept at face value the existence of this second level of reality. To the extent that the myths constitute a form of belief, they indicate the state of affairs that existed in the distant past. But the myths also explain the origins of the hunting rituals that are used today. Ritual action is primarily symbolic in nature. We may say that the hunting rites are believed to constitute an effective form of magical action, and that they depend to some extent on reconstituting the world 'as if' the conditions of mythic times were in place.

One of the more significant results of the idea that game animals are, from this magico-religious perspective, living in social groups similar to those used by Cree hunters, is that social interaction

between humans and animals is made possible. Three major models
for this interaction between hunters and game animals, based on three
types of social relationships, can be identified in the symbolism of
hunting rites: (1) male-female, (2) dominance-subordination, and
(3) equivalence.

The first of these usually suggests that the victim can be represented
as the female lover of the hunter. Several examples of this, particularly in the context of divinatory dreams, were referred to in Chapter
6, and this subject will be further elaborated in the next chapter.
Preston has recently made a similar point in a study of the Cree of the
East Coast of James Bay. By using material from hunting songs, myths
and accounts of divinatory dreams, he concludes that there is a love
relationship between the hunter and his prey. In the case of the
caribou this love is analogous to the sexual love between a man and his
lover, or the love of a father for his daughter, but in the case of the
bear the love is analogous to the love a man has for his son or for his
grandfather (Preston 1976:215-16). In the case of bear hunting which
he cites, however, the divinatory dream is about an old woman, for
whom the dreamer feels very sad (ibid.:232). According to Preston,
the relationship to the beaver is also analogously sexual, but whereas
the caribou gives itself to the hunter eagerly (analogous to sexual lust)
the beaver gives itself to be killed with the more decorous attitude of
generosity (ibid.:230).

A relationship of dominance-subordination is often suggested in
cases where magic is used to compel an animal to approach the hunter
or to in some other way allow itself to be caught. As we have said,
ritual preparations for hunting are primarily divinatory in nature.
However, shamans are said to have the power to make game animals
come to them. In the 'Shaking Tent' a battle may take place between
the spirit of the bear and a spirit helper of the shaman who performs
the rite. If the spirit of the bear is defeated the hunters of the group
will be able to kill bears during the following season. In this case, the
subordination of the bear in the preparatory rite can be followed by
the actual killing of the bear, in which the emphasis is not placed on
the subordination of the prey by the hunter, but of the generosity of
the bear, and the warm relations between the victim and the hunter.
This same model of a preliminary subordination of the bear to the
hunter by means of magic (in this case by the use of a song), followed
by the actual killing, in which the bear allows himself to be killed, as
an act of someone who is an equal of the hunter, may be found in the
myth of 'The Boy who was Kept by a Bear', which is given in the last
section of this chapter.

A second context in which the model of a dominant-subordinate
relationship is applied to game animals is contained in the idea that
some species, or groups of species, have an entity which has control
over them as a group. This entity is usually one of the 'Animal

Masters', although this concept is not as thoroughly applied by the Mistassini to all game species as it is elsewhere in the Algonkian world. The most common analogy used in speaking about the relationship between the controlling entity and the animals over which it has control is that these animals are its 'pets'. It is not known if the keeping of animal pets by the Cree has a long history, apart from domesticated dogs. The Cree term (*awhkaan*) used for 'pet' refers to a whole class of domesticated animals, and this includes dogs. In the case of the Master of the bear, *memekwesuu*, the bear is usually specifically stated as being *memekwesuu's* dog. In fact, although Cree dogs do work, they are usually treated very much like 'pets' in the ordinary sense of the word, except that they are not usually allowed inside the dwelling. In short, the Animal Masters and the other controlling entities are thought of as being in a dominant relationship to a particular class of game animals. They both look after the animals and influence their actions, in the same way that a hunter looks after and controls his own dogs.

The third type of model used in religious symbolism to refer to a relationship between a hunter and the animals he kills may be referred to as 'animal friendship'. This refers to a situation in which a particular hunter has developed, over some period of time, a special relationship of privilege with respect to a particular species. The accounts we have of such a relationship concern known historical or living individuals, although some myths contain analogous incidents.[1]

The most common use of this idea of friendship between a hunter and an animal is in stories about men who have the reputation of having killed a large number of animals of a particular species. Such a man is said to have a particular member of that species as a 'friend' (*uwiicewaakan*). This term denotes a co-resident, and might also be translated by the term 'partner', except for the rather formal connotations of the latter term. Sometimes this animal, which the man must never kill, is spoken of as being the man's 'pet' (*awhkaan*). Generally, the man who has such a reputation is already past the age of peak hunting abilities, so that while his reputation rests on past kills, the significance of his ability is that he is believed to be able to help the younger men of his group make kills of that particular species.

An example of an event which illustrated for me the nature of animal friendship occurred during the field work at Mistassini Post. One Thursday in October an old man, William E., died on his way to hospital in Chibougamau, and his body was returned the same day to Mistassini. The next day a goose from one of the several high flying flocks which fly south at that season descended to the village and began flying low between the houses. Several men ran out with guns, but only one or two shots were fired. At the time the event was explained as due to the bird having been wounded some time earlier, and having had to leave the flock. Some people thought it was finally killed, but others told me it had got away. The following Monday a similar incident was reported to me as having occurred that day, but in this case I was told that the young men were instructed not to kill the bird because it was William E.'s 'pet'. The concept of 'animal friendship' was then explained to me, as just outlined. I was told that some old men have 'pets' of several species, but never more than one of each species. It is also possible for a married woman, who may never have been hunting in her life, to acquire animal friends.

When a man who has an animal friend dies, it is said to mourn for him. If it is very sad this species may leave the area entirely. As a result, the deceased man's hunting group would no longer be able to kill animals of this species. For this reason offerings are made at the funeral feast as an attempt to persuade the deceased not to take his animal friends with him. In order to discover if any animals will leave the area divination rites are used to reveal this information, and these are often used after the death of a successful hunter or a powerful shaman. After the burial, a watch is kept each night at the grave. If an animal is seen approaching the grave it is taken to be one of the man's animal friends, and this event is taken to indicate that the animal is sad, but that it will not leave the area. Another technique used is to perform a 'Shaking Tent' ceremony. The shaman faces *west* while in the tent, the opposite direction from which he faces in an ordinary performance. The shaman sees the dead man travelling towards the west, and any animals which are seen following in his path are animal friends, which will leave the area, and which the group will not be able to kill for some time. In the case of the goose mentioned above, I was told that this unusual event was also an indication that this species was sad, but would be returning to the area in subsequent years. In such a case where an animal friend does stay in the group's area it is often said to be because someone else in the group has become a friend of that species. I was told that William E.'s friendship with the goose was taken over by one of his sons.

2. *The ritual aspect of killing*

In order to give a hunter the magical power to kill game animals successfully, especially on hunts considered particularly important, such as those which follow divination of any kind, charms of various kinds may be worn. These include neck charms, garters, a special skin coat, specially decorated mittens, moccasins, a decorated ammunition pouch, a decorated rifle case and beaded charms attached to the rifle butt and trigger guard. These luck charms are of two basic kinds: those made from a part of an animal or a peculiar shaped natural object felt to have intrinsic power, and those made entirely of decorative material such as beads or ribbons, in which case the power is felt to reside in the design, which normally comes from a dream. The design both transforms a utilitarian tool into an object that indicates 'respect' for the animal that is to be killed, and it ensures that the tool functions properly. The use of a special part of an animal carcass in a charm is part of the complex of rules concerning the proper disposal of all parts of game animals, a subject that will be discussed in the next chapter. The basic idea is that particular inedible parts of a game animal have intrinsic power, and this power is used for a person's benefit in one of three ways: it is kept near the place where the person's head rests at night, thus promoting divinatory dreams; it is displayed outside the dwelling to decorate the camp and please those spirits which aid in hunting; or it is decorated and worn as a hunting charm, in order to show respect to the animal about to be killed, and to give power to the hunter who wears it.

The extent to which those hunting charms which are worn are actually used today is hard to assess, and it may well be that they are now used less than in the past. It is not difficult to obtain descriptions or to be shown such charms.[2] However, their use is semi-secret, in the sense that they may be worn underneath clothing, or kept in a pocket. Few of them were in use by members of the three hunting groups with whom I stayed for extended periods, or they were kept hidden from me during my visit. Most charms today are of the type made of animal remains — a duck beak, the head of a goose, an otter paw, a marten tail, a bear chin, or something else the composition of which was dreamed about — and in most cases these are merely kept in the dwelling with an individual's private possessions, and less often worn as a necklace. Several informants spoke of using various lumps of material found in game animals as charms. In this category are lumps of bony material and hair found under the skin or in the stomach of an animal (Banfield 1958), peculiarly shaped bones found in the crop of a bird, and a bony disc sometimes found in the region of the sternum of a caribou. It will be recalled that other similar 'found' objects sometimes have divinatory significance also (see Chapter 6). When used as charms, these objects are usually sewn in a small pouch, or given a decorative trim.

While charms are believed to give power to the wearer, the decoration of utilitarian objects used in the hunt is for the purpose of showing respect to the animal about to be killed, and to ensure the object performs its function properly. An exception to this is the special coat or parka made of the skin of an animal, which gives to the wearer the animal's power. Today hunters no longer wear such garments, and they are now only made for children. The hide of a caribou or a young moose is used, and the hair is left on. The hood of the garment is made of the head skin, with the ears left in place. Since they are only made for children they are not worn for hunting purposes, but the wearing of one is said to increase the child's later hunting ability. Children sometimes have parkas made of woven strips of rabbit skin, and ears may be made in the hood.

The decoration of clothing and hunting equipment is explained by the Mistassini from two points of view. As I have said, the decoration is said to show respect to the prey, but it is also designed to ensure that the 'spirit' (*aataacaakw*) of the object does its proper job in the hunt. Thus the decorations on moccasins and snowshoes are said to guide the hunters' feet swiftly to the game; and the decorations on the ammunition pouch (*piitsinaakan*), the gun, and the gun case (*spitsinaakan*) ensure that they function properly. In the Willie J. group I also observed garters (*ciisceypiinaan*), which were woven using the fingers and made of coloured wool, being worn at Easter time. All hunting ceases between Good Friday and Easter Sunday, and during this period certain animals, such as the porcupine, are said to fast. The garters are worn as soon as hunting recommences. They were, in the above instance, worn only once, after which the garters were made into a new carrying strap for the hunting bag (*niimuutaan*). The hunting bag itself is another piece of necessary equipment which is always decorated.[3]

Other items of hunting equipment which are often decorated are the top board across the front of a toboggan, and the special string (*niimaapaan*) used in carrying or dragging on top of the snow certain kinds of game which they are taken back to camp. In both cases the decorations are designed to show respect towards the slain animal.[4] The decorated toboggan is seldom seen now, but the ceremonial carrying string (*niimaapaan*) is in common use. The string is woven from strips of caribou or other animal hide, and dyed red. A loop is made at one end to attach it to some part of the animal, and sets of ribbons are attached at intervals along the string and at the loop end. In Speck's description it appears that each *niimaapaan* was made for use with only one kind of game, so that presumably his informants would have owned several of them. Hunters whom I have observed used the *niimaapaan* mainly for carrying beaver, porcupine, caribou legs (I observed one occasion when a whole young caribou was dragged back to camp using a *niimaapaan* and one other rope) and bear, but the same *niimaapaan* is usually used by a hunter for all animals.

The instructions for making the decorations on the various charms and items of hunting equipment are said to be dreamed by the hunter who owns the item, although some also say that their wives may decide the correct design. There is no inheritance of designs, but a limited number of design elements, colours and materials characterize all the decorations. My informants were reluctant to give the kind of direct symbolic interpretation of the shapes and colours which Speck had earlier obtained. Table 12 summarizes Speck's data on the colour symbolism of the *niimaapaan* from several informants from three bands (Speck 1935:203-12).

In reading this table it is useful to remember that in the Cree

Table 12.   COLOUR SYMBOLISM OF THE *NIIMAAPAAN*

	Lac St. Jean	*Mistassini*	*Nicbicun*
Red	Small game	Beaver	Beaver
Yellow			Red Fox
Black	Bear		
Green	Large game	Small game	Beaver
White		Caribou	
Blue		Bear	Bear
Pink		Lynx	Caribou, Lynx

Source: Speck 1935:203-12

language there is one term (in the Mistassini dialect *asawaaskasew*) which overlaps that part of the spectrum where Canadian English makes the distinction between blue and green. If what Speck calls blue is actually a dark shade it might, in Cree terms, fall under the general range of colours classified by them as black. Also, it is possible that 'pink' and 'white' were placed in the same general colour class by Speck's informants. These assumptions would permit the speculation that there is a simple general system of colour symbolism of major animals, particularly if Lac St. Jean classify beaver as small game. This proposal leaves unsolved the significance of the animals symbolized by the blue-green colour.

Beaver	*Bear*	*Caribou, Lynx*
Red	Black	White

Although it appears that detailed identification of the colour symbolism of animals in *niimaapaan* decorations may have faded since Speck's time, other kinds of evidence suggest that the above scheme does accurately summarize the association between these animals and colours. 'Dark' and 'Black' are found in the various circumlocutions for the bear, as well as for bear meat. The caribou is often symbolically linked to snow, as are the lynx and the hare. In a myth told by the Montagnais and Naskapi the leader of the caribou is a man married to a caribou. However, the Mistassini, who know this story, say that the leader of the caribou is married to the spirit of the snow. The ceremonial hide which was displayed during the winter towards the east is made as white as possible in order to be as attractive as possible to the spirits that control the 'winter animals' — that is, the animals like the caribou, the lynx and the hare which are not slowed down by the snow. In the case of red, several informants stated that the spirit of a beaver liked the colour red. These three colours also correspond to the approximate predominant natural colouring of the bear, the caribou and the beaver, respectively.

3. *Beaver trapping*

The animal which may be said to be the staple resource of the Mistassini hunter is the beaver. For most of the animals killed by the Mistassini, all techniques, skills and hunting magic are directed towards the single moment when the animal is killed, either by it coming in range of the hunter's gun sights, or by it stepping into the hunter's trap. But in the case of the beaver there are two critical moments: first, when the hunter finds the beaver colony, and second, when the animal is caught in his trap. Both of these events are highly dependent on knowledge and skill, and less subject to factors over which the hunter has no control, than is the case with most other game. The finding of a beaver colony is an event which has an importance analogous to that of the final kill of some of the other animals.

The killing of all the other major game animals is announced by the hunter bringing back to camp some token part of the kill. These are left to be found when his bag is unpacked by the women (see Chapter 8). Analogously, when a beaver lodge is found the hunter selects pieces of wood from the lodge which have clear impressions of beavers' teeth marks on them. These are used to estimate the size of the adult beavers. One such stick is usually brought back to camp, where it is shown to the others, and placed at the wall where the hunter's head rests at night (*taawpwaataakan*), in order to promote dreams that will give the hunter power. This stick is called a *cimutuwaan*.

Several kinds of explanations, beyond its practical use in estimating the size of the beavers in the lodge, are given for the significance attached to the *cimutuwaan*. One of its uses is in enabling the hunter to be successful in killing beavers, not only by promoting divinatory dreams, but also with the idea that if the stick is put into a plate, or in the past on a special decorated birch bark feast dish, the hunter would be able to kill all the beavers in the lodge. I was unable to confirm if any hunters still follow this practice.

A practice which links the *cimutuwaan* with the ability to kill beavers is found in another idea, in this case also involving the muskrat. The muskrat is known to have a symbiotic relation with the beaver, and furthermore it is said that the muskrat has an insatiable curiosity about the beaver. Thus, when the hunter comes and takes the *cimutuwaan* from the beaver lodge, the muskrat notices this, and follows the hunter back to the camp. He then returns, and reports to the Master of the Water Animals (*Wiisinaak*) that he has seen the men putting the *cimutuwaan* in their mouths, and in the dish. It is for this reason that, while the men are first examining the *cimutuwaan*, they call out, 'All right, Muskrat, you can go back and tell your boss that there are lots of us here and we are hungry.' The fact that this is a joke intended to amuse children, rather than a serious belief, places it in a similar category to those myths which may not be taken literally, but which nevertheless give insight into the structure of religious ideas. An informant from Rupert House gave me another viewpoint on the use of the *cimutuwaan*. He told me that the stick represents the beaver lodge, and it is brought back to camp so that the hunting group leader may assign that particular lodge to be trapped by a particular hunter. The stick is most often given back to the man who brought it, as a sign of the handing over of the rights to all the beavers in the lodge. He might, however, give the stick and the trapping rights to another man. My observations on the use of the *cimutuwaan* among the Nichicun and Mistassini groups with whom I lived are not inconsistent with this interpretation, apart from the fact that I do not believe that the stick was brought back for each and every beaver lodge found. Clearly, the practice has several functions, and these may include a juridical one, as well as having ritual and technical aspects.

The beaver is usually taken back to camp by dragging it over the snow by a string or *niimaapaan* attached to a sharpened wooden peg pushed through the animal's nostrils. Even when the animal is not dragged back, but is carried on a toboggan, the nose peg is used. The explanation for the use of this peg is given in practical, non-ritualistic terms: it is said that although the beaver trap usually grips the animal's body or its leg, it will bleed through the nose after taken from the water if the nose peg is not used. It is not clear to me what is the basis for the fear of this bleeding, or if the nose peg would be an effective prevention. It does not appear to be given any religious explanation, apart from the general injunction against leaving the blood of game animals showing on the snow. It is possibly a customary practice, the religious rationale for which was not known by my informants.

4. *Bear hunting*

Bear hunting for the Mistassini is analogous to beaver hunting on a point previously mentioned, that is, it is a hunt which normally has two separate phases, the first being when the bear is discovered, and the second when it is killed. In winter the discovery phase is a matter of finding a den, and establishing the essential fact that the den is occupied, a fact which is signalled by the presence of frost around a hole in the snow, caused by the animal's breathing. In summer, bears follow the same paths year after year, particularly during the blueberry season, so that their presence is often known before they are first seen. They are also attracted by the garbage at old camps, and fish is sometimes put out as bait for them. Thus, whether the bear is to be shot, or to be killed while in a trap, the expedition to kill the animal is normally quite separate from the expedition during which the bear is discovered, and the kill is consequently often well prepared for.

Divination can in this case be seen as one ideological aspect of this preparation.

Because when he sets out to kill a bear the hunter already knows where he can expect to encounter the animal, the bear hunt epitomizes the kind of hunt which is idealized in the concept discussed in the last chapter, regarding hunting divination. In other words, hunting by divination in general, and bear hunting in particular, is characterized by the outcome being known in advance, or known with some degree of certainty once the animal has been located. Along with this relative predictability, the animal has sufficient size and ferocity with which to attack the hunter, but since such an attack, in fact, seldom happens, the killing of a bear exemplifies another Cree ideal of the hunt: the animal is believed to lose the 'natural' inclination to hide, to flee or to attack, and instead to 'offer' itself to be killed. In a sense, bear hunting epitomizes the ideals on which the religious aspect of all hunting is based.

The killing of a bear is surrounded by rules. The taboo on going after other animals has been mentioned. If the bear has been caught in a trap, a charm necklace may be placed on the leg which was caught, after the killing. Prior to the killing the hunter talks to the bear, and it is believed that the animal understands. After the killing the bear is placed on its back with the legs in the air, and tobacco is placed on the chest, and then it is smoked by the hunter.

The killing of a bear is marked by the observation of two kinds of rites. These are a special emphasis on general hunting rules which apply to a greater or lesser extent to the killing of any game animal, and, secondly, rules which apply only to this one kind of hunting. In the first category is the taboo against killing other game while on the way to killing a bear, as well as the use of charms, of clean clothing, of decorations, and of the *niimaapaan*. Another such rule, which may also apply to other hunting, is that women must keep the camp neat and clean while the hunting is underway, since it is believed that the animal will not allow himself to be caught otherwise. Some Mistassini disapprove of whistling while hunting, since this is believed to cause strong winds which would interrupt hunting. Other special practices, which apply only to bear hunting, include talking to the animal, offering tobacco to the corpse, and carrying the whole carcass back to camp before butchering. I was unable to discover the extent to which any of the rites are actually practised, since no bears were killed by the groups I accompanied.[5]

5. *Other ritual aspects of killing animals*

While the main tenor of all special behaviour during a hunt is directed towards the animal, and to the idea of paying respect to the victim, there is also some attention paid to other entities which are felt to inhabit the 'bush' (*nuhcimiihc*). By remaining silent in the bush a hunter sometimes is able to hear helpful spirits which may whistle to him from the trees, thereby indicating which is the right path for him to find the game. Once a hunter is following the tracks in the snow made by an animal there is an injunction against him stepping into the same tracks as the animal. It is said that the animal is offended by this, and will not allow himself to be caught.

One entity which must be taken into account during winter hunting is *Ciiwetinsuu*, the spirit of the North Wind. In some ways *Ciiwetinsuu* acts as a 'Master' of the winter animals. This entity may visit the site of a kill, and if there is blood on the snow he becomes angry, and sends a snowstorm. Therefore, after killing and cutting up the animal, the hunter is careful to cover all traces of blood with clean snow. In the case of big animals like moose and caribou, the animal is usually skinned and cut up for transportation. The animal is said to be offended if anyone but the hunter who did the killing cuts off the head, a job which is done with the use of an axe.

After the killing, as we will detail more fully in the next chapter, the hunter returns to camp with a number of special parts of the animal, which are used as tokens to announce the kill that has been made. A meal is prepared with these parts, and the following day every able-bodied person returns to help transport the meat back to camp.[6] One of the token pieces of meat which are used to announce to the group that a moose or a caribou has been killed is the foetus.

Those female animals that are killed during the winter are usually found to be carrying young, and the foetus of the moose or caribou is the subject of special attention when one of these animals is cut up at the kill site. A piece of intestine fat (*wiikw*) is taken and placed into the mouth of the foetus. This rite is directed at the Master of the particular animal species involved, and its purpose is to ensure that any such animals killed subsequently by the hunter will have plenty of fat on it.

The foetus is later given further special treatment. After it is brought back and displayed with the other tokens of the kill, it is skinned, and eaten. It may be boiled, or first partially dried and then boiled. Informants differed about who should eat the foetus. Some said it was only for the old people, and others said it was only eaten by men. In the camps I visited foetuses were sometimes eaten only by the old people, but in other cases they were served to all the adults of both sexes. It is believed to be important that the foetus is treated as much as possible like a full grown animal; that is, it should be skinned, and the bones treated with respect, by hanging them up, as is done with a normal animal. This particularly applies to the leg bones of the moose or caribou foetuses, which are sometimes seen hanging on a wall or tent pole, and which are often used as buzzers on a drum.

6. *Killing as a social transaction*

In the last chapter the point was made that the hunting rites of the Mistassini make up a set in which the hunting production is presented as a form of transaction between the hunter (and often including others in the hunting group) and a group of entities said to be associated with the game animals. As might be expected, the symbolic and ideological expression of this concept of hunting is, to a large extent, to be found in rites and oral materials which are not evident during the actual activity of hunting. Most hunting ideology is found in the rites which regularly accompany the preparation for killing and the disposal of the meat afterwards, or in the accounts of hunting in the form of myths, and of stories about past events. Nevertheless, in this chapter we have seen that there are some aspects of the actual process of killing, such as rites and other symbolic material, which carry this same ideology of a social relation existing between the hunter and his prey. One possible reason why these rites and beliefs play a relatively minor role in the total symbolism of the hunt is that the kill tends to be a solitary task, while the other aspects of the hunt are conducted more on a communal basis.

Hunting magic, and stories stressing the religious aspect of killing animals, while they tend to present the human-animal transaction as a kind of social relationship, are not restricted to a single stereotype of this relationship. Most of the rites contain elements suggesting that an exchange relationship exists between the hunter and the animal, or with a person or an entity who has control over the animal. The typical man-animal relationship may be described as based on a folk model of either 'friendship' or 'love'. In most of these rites the hunter symbolically places himself initially in a subordinate position to the animal, making offerings and obeying taboos, and is later rewarded by the animal 'giving' itself to be killed. However, the oral material about past hunts and about mythical encounters with animals usually carries this exchange process to a further stage, in which the hunter, using magical power, establishes, in a coercive manner, his ability to cause the animal to come to him against its will. We may refer to the first attitude as the *friendship* approach, and the second as following a tactic of *coercion*. In the following myth there are examples of relations between men and animals of both these types.

The Boy who was kept by a Bear

A bear found a child and kept him like a son for several years. Every summer the bear would hunt for all kinds of food — beaver, porcupines, other animals — and in the fall the bear and the child would collect blueberries. Then they gathered their food and took it to where they would spend the winter.

One fall the bear told the child he could sense the boy's father starting to sing. The bear tried to sing his own song to oppose the father, but the power of the man's singing was too strong for the bear, and it made him forget his song and stop singing.

Later, during the winter, the child's father started to sing again, and again he succeeded in defeating the bear's song. The next day the bear told the child that he could sense the father preparing himself and setting out to find them.

The father began walking straight towards the place where the bear and the child were staying. The bear tried to lead him astray. First, he threw a porcupine out of his den. At the same moment the man noticed the marks where a porcupine had been gnawing at a tree off to the side of his path. But the man just kept on walking straight, intending to kill the porcupine on his way home.

The bear called out, 'I cannot defeat him! Straight! Straight! He comes walking to me!'

Next the bear threw out a beaver. At that moment the man was passing a lake, and he noticed it contained a beaver lodge. But he kept on walking ahead, meaning to investigate the beavers on his way home. The bear uttered the same cry, 'I cannot defeat him! Straight! Straight! He comes walking to me!'

Finally, the bear threw out a partridge. At the same instant a bird flew out from under the snow near the father, and landed on the other side of his path. But the man kept on straight, meaning to kill the partridge later. The bear again makes his cry, 'I cannot defeat him! Straight! Straight! He comes walking to me!'

Realizing the man's power was stronger than his, the bear used magic. He lay on his back with all four legs in the air [in another version, he stood upright on his hind legs] whereupon an object [the Cree version used the inanimate form] came crashing out of the sky, causing a huge storm. But still the father kept coming towards the bear, and for the last time the bear called out, 'I cannot defeat him! Straight! Straight! He comes walking to me!'

Knowing that he was about to be killed, the bear gave the son one of his forelegs, telling him to keep it wrapped up and hanging in his tent above the place where he always sat. He told the child that if he wanted to hunt bears he was to climb to a place where he could get a good view of the surroundings, and look for the place where smoke was rising. He was told that only he would be able to see it, and if he looked at that place he would always find a bear.

Then the child's father began to break through the snow covering the bear's den, the bear went outside, and the man killed him. He took his son home, and the boy looked after the bear's foreleg as he had been told to do. Later the boy got married, and was an extremely successful bear hunter. His hunting group lived almost entirely on bear meat. Sometimes he would tell another hunter where to look for a bear, and the man would look where he was told, and would always kill a bear.

The hunting group was visited by another group. The women of this group were very jealous, because the hero could find bears whenever he wanted, and their own husbands were never able to kill any. While the hero was off hunting for bears of which he had previously found the location, one of the women of the second hunting group decided to look for the source of his power. She went into his tent, took down the package, and started to unwrap it. At the same moment the hero became aware of what was happening, and immediately returned to the camp.

For a while he could be heard outside his tent. Then he entered, but stayed sitting on the doorstep. He asked for the culprit; the woman admitted it was her. He told her that the following day she could find a bear by going to a particular place which he described.

He then removed his ammunition pouch, took off all his clothes, and went to sit at his accustomed place. Immediately, the leg fell down, and both he and the leg disappeared underground, leaving no trace behind. It was said that he had become a bear. [Told by Charlie Etap.]

This myth is important from several points of view, but we will limit ourselves to a few comments. Three major types of social relations between men and bears are presented: first, there is the relationship based on a father-son dyad; second, there is a sorcery fight between the father and the bear; and finally a model of generalized symbiotic relationship between the hero and all bears, which we may see as most similar to 'friendship'. Other kinds of relationships are hinted at: the human hunting group and the population of bears seem to be treated as two groups of equivalent status to each other, who cannot interact except through the mediation of the hero who is symbolically a member of both groups.

To make the above suggestions clearer, a few details of the myth should be expanded. First, the incident of the song fight between the bear and the father is a typical example of such fights which are often reported, outside the context of myths, as taking place between two human shamans. In fact, the whole encounter between the father and the bear refers to magical techniques which are more associated with sorcery than with hunting. At the same time, the myth gives the origin of the taboo which is now observed against a hunter going after other game while engaged in a hunt in response to information obtained by divination or in dreams.

The various relationships between men and bears in the myth cover, as we have said, three focal relationships: (1) parent-child, (2) friend, (3) enemy. The third differs from the others in that the transaction is conducted by means of *coercive* behaviour, as opposed to cooperative or *exchange* behaviour. The first differs from the others in that it is *hierarchically* structured, as opposed to an equivalence or *reciprocal* structure. The interpretation of this aspect of the myth is developed in the next chapter.

The myth implies that bears have a society parallel to, but invisible from, man. The hero's technique of finding bears, by looking down from a hill for smoke rising from their dens is a reference to the technique which a stranger would use upon arrival in a new area, in order to discover, from the smoke of their fires, where any resident hunting groups were located. Also, the references to the bear collecting representative species of the three classes of animals (of the land, of the water and of the air) hunted by men indicates the same human/ bear parallel. The society, modelled on a hunting group, is invisible not only because ordinary men are unable to see their smoke, but because they have an underground existence.

The myth establishes the taboo against a hunter revealing the *source* of his knowledge and power with respect to hunting, although at the same time he may reveal the *content* of the knowledge. This is a significant distinction, since in the practical world it is the old men who have most of the magical knowledge and power, and the young men who do most of the hunting. The myth provides ideological authority for this state of affairs, by showing a division of labour between magical power, and the use of divinatory knowledge.

Myths such as this one, and others involving such incidents as marriage with animals, along with the rites which accompany hunting, present not only what we may call this dominant ideology of hunting, that is, that the animals are like friends or lovers of hunters, and the elders hold the key to this relationship; at the same time the elements of a 'counter ideology' are present in the same symbolic material. However, it is the dominant ideology which is the interpretation most often given by the Mistassini themselves.

In this chapter we have dealt, for the most part, with the nature of ritual relations between hunters and game animals in general, rather than with each particular species. However, it has been clear, at least for the small amount of material specifically relating to the caribou, the bear and the beaver, that each game animal species, or in some cases groups of species (often grouped together on ecological criteria), have a special symbolic character which gives them a special kind of ritual relationship to the hunter. From the perspective of this study, giving a special place to each animal species in the ritual symbolism presents problems, some of which lead beyond the scope of the study itself. Rather than attempting to cover all aspects of religious ideology, I have concentrated on the hunting rites, and dealt with such matters as sorcery, mythology and semantic categories as ancillary material. However, a close examination of the ideas surrounding animals beginning from one of these perspectives must include more than the ideology of production, where my own studies began. The primary reason why I do not attempt such an excursion is that my data is not yet adequate in these other areas.

An excellent example of the contribution which the study of semantic categorization of animals can make to the problems of the different symbolic significance attached to various animals, both game animals and others, is found in a recent study by Bouchard and Mailhot. They have shown that among two Montagnais groups, culturally and linguistically related to the Mistassini, there are at least four distinct overlapping systems for the classification of animals. The first is equivalent to species, while the second divides all animals into winter and summer animals. The third classification divides game animals into groups, each of which is ruled over by an 'Animal

Master', Finally, all animals can be ranked on a scale based on the relative amount of evil power they possess. Each of these classificatory systems is a structure which opens out onto the next overlapping system, so that together they lead from the more concrete structures, directly related to hunting production and the direct observations of hunters, to successively more abstract levels of religious thought (Bouchard and Mailhot 1973:65). Although I did not obtain any indication of the existence of the hierarchy of evil power at Mistassini, such a system may exist. Other classifications of animals include domesticated, as opposed to wild, and 'big game' animals (meaning the larger animals of ritual importance) versus smaller game animals. As with the Montagnais, the species are sub-divided into broad groups, generally on the basis of anatomical similarities. The Mistassini sub-divide many of these categories again, on the basis of the ecological zone occupied by the group, or the usefulness of the group to man.

Broadly speaking, then, we may say that Cree semantic classification does not exhaust the significance attached to animals, but that it follows the same form of thought as do ideas about hunting generally. By this I mean that it relates to two different aspects of the phenomena of animals. In the first place the categories reflect the relevant distinctions in qualities possessed by the animals, qualities which are perceived and used by the hunter in his work. In addition, other categories introduce cross-cutting qualities ascribed to the animals, qualities we may describe as 'totemic', in the sense that they establish relationships between animals and humans, either with human groups, with human individuals or with human characteristics. Within the context of this second set of animal classifications ideas about particular encounters with animals develop; these encounters are framed as encounters with persons, and the interpretations use, as analogues, the commonplace social mechanisms, such as coercion, sexuality and gift exchange.

8
Respect for the Animals Killed

1. *The hunter's return*

With this chapter I complete the presentation of the cycle of rites associated with hunting. In this phase the dead animal is worked on in the camp, and the woman takes charge of most of the tasks of butchering, skinning and cooking. The active hunter spends only the evenings in camp, at which time he is often exhausted. At feasts, which formalize the ideological expression of the proper final disposition of game, men again move to the centre of the rite. But effectively the man gives away the animal to the woman as soon as he gets to camp.

Along with this transformation of the animal from being the hunter's friend to the woman's property, there is another transformation in the hunter-animal relationship. We have seen that, at the stage of divination, the animal is on friendly terms with the hunter, but is far more powerful than him. The act of killing, on the other hand, becomes an exchange between 'persons' at a reciprocal or equivalent level. Finally, after the kill, in addition to giving away the food, which is then consumed, the hunter must observe rules regarding the disposal of the inedible parts of the animal, rules which are used for the purpose of regenerating further animals, but which also symbolize a final shift in the social model of the man-animal relationship. It is the nature of this shift whereby the animal becomes turned into food, offerings and sacred remains, and the relation of this shift to the whole question of the reproduction of the hunting cycle which will concern us here.

We can note three quite separate occasions when ritual is in evidence following the kill: in the first place, when the meat is first brought into the dwelling; secondly, during the eating of the meat; and thirdly, when the inedible remains are disposed of. By grouping these three occasions together in this chapter, I have chosen to emphasize one particular aspect of these various rites. The Cree say that the rites are all intended to show gratitude for the meat, and also to express the hope of extending their good fortune to future hunts; but the expression which best states their central attitude following the kill is the desire and the necessity to show *respect* towards the animal. This is achieved by treating its carcass properly.

Much of the symbolic behaviour associated with the arrival at the camp of hunters is in the form of taboos. Returning hunters must be quiet; they must never shout greetings or brag about what they have caught. The camp people must not run outside when the hunters are heard to be approaching. If the hunters are hauling toboggans the women will go outside when the men are heard at the door taking off their snowshoes, to help them unload the toboggans and take the catch inside. Otherwise, the women wait for the men to enter and to hand them the hunting bags, which they then unpack. In either case, the men and the women say little if anything, the women silently unpacking what the hunter has killed. If the catch is of considerable importance, it is laid out and is silently admired for some minutes. Visitors from other family groups may come and make an admiring comment, and perhaps stroke the animal's fur, but conversation does not begin until the man finally starts to talk.

Strong emotions are felt when hunters return. The strength of the feelings is greatest if a bear, moose, caribou or beaver has been brought back by the hunters. The taboos or other rites used on this occasion do not symbolize these feelings, but on the contrary they restrict their open expression. Also, for the people who are in the camp, there is an intense curiosity and excitement about the prospect that the hunter has made a significant kill, but they are not permitted to show these feelings openly. An injunction is specifically placed on children running out and greeting the hunter, a taboo called *asawaapin*. At the same time, the returning hunters, if they have been successful, feel very proud of themselves, but they also are not permitted to show this feeling openly. For them, a taboo is placed on bragging about their success, and so they must reveal what they have caught slowly, by non-verbal means.

The explanation given for the *asawaapin* taboo is by means of a myth (although all of the several versions that I was able to collect appear to be abrupt and incomplete) which is used to frighten the children into obeying the rule. It tells of a hunter who returned home without having killed anything, to find his small son waiting outside the door. This happened each day for several days, and the father became angry each time he saw his son waiting, because he had not been able to kill anything. He blamed his bad luck on his son. Finally, as he returned one day to again find his son outside waiting for him, he shot the boy with his bow and arrow. After this he was able to kill game again.

A more specific explanation of the taboo is sometimes given. It is said that children must not be the first to see game being brought into the camp. Instead, it must first be seen by the old people. One man told me that the returning hunter must pass directly through the doorway to the old people inside to show them his kill, and any children outside the door are like a plug in a hole the hunter must pass through. According to Fred Georgekish, at Eastmain dogs must not be tethered near the doorway, since they act as a blockage to the path of the game (personal communication). This plug not only impedes his progress in bringing his game to the old people, but it represents an impediment to his hunting, which is why in the myth the child outside the door is said to be responsible for hunting failure. This notion is one of a number of ideas about clearing the passageway through the door, and is a subject which we will return to later in this chapter.

These folk explanations of *asawaapin* leave some questions regarding the significance of the taboo and of the myth. I am reluctant to offer any kind of analysis of the myth in this form, as I have been given some hints that a longer version is in existence. However, the myth does make clear something that is probably also the case in real life: failure on the part of the hunter can be the cause of resentment by the people of the camp who are dependent on the hunters, and this resentment must be carefully hidden. The *asawaapin* taboo is thus parallel to the injunction against a hunter bragging about his kill. When he is successful he must hide it, and when the members of the domestic group are disappointed they must also hide it.

2. *Announcing the kill*

Game is brought back to camp by one of three methods, depending on its size. (*a*) Small game and fish are carried in a container. For fish, a birch bark wrapper is used, or more commonly today a metal tub. Other small game, such as birds and animals smaller than a beaver, are carried on the back in a hunting bag. (*b*) Intermediate sized game, such as beavers, otters, and porcupine, are also brought in whole, but without a container. In the case of beavers, they are dragged behind the hunter if there is snow on the ground, using a *niimaapaan*, a cord attached to the nose. Otters and porcupines, and beavers killed in summer, are tied across the hunter's back. A similar carrying method is sometimes described for the bear, as was previously noted. (*c*) The largest game animals are butchered where they are killed, and the hunter normally first returns to camp with only a few tokens of his kill; these are carried in the hunting bag.

In the last chapter it was mentioned that the discovery of a new beaver lodge is announced by a token brought back to camp, in the form of a stick from the lodge. When a moose or a caribou is killed edible tokens of the kill are also brought back. Thus when a woman unpacks the hunting bag she may find either only small game, or there may be tokens to indicate that larger game has been killed. The tokens do not, however, consist of any of the principal kinds of meat which are eaten as a staple food from either the moose or the caribou. That is, the tokens are not muscle meat (*wiiyaas*), or the type of fat found attached to muscle meat (*wiikuw*). Instead, tokens of a big game kill come from the region of the abdominal cavity, and usually consist of two organs, the heart (*utehii*) and the lower intestine (*utacii*), and two kinds of fat. The first kind is called *wiis*, and consists of a thin

Plate 12. 'Tokens' used by a hunter to announce a moose
kill: the foetuses, the kidneys and intestine fat.

lacy sheet of fat found across the rib cage, underneath the skin. The
second kind is called *wiikw* and is a thick white fat found in lumps
around the internal organs, particularly the kidneys. This kind of fat is
sometimes spoken of as being like bear fat. Female moose or caribou
killed in late winter and early spring are often found to have foetuses
(*umaanciis*). As was mentioned earlier, these are subject to special
treatment, in that a piece of *wiikw* fat is put in their mouths during
butchering, and they are always brought back to camp with the other
tokens of the kill. In a few instances I observed that the lower part of
the legs of caribou or moose were also brought back with the first
tokens of a kill. The significance of this part of the animal is that it
contains another highly prized kind of fat called *wiin*, which is found
enclosed by the metapodial bone. This kind of fat is made the focus of
the most important feast among the neighbouring Naskapi; among
the east Cree it is eaten as a delicacy, but no particular ritual is
attached to its consumption.

If the tokens of a large kill are found when the women unpack the hunting bag there is much restrained excitement, and the tokens are laid out for everyone to admire. Later the same day a meal is prepared from them. This meal appears to be obligatory, since if the hunters arrive at the camp after the evening meal has been prepared, a second evening meal made from the big game tokens will be eaten later that same night. The foetuses are not always eaten at this meal. However, they are skinned and butchered as if they were full-sized animals.[1] I was told it is pleasing to the animal species if the foetuses are treated in the same way as the full-sized animals which are brought into camp. In some cases the foetus meat is allowed to dry by hanging it in the rafters above the stove. It is then later boiled and eaten, each person at a meal getting a tiny piece.

3. *Displaying the kill*

The pattern of laying out the tokens which are brought back as soon as a large animal is killed is one example of a general pattern of displaying the game that has been killed soon after it is brought into the camp. The degree of importance evident in the way this display is handled reflects the three categories of game mentioned earlier. Game smaller than the beaver is given very minimal attention when it is first taken out of the hunting bag. However, if it happens to be the first of such game killed by a young person it will be treated with far more importance, and will be admired by everyone in the hunting group before it is skinned and butchered. Animals like the beaver, porcupine and otter which are not usually brought back in a container often, in winter, become frozen by the time the camp is reached, and these are hung up in the dwelling to thaw out before they are skinned and butchered. Otherwise they are laid on the floor of the dwelling in the middle of the family area, facing the door. This rule of facing the dead animal carcass towards the door applies to animals when they are first displayed after being brought inside the dwelling. The reason given is in order that the animal may see out through the door, and see how the hunter went out when he left to go hunting. Here again, we see the idea of the symbolic significance attached to the path which the hunter takes through the doorway of the dwelling both when he leaves to go hunting and when he returns.

The display of the meat of the largest animals — the moose, the caribou and the bear — is of the most importance. These animals are usually skinned and the meat cut into convenient portions (for the purpose of transportation) as soon as the animals are killed. The hunters then bury the meat and the hide in the snow, or in mild weather, cover them with spruce boughs before they return to the camp with the tokens. In the recent past it was necessary to build a cache of logs or for one hunter to set up camp at the site of the kill to

Plate 13. A hunter with a young caribou he has killed shortly after it was
brought into camp.

protect the meat from scavengers, especially wolverines. However,
wolverines have now disappeared from this area, and the covering of
snow or spruce branches is usually enough to protect the meat from
other scavengers, such as wolves and ravens, at least for a few hours.
On the day following the return of the successful hunters, every able-
bodied person in the camp would be engaged in transporting meat
from the kill site to the camp. The major display of a big game kill is
made as soon as this meat arrives in camp.

Preparing the display of moose, caribou or bear involves taking all
the meat into the dwelling of the hunter who killed it, and piling it at
the back of the tent, opposite the door. Again, heads of the animals
are always carefully positioned to face towards the door. After about
half an hour, during which time the whole group admires the huge
pile of meat, the family of the owner will begin to distribute various
pieces of raw meat to the other families in the group. In the case of a
bear, this animal is often brought to camp and displayed before it is
butchered, and the meat is usually distributed in a cooked state at a
feast. Feasts are often held to celebrate the killing of moose or caribou,
but for these animals only the head, and sometimes also the small
intestine, are eaten at the feast, and the rest of the raw meat is
distributed beforehand.

Meat distribution is accomplished in up to three separate processes,
the first taking place before the meat has been transported to camp,
when a successful hunter may present a whole carcass to an unsuccessful

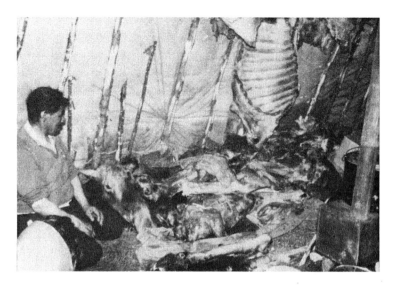

Plate 14. Display of the meat of two moose, soon after it had been transported into the camp.

one. This man is then in the position of 'owning' the animal, in the same way as if he had killed it himself. That is, he is responsible for organizing the transportation of the animal to camp, for the display, and for the final cutting up of the meat into portions, and he may keep the hide for his own use. However, after the display this meat will then be subject to the second process of distribution of raw meat, as also will the meat of animals brought into camp in the charge of the hunter who killed them. The rule for this second distribution is basically that the muscle meat is distributed roughly equally among all families. However, this distribution process may be overlooked if all families in the group already have a store of meat, and thus some hunters may build up much larger surplus than others. A third distribution may then take place if one family runs short while others in the group still have some. This third kind of distribution, unlike the others, is conducted in a way that does not draw attention to the transaction.

In winter, after the meat has been distributed following the display, most is taken outside again, and is stored on cache platforms where it is allowed to freeze. In spring, the meat is stored by cutting it into narrow strips, which are then placed on a rack over an outdoor fire to dry, after which the meat is pounded into a fine powder and stored in flour sacks. Some of the meat that is displayed is not put in storage afterwards, but is cut into pieces of a suitable size for cooking, and the first meal of muscle meat usually follows the display. As in the case of the meal which is prepared from the tokens which are brought back first of all to announce the kill, the first meal of big game meat following the display is obligatory, in the sense that a meal is eaten, even if what would ordinarily be the final meal of the day has already been served.

4. *Food offerings* (mistashamaawin)

In winter, Mistassini hunters normally eat three or four meals each day, each meal consisting of a serving of meat or fish, accompanied by some form of baking-powder bread (*ayhkunaaw*) and tea. If meat is in short supply, the main dish may consist of beans, macaroni or rice, sometimes with a little bacon or salt pork; very occasionally if the supplies are low the meal consists of only a flour preparation, such as fried pancakes. However, in normal circumstances the main part of a meal always includes a large quantity of meat. An average over the whole winter of almost three pounds of meat per person per day is eaten. At all feasts and quasi-feasts, which we will describe later in this chapter, offerings of morsels of all food to be eaten or drunk, as well as tobacco, are first placed in the fire. At other meals offerings of meat are often put into the fire in a less formal way, particularly when it is a special meal which meets some of the criteria of a feast. Thus, an offering is often made at the first meal consisting of the meat of a particular species which has not been killed for some time, or the meal of the 'tokens' which are brought back to announce that big game has been killed, or merely if the animal served is particularly large, or has a particularly large amount of fat on it.

Offerings of food may be put in the fire by the male head of the commensal group when he is serving the food for a meal. If beaver meat is served the offering made by the server would include a small piece of chest meat cut from just below the neck. These offerings by the server are always made at a feast, and include bits of meat from all the major sections of the carcass of the animal being served. In addition to this kind of offering of the server, any individual may also make his own small offerings of food into the fire before he begins to eat. At a feast such individual offerings are usually made by those persons who are served with the skull or the jaw of a beaver.

The reason why the throat meat of the beaver is used in offerings is explained by reference to the myth of 'The Child who had Lice in his Hair'. In this myth the child is abandoned by his parents, but is adopted by a giant, sometimes identified as *Mistaapew*. The giant hunts on behalf of the boy, but refuses to eat all but a small specific portion of the meat he kills. In the Mistassini and Waswanipi versions the giant always hunts for beaver. In the Waswanipi version collected by I. E. LaRusic, the giant refuses to eat anything but a piece of meat from the beaver's throat (personal communication). In one of the versions which I collected at Mistassini, from a man of the Nemescau band, the giant asks for the head, the forearms and for the meat from under the chin of the beaver. In this version the giant is specifically identified as a bear.[2] As we will see later in this chapter, the chin of the bear is also an object of ritual importance. The available evidence suggests that the beaver is a ritual substitute for the bear, and the throat is used as an offering because it is identified with the bear's chin. Like the forearms and the skull, this is a sacred part of the bear. Later in this chapter we will note that both the rules of serving at meals, and the rules for the disposal of animal parts, treat the bear and the beaver in parallel manner.[3]

I found that it was not always possible to obtain a clear idea of who or what were thought to be the recipients of the offerings of food put into the fire. It was generally agreed that the purpose was to improve hunting success in the future. Specific persons or spirits who received the offerings were usually spoken of as *cumusum* ('your grandfather'), a general term of respect applied to several spirits. Where it was possible to obtain the name of a specific spirit for whom the offering was intended, I was, on different occasions, told: the bear, *Mistaapew*, the spirit of the 'outside' (*wiiwiitimiskew*), the master of the animal that was being eaten, and the spirit of an old man who no longer went hunting but lived in Mistassini Post. When the offering is put in the fire I was told that it is proper to address the spirit intended to receive the food. However, such addresses are not always made aloud; the few I have overheard only contain a short statement presenting the offering. In the course of one myth in which the hero, *Ciisaa*, rescues two girls who have been captured by two *atuus* monsters, he is aided in his task by an old woman who, at one point in the story, instructs him to make an offering by putting it in the river and saying, 'Grandmother of the clouds, I offer this to you'. This phrase in the myth is the same one which is sometimes used when food is put in the fire.

5. *Rules of serving food*

There are two kinds of rules which must be followed when game meat is served: first, certain parts of the animal connote honour to the recipient, and thus are only served to suitable persons; second, but only in the case of the beaver and the bear, certain portions of the animal are referred to as 'man's food' (*naapew miicim*), and other parts as 'woman's food' (*iskwew miicim*). Among the Fort George band the restrictions are sometimes also applied to the caribou. It is believed that a person who eats any food which is restricted by taboo to the opposite sex will become ill, usually suffering pain in the part of the body corresponding to the part of the animal from which the offending food portion came. As a practical everyday matter, both of these kinds of rules apply principally to the beaver, which is eaten almost every day, the whole animal normally being cooked and served at one time. The serving rules apply most strictly to the bear. However, the bear is seldom eaten in winter. When a bear is eaten most of the meat is consumed at a feast, when the sexes are often segregated, and all the parts of the animal which are subject to the special rules of serving are served at this first meal.

The principal part of the animal which connotes honour is the head, and this is always given to one or more male hunters. This rule applies to the bear and to animals the size of a beaver or smaller. However, in the case of the muskrat, and sometimes other small animals, the head is often given to a young boy.[4] The bear's head is shared by adult men only. In the case of fish, the head is not restricted to male hunters, but it is usually served to an older man or woman, because it contains the choicest parts of the fish. There are other choice food portions which I was told are often reserved for old people, e.g. the foetuses of any animal and the tail-bone of a beaver. The tail is usually divided up and a portion served to everyone at the meal, but the bone and the meat attached to it is often served for an old person.

The principal items involved in the distinction between man's and woman's food are the feet and the lower part of the limbs of the beaver and the bear. The front limbs are served only to men, and the rear ones to women. Several folk explanations for this practice were elicited. In the myth of 'The Boy who was kept by a Bear', the bear gives to the boy his forelimbs when the boy's father arrives to take his son away. The bear tells the boy that he will always be able to find bear dens as long as he keeps the gift wrapped up (see Chapter 7). This explains why this part of the bear is wrapped and hung in a tree after the bear is eaten. Mention has already been made of one version of the myth of 'The Child with Lice in his Hair', in which the giant only eats the chin, skull and forelimbs of the beavers he catches. I was told that it makes the bear angry to have his forelegs cooked and served with the rest of the meat, and a hunter who does this will be attacked by a bear. One man said that the forearms of the bear are man's food because they contain the strength, and man is the stronger of the two sexes. Another said that a man eats the forearms because he wants his shot to hit the forepart of the animal, and not to fall behind, as it can do if the animal is moving. At the same time, it was said that women have the rear feet because they are the ones that stay behind.

6. *The feast* (makusaanuu)

So far in this chapter we have been concerned with activities involved with the bringing of game meat into camp and its use as food, activities which could not in themselves be called 'rituals', but which, because of their symbolic content and their associations with religious beliefs, must be seen as having a ritual aspect. In the case of the feast, however, there is a self-conscious awareness by the participants that this meal as a whole constitutes a significant event, and one which results in important effects for the whole group through supernatural means. For example, I was given spontaneously the following statement by a man as an explanation for a case of starvation which he had just related to me:

This sort of thing [starvation] was due to things that happened while people were having a feast. If someone did something wrong at a feast, things might go badly for him in the future. And if nobody did anything wrong at a feast, then they would kill plenty of game, even if they were almost out of food. They would usually be able to kill some kind of animal each day.

The following description is based on a series of nine feasts which I attended during the winter I spent with the Nichicun local band; three of the feasts involved the whole of the Nichicun group, and each of the others was with one of two separate hunting groups. Three principal categories of feasts can be identified according to the particular occasions which prompt the feast to be held (see Table 13), but the specific reason for the feast does not change the basic similarity of all feasts held in the bush camps in winter, and it is these general characteristics which our description will be centred on.

Table 13.   FEAST OCCASIONS

(1)	*Passage rites*
(a)	Soon after the birth of a child
(b)	After the 'Walking Out' ceremony (see Chapter 4)
(c)	The *usciiminhun* feast, which is held when a young person kills one of the major game animals for the first time
(d)	On a child's birthday (although this is not observed by all families)
(e)	After the marriage ceremony
(2)	*The conclusion of a particularly successful hunt*
(a)	The first kills of each major game animal made at the beginning of each season
(b)	Particularly large kills
(c)	Generally after the killing of an adult bear
(3)	*Calendrical events*
(a)	The start of winter when the group moves into its first winter camp
(b)	Christmas
(c)	New Year
(d)	A feast for the end of winter

In addition to the occasions shown in Table 13 a number of feasts were noted in the settlement which seem to be recent innovations: a feast was held when a family moved into their new government-subsidized house in the village, and another was held in the nearby town of Chibougamau when an Indian Friendship Center was opened. Recently, the Mistassini have begun to hold a regular mid-summer 'Pow-wow', an event which includes a feast. The present account, however, is concerned mainly with the feasts held in the hunting camps.

The basic similarity of all feasts can be summarized in the form of a number of invariant features by which a feast may be contrasted with what happens at an ordinary meal. The following are the eleven most important of such contrasting features, which can be seen as the rules by which a feast operates.

In the first place feasts, in contrast to ordinary meals, are communal, in that everyone in the residential group, which may be anything from the hunting group to the whole band, may attend. At other times meals are never eaten with people who are not from the same commensal family, not even when several commensal families share the same communal dwelling, although cooked food may be sent to others at meal times. The exception to this general statement is that a meal is shared with strangers when they first arrive in camp, a meal which has many of the qualities of a feast. According to some accounts, only men eat at bear feasts. In the bear feast which I observed women ate at a second sitting. At other feasts it may be the unmarried and widowed persons who eat at a second sitting. Because of the size of the settlement of Mistassini, there are some less important feasts held there which are only attended by kin and close friends, but in these cases communal food sharing is expressed symbolically by a distribution by children of the family of feast food around the village afterwards.

At a feast, unlike a normal meal, a surplus of food is prepared and served; all of it is served, but nobody finishes what is served to him. This practice is in contrast to many descriptions of feasts found in historical sources, as well as among contemporary neighbouring groups, and even from some Mistassini informants, who speak of an 'eat all' feast at which very large amounts of food are served, all of which must be eaten at the one sitting. Le Jeune, who lived with a Montagnais group in the early seventeenth century, noted both 'eat all' feasts, and feasts where surplus food was taken away afterwards, although he did not say under what conditions one was undertaken rather than the other (Thwaites 1896-1901, 6:281). Mistassini informants say the 'eat all' feast used to be associated with the first kills of major game animals each winter.

Special recognition is paid at feasts to the status of each participant, by means of seating position, by the roles they take in the proceedings, by the portions of meat they are served and, if there is more than one sitting, by which of the sittings they attend. As we have mentioned, certain parts of bear and beaver meat are 'women's food', other parts 'man's food'. The head of an animal connotes honour, and normally

Plate 15. Burning the fur of the first beaver caught in the winter, in preparation for a special feast.

those of animals the size of the beaver or smaller are served to a male at least old enough to hunt the species in question. At ordinary meals no great emphasis is placed on serving rules, as any unequal honour bestowed on hunters of similar status equalizes over a number of meals. At a feast, however, the server and his helpers spend large amounts of time making sure that each person is properly served. The skulls of beavers and smaller animals are separated from the jaws, something not done at ordinary meals, and the latter are given to hunters of lower status than those who are served the skulls.

Offerings of food are always made to spiritual entities at feasts. A little of each kind of food served is put into the fire. The recipients may be identified as the spirits of living or dead persons with kin ties to the group; more often they are the spirits who aid in hunting, or game animals such as the bear. Other offerings, apart from feast food and tobacco, include drumming, songs addressed to particular spirits, and dancing. These latter performances take place after the feast meal is finished and are not done in every case. As we have noted, offerings of food are also made at some ordinary meals, usually to mark an occasion of significance not, however, important enough for a feast. Drumming and singing are forms of 'offerings' intended specifically to ensure successful future hunting, and are most often performed at feasts early in the season, such as the First Beaver Feast, and the Winter Feast.

Guests at feasts are expected to behave in a restrained, respectful manner. If beer or home brew is to be consumed as part of the celebrations the person in charge of the feast forbids its consumption before the meal is finished. Young people are told to speak quietly and eat slowly. They may also be told to remove their hats on entering the feast tent, although I have observed at the same time older people who kept theirs on.[5] Respectful behaviour is most in evidence at a bear feast.

Cleanliness is also a feature of feasts. A clean, decorated birch bark sheet, or a decorated cloth, is laid down, usually a sheet kept for such occasions; in most cases the floor is first given a new covering of fresh spruce or balsam boughs. The bush in general, and things from it such as boughs, are considered clean, in contrast to the settlement and the camp. This concept of cleanliness implies that what is 'clean' is more attractive to the spirits. For instance, it is said that a 'Shaking Tent' ceremony ought to be performed in the bush, because it is not clean around houses. Clean clothes are worn to a feast if possible. Earlier sources often mention a special feast tent set up some distance from the dwellings; possibly this was related to the requirement of cleanliness.

At feasts a rule of clockwise movement can be observed. The seating forms an almost complete circle, usually around the fire, and food, tobacco, etc., must pass in a clockwise direction, although empty dishes may pass in the reverse direction. The drum is passed to those who will play it in the same direction, and dancing around the fire moves the same way. This clockwise rule occurs in other contexts, all of which involve the idea of communication between men and spirits.

A special feature of feasts is the meticulous attention given to the final destination of all food served there. At ordinary meals food is never wasted, and scraps may be included in what is fed to the dogs. Care is taken not to allow dogs to eat the bones of game animals, but this rule is not always applied to the bones of immature small animals. At feasts, on the other hand, it is as if every morsel that is served must be accounted for. The individual in charge of the feast is careful to wipe out every serving dish with his fingers and lick them clean. Any crumbs which fall are carefully gathered in the sheet and thrown into the fire at the end of the feast. The rule is often expressed in terms of making sure that the dogs never touch any part of the feast. Food served at a feast can be said to be in a 'sacred' condition, and must be either consumed by the participants or given to the spirits, either by putting it in the fire, or, as in the case of the inedible remains, by placing them in a cache, hanging them in a tree or dropping them in a lake. In the case of the first beaver killed, this principle applies also to the animal's skin. The animal is prepared and cooked by a special method, involving first the burning of the fur and then the boiling of the carcass whole. The skin is eaten with the meat. Unlike subsequent beavers, the fur of which is traded, literally every part of the first animal killed except the bones is eaten at its feast.

The next rule follows from an earlier point about the surplus of food: food that is taken away from the feast must be wrapped up. Each guest takes to the feast his plate and cup, wrapped in a clean cloth. Before he leaves he wraps the uneaten portion in the plate with this cloth. If this is not done it is thought that game animals will move away from the area. It is thought that *Ciiwetinsuu*, a spirit associated with the cold, and the winds of the north and west, sees the food leaving the tent and withdraws the animals he controls. It is said that any food which is carried from one tent to another should be wrapped for this reason, but in practice the rule is applied mainly to food taken home from a feast, and to gifts of cooked food. The feast food brought home in this way is eaten along with regular meals over a period of a few days. Wrapping of feast food to be taken outside the feast tent may be related to a practice mentioned in earlier sources of sealing up the feast tent, a practice no longer observed by the present-day Mistassini. Clouston (Davies 1963:37) describes a caribou feast held near Kaniapiskau Lake, northeast of Nichicun, in 1820. As soon as everyone was inside the tent, all holes were carefully sealed up. Speck says of the Montagnais-Naskapi feast, 'The openings of the feast lodge are all kept closed lest the animal spirits who are thronging outside enter or obtain a glimpse of the procedures inside ... ' (1935:202).

Another distinctive aspect of feasting is the emphasis placed on male roles in the proceedings. There are two specific central roles, 'The one who gives the feast' (i.e. who supplies the principal animal food), and 'The one who is in charge of the feast'; both are males. Cooking at an ordinary meal may be performed by both men and women, but if women are present they are in charge. At the feast the men cook and serve the meat, while women look after the sweet food. The contrast between the activity of an ordinary meal and a feast is not simply that the focus of the preparation passes from a woman to her husband. Rather, a group of men from several commensal groups emerges around the informal leadership of the man in charge of the feast.

The final item in this list of the elements of a feast — a list which may not be exhaustive — is that special foods are served. For the meat, there are a number of special cooking methods employed, not all of them exclusively confined to feast occasions. For beaver, the cooking methods include 'burnt fur-boiled whole' method (*ptaaw amisk*), already referred to as being used for the first beaver of the season, and a method in which the beaver is first divided into two parts, one containing the fat, the other containing the muscle meat, both of which are skilfully butchered and sewn up so that each retains the body outline of the animal. In the latter method the fat part is turned inside out and roasted, while the lean part is boiled. A third method of serving beaver at a feast is also a method commonly used at other times; the beaver is suspended by a cord next to the stove and roasted

Plate 16. A feast, held to celebrate the birth of a child (centre).

whole. Geese and other birds, as well as fish, are also roasted whole. Feasts utilizing moose or caribou usually focus attention on the head, which is boiled. Other meat from the animal is roasted and served. When boiled meat is served at a feast the cooking liquid may be used as a cold drink.

To summarize the main points from our material on the cooking of meat at feasts, the following are important. (1) The cooking method used is one which is designed to preserve the fat in a solid state, or it allows it to be collected and served separately, as is the case for bear fat. Fat is always the most significant part of an animal for the Cree; it has a symbolic significance at feasts, particularly the winter feast. This feast is held after the hunting group first moves into its winter lodge, and during the feast fat is smeared on the walls, doorpost and the guns, as well as being placed in the fire with the other food offerings. Fat is thus presented both to the spirits outside the dwelling, and to the domestic spirits and those of the hunting equipment. (2) In the feast the responsibility for the cooking of the meat is transferred from women to men, who use more elaborate methods, but still follow in outline the principles of everyday meat cooking practice. The cooking of the rest of the meal (i.e. items based on flour, and tea) is under- taken by the women, but in this case they invert the practice of every- day cooking. The bannock, or baking powder bread, served everyday, is white and not sweet. At feasts, instead, bannock is not served, but a number of puddings, pies and doughnuts are, all of which are sweet and dark in colour. Tea, at ordinary meals, is served black, and individuals may add milk or sugar; at a feast it is served already sweet and white.

(3) Finally, it is most noticeable that the method of cooking the central meat item is one which usually preserves the animal, either in its body outline or one part of the animal being used at the feast, like a moose head, and this is maintained in a whole state during the cooking process. This is especially significant in the *apuutina* method, where two body forms of the animal, one of fat and the other of lean meat, are preserved during cooking. The feast animal is, so to speak, preserved for as long as possible in the form of an animal-person, rather than as a quantity of meat, before it is actually cut up and served. This also results in the division of the animal corpse into parts at the feast itself, and this has symbolic importance, becoming an integral part of the rite, and thus the focus of the whole group's attention.

7. *Quasi-feasts*

We have seen that a feast differs from an ordinary meal on a number of points. Some of these rules for feasts are not closely adhered to under certain circumstances, particularly in the summer settlement and among those Mistassini who no longer engage in full-time hunting. It is also the case that, in the hunting group, there are occasions on which a meal is eaten which cannot be described as a feast, as this term has been used here, but which shares some of the elements of a feast. Rogers refers to a 'little feast', at which each commensal group eats in their own quarters, but in which the family which provides the 'feast' sends around cooked food to each of the other commensal groups in the residential unit (1972:130). I observed several meals with special religious significance. For example, three hunters came home, each having killed an otter, the first of this species which the group had killed that season. The animals were cooked together, and the cooked meat carried to each family. On another occasion a beaver was found in a trap where it had become completely frozen in ice; this caused the hair to fall out, after the animal was thawed out. I was told that this was offensive to the animal, and the hunter who had caught it presented the animal to the hunting group leader, who prepared and cooked in the standard manner used for the first beaver caught each season, that is, by burning off the fur and boiling it whole. This was then eaten, employing some of the rules of a feast, but without the whole group eating together.

Earlier in this chapter other references were made to meals which share some of the features of a feast; the first meal offered to newly arrived strangers in camp, and the meal which follows the displays of the 'tokens' of a big game kill, and that which follows the bringing of the meat of a moose or caribou to camp. Other examples of ritualized eating include the drink of the blood of a freshly killed caribou, which in the past was shared by all men engaged in the hunt. At present, a food preparation is cooked using the stomach contents of a freshly-killed caribou. When the fat which is found in the metapodial bones of the moose and caribou is eaten it is shared around carefully. A number of such special foods are prepared from time to time, and eaten without a formal meal. One example of particular importance is called *muuskamii*. This is a soup made from boiling the cracked long bones of moose or caribou. The same term is also used for the cooking water in which meat is boiled, and which is served as a drink at any feast at which boiled meat is also served. *Muuskamii* made from bones is served cold, and is usually drunk between meals. It is cooked in a large pot and cooled with clean snow. The pot is carried around to each family in the hunting group. It must be served first to the oldest male, followed by the other men in the family, after which the women are served. When the soup is first made an offering of a spoonful is put in the stove.

All the above examples of practices involving food consumption have something in common with feasts, although they lack the formal occasion of commensality. What they all do stress, in common with the feast, is the idea of ceremonialized group-sharing of food.

8. *Decorated animal remains* (intucikan)

After everything edible has been consumed from a game animal, care must be taken that the inedible remains are not thoughtlessly neglected. Some particular parts of certain animals may be kept by an individual hunter, while other parts are set aside, and carefully hung up together as a display for the spirits. In the first category there are such items as the bear's chin, the ceremonial caribou hide, and the goose head. The chin skin of the bear is decorated symbolically and is said to represent the entire bear; it is sewn into a triangular container in which a small wormlike piece of flesh (lingual frenulum) from under the bear's tongue is kept. Some men are said to have kept all the chins of every bear they have ever shot. 'Ceremonial hides' are probably no longer made, although some men still keep them. The one shown to me was made of an entire caribou skin, in which the head, ears and much of the leg skins remained attached. This skin, which according to some should be from the first animal killed in the fall, was prepared as carefully as possible, so as to be free of holes, and, in processing, it was made as white as possible. Hair was left attached at the edges, and the hide was cut to form ribbons at seven places around the edge, to represent the four feet, the tail, and the two antlers. These ribbons of skin were decorated with dots of red paint.

Plate 17. Antlers decorated with coloured ribbons, and the skulls of small
animals, at the site of an abandoned camp.

The ceremonial hide is displayed at the doorway facing the rising sun
at dawn, once or twice during a winter. The display is done, according to different informants, for the spirit of the 'outside', for 'our
grandfather', or for a spirit called 'caribou woman'.[6] Among the
Fort George Indians the skins of many medium and large-sized
animals were decorated and displayed as 'ceremonial hides'. The first
goose which a young man kills is given to a woman, who dries it, stuffs
it with grass, and decorates it. It is then kept by the young man. A
hunter may also keep a bone disc from the sternum region of the first
caribou he kills.

We have seen that the ceremonial hide was sometimes temporarily
displayed at the campsite; some of the bones of animals killed during
a group's residence at a camp are erected as a permanent display when
the group moves on. Like the hide, these are oriented so that the skulls
face the rising sun or can be seen from that direction. The bones
displayed are skulls, except those of the moose and caribou, as these
skulls are broken up during the serving. However, any antlers of these
animals are carefully displayed, as are the scapulars. In addition, the
forelegs of bears, beavers, and sometimes other animals such as the
otter, are tied in a tree, usually wrapped in birch bark or cloth first.
Coloured ribbons may be used to decorate the skulls and the antlers,
and the bear skulls are sometimes painted, or marked with burnt wood
from the fire. In the past, many of the displayed bones were hung
from a tree which was prepared by stripping off the branches, except
for a few at the top, and decorating the trunk with horizontal bands,
which were sometimes painted. As was mentioned in Chapter 4, this

Plate 18. Bear skulls. Offerings of tobacco may be placed
in the nasal cavity.

pole, called *mistikukaan* appears to have been replaced by a flagpole,
or a combination of flagpole and weathervane, which I have only
observed at permanent campsites. I found that only a few informants
knew if there was a collective term for the bones and other decorated
animal parts that are used for display, but some older informants used
the word *intucikan*. [7]

9. *Disposal of ordinary bones*

As we have seen, an important aspect of the proper treatment of game
is to dispose of the bones (1) so that these are not touched by the dogs,
and (2) so that the abandoned campsite is left in a 'clean' condition.
Bones of both land animals and birds are placed on an elevated platform, while those of water animals are returned to the lake.

10. *Concealment and display*

The analysis of the rites involved in the concluding phase of the hunting cycle has shown that they are all designed to demonstrate 'respect' towards the game animals brought into the camp. As the corpse is separated into food material and the inedible remains, sacredness accumulates in these remains, and the 'respect' of the hunter is directed at them, until each category of animal material has been returned to its proper place around the camp, and the camp itself is allowed to return to the bush.

These ritual acts of respect to the animals, like those concerned with the preparatory and actual hunting phases, are part of a system of ideas which offers two fairly distinct ideological interpretations of the whole process of hunting. In the first place, the rites give a supernatural, magical interpretation of how game animals behave in relation to man, and specifically how this relationship is crucial to the actual process of harvesting game animals. At the same time, in a less direct way, the symbolism in the rites provides a model, and thereby a validation, of the social relations between those men who hunt and those who consume the animals. The most obvious interpretation of the ideology of the relationship between man and prey presents a 'positive' view of it (i.e. relations between hunters and the animals, or their controlling spirits, is one of a series of prestations and counter-prestations). However, in this section we will also look at some evidence which does not fit neatly in such an interpretation. At the same time, we will see that the symbolic expressions which mark the sharing of meat involve more than the straightforward social ideology of 'generalized exchange' (see Sahlins 1972) among hunting group members, and appear sometimes to represent the perspective of the hunters, while at others they stress the ideology of the elders who are no longer the active hunters.

As far as the ideology of man-animal relations is concerned, much of the explicit expression throughout the hunting rites is one of a series of prestations and counter-prestations. Men make gifts to the animal world, that is, to the bush, and in return are the recipients of gifts of game animals killed by the hunters. During the third phase of the hunting cycle great stress is laid on the boundary separating the human domain (the inside of the dwelling) from the animal domain (the outside, and the bush). The *asawaapin* taboo keeps the domestic group inside as the hunter brings in the animal. During the feast it is sometimes the practice to seal any holes in the tent. Given that this separation between the domestic and animal domains is established, the rites also draw attention to the two pathways that remain between these domains, the doorway and the chimney. The doorway, kept clear by the *asawaapin* rule, permits the entry of the gift animal, while the chimney is used to send the offerings of food put in the fire back to

Plate 19. A platform for the bones of land animals at the
Nichicun camp.

the outside. This gives a model of exchange between man and animal,
between inside and outside, as shown in Figure 13.

However, this 'positive' account does not take into account some of
the negative aspects already encountered in the relations between the
hunter and his prey, for example the negative treatment shown to
Ciiwetinsuu, and the idea that if feast rites are performed improperly
starvation may result. Coercive relations between man and animal
were shown in the myth of 'The Boy Kept by a Bear', where the way

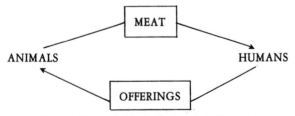

Fig. 13. Hunter's ideological model of hunting

the boy's father overcomes the bear is the model for the use of magic to subdue an animal. Similarly, the fight between *Mistaapew* and the bear in the 'Shaking Tent' which results in good hunting for men a positive exchange ideology is not adequate in itself. Although the feast appears to convey the positive exchange model, one myth which gives the origin of the feasting ritual among the Cree also suggests that hunting does not rest on positive relations alone. This myth, of which a short outline follows, is the story of *Kaamakuset*, 'he who feasts'.[10]

There is a famine. Two brothers who live with their sister set out to try to obtain food from *Nanimsuu*, a powerful man who keeps alive all the game animals inside his huge house [in one version it is said to be so large it covers a lake]. *Nanimsuu* says he will feed the brothers, but they must eat all they are offered, or they will be killed. They agree, are unable to eat the huge amounts offered, and are killed. *Nanimsuu* burns their bodies, as he does with all such victims. The sister has a son supernaturally, and he becomes a mature man in a matter of days, and magically returns his mother's brothers to life. Together the three men visit *Nanimsuu* again, the young man accepts the challenge, and is offered one after another of each of the largest game animals, cooked whole. He consumes each one, cooking liquid and all, and each time throws back the empty cooking pot to *Nanimsuu*. Although he manages to eat everything he is offered, *Nanimsuu* still tries to kill him, but he escapes [in one version, by cutting an exit through the rear wall]. The hero then took the name *Kaamakuset*. [Told by Sinclair Rubin]

In one of the many versions of the story of the caribou house, or the caribou mountain, which is also known to the Mistassini, there is a passage with some striking similarities to the foregoing myth. Most versions explain how a hunter married a caribou and went with the herd to live inside a mountain to the north, from where he now controls the caribou. A myth, collected at Northwest River, Labrador (Lefebvre 1969), concerns a visit made to the caribou master.

There is a famine. A shaman decides to visit the master of the caribou, inside his mountain house in the far north. He takes a friend, whom he instructs to watch carefully, and follow all his actions. When they are inside the huge house, the caribou master offers the shaman a quantity of food, which he consumes entirely, after which he throws down the vessel it is served in, saying, '*Ninimish*,[11] here is your pot!' His companion is also offered food, and he does exactly the same. Following this they are allowed to leave. As they journey south they are followed by a caribou herd, which ends the famine for their group.

There are several clear references in these myths to feasts: there is the name of the first hero, and references in both myths to the 'eat all' feast. Feast conditions are implied when they specify a surplus of food held inside a sealed dwelling. The sealed nature of the dwellings is stressed. The caribou house is inside a hollow mountain with stone doors, while *Nanimsuu's* house is described as having three doorways,

one inside the other. We have seen that the sealed dwelling is characteristic of feasts. Also in the myth there is an inversion of many of the
conditions of a normal hunt. The shaman, or man with spiritual
power, is like a hunter, except that he is required to go inside to get
the animals (or food) and bring them out. Rather than receiving the
animal as a free gift, he must take it by coercion.

These examples of a model of negative or coercive relations between
men and animals are at odds with the model of positive exchange
relations as shown in Figure 13. The hunting religion includes both a
divinatory aspect, in which the hunter tries to foretell future hunting
and to make the proper prestations, and a magical aspect, in which
shamanistic power is used to invert the normally superior position of
the animals over men and to acquire game meat by outwitting the
animals, and then concealing the results.

We turn now to the ideology of social relations, and particularly the
relations between the hunters and the others in the hunting group, as
this is expressed in activities involving the animal after it has been
killed. The predominant expression given to these relationships in the
distribution of game meat is of positive relations characterized by the
free sharing of meat by the successful hunters to the other families in
the hunting group, both with quantities of raw meat, and through
symbolic distribution of a surplus of cooked food at the feast. No
specific repayment is expected, and moreover the hunter who gives the
meat is expected not to brag about his prowess as a hunter. Within the
family positive relations are also expressed, including the idea of an
exchange between the men who bring in the game meat and the
women who supply the men with clothing. The division of the animal
corpse into parts many of which must be given to particular individuals or classes of individuals in the domestic group (the head for a
senior hunter, the prized parts of the intestines (the 'tokens') for the old
people, and, in the case of the beaver and the bear, special parts for the
males and for the females) suggests that the hunter does not so much
give the meat to the family as bring to the camp meat which is already
destined to be consumed by particular people, since the body of the
animal is structured so as to reflect the form of the domestic group.[12]

However, there are additional aspects to the Cree social ideology of
sharing; one concerns the 'surplus' which is characteristic of a feast,
and the other concerns the relationship between a hunter and the old
men who remain behind in the camp. The surplus of meat is a central
characteristic not only of the modern feasts, when food is taken home,
but also of the historic 'eat-all' feast. This central idea of surplus
suggests that the differentiation between these two kinds of feasts
results from the fact that one is a simple transformation of the other. In
both cases the initial situation is the same, that is, there is a surplus of
food distributed. While, in the case of the 'eat-all', people remain
inside the sealed tent until all the food is eaten, in the case of the

other kind of feast the surplus itself is sealed, and carried out of the tent by the guests. Given the 'problem' that a surplus presents to the nomadic group, these feasts symbolize two solutions: in one case people overfill themselves, and in the other people overfill their plates. In both cases there is an initial surplus which subsequently is hidden, either by overeating, or by wrapping it so as to hide it.

We turn now to the way hunting rites also involve an ideology of the social relations between the hunters and the old men. The religious ideology of hunting proposes that old men have, by their past hunting activities, established permanent positive relations with animals, and this gives them divinatory and magical power to bring success to others in the group. The following diagram outlines this representation of hunting.

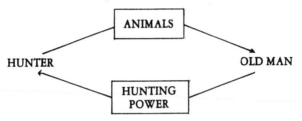

Fig. 14. The ideology of hunting held by old men

The old man is symbolically given priority over the meat of the animals brought to camp, as can also be seen in the 'Walking Out' ceremony (Chapter 5), and in the *asawaapin* taboo. This priority is given by virtue of the power of his songs and charms, power which accounts for the success of the hunter. At the feast it is the old man who acts as host, and redistributes the meat in amounts surplus to everyone's needs. The feast in this way allows the old man as host to preside over the distribution of food, and thus be given credit for the surplus.

A real surplus of meat is, however, rare, since a store of meat is continually required to see the group through periods of poor hunting. Moreover, rather than there being a communal hunting group larder, from which everyone helps himself, meat is the object of prestations and counter-prestations between hunters after every kill. Each commensal family has a larder from which members may draw without any accounting, but all adjustments of food supplies between these larders take place exclusively through gifts, apart from the relatively small amount of food redistributed at feasts. Gifts of raw food carry the slight stigma of the implication of being from a successful hunter to an unsuccessful one. This competitiveness between hunters is always denied, but the potentially awkward situation when raw meat presentations are made is usually muted through the mediation of children, who carry the gifts.

While meat is actually owned by specific family groups within the hunting group, and differential hunting success is adjusted through a system of generalized exchange, the ideology, as expressed at feasts, suggests to the contrary the existence periodically of huge supplies, redistributed so that everyone has a surplus.

But in day to day living, meat is not a free commodity owned by the whole group, nor are the quantities of meat stored in the camp useless surpluses. Each family owns its own stored supply, and these stores are continually changing, due to differential hunting success and to different rates of consumption. Readjustments are made, by means of gifts given to families with less than the others, before they run short, and without them having to ask. In other words, each family must be aware of the stores kept by the others in the group, stores which are, for the most part, kept outside on cache platforms.

By symbolically inverting some of these conditions, the feast indicates an awareness of the possibility of hostile feelings by some hunting group members towards the normal system of food exchange. One noteworthy feature of the distribution of food at a feast is that, although each person is given an amount which is surplus to what he can eat, he cannot give any away, but must keep it to himself, and even must hide it as he leaves the feast tent. The feast in this way, by stressing concealment and danger, reveals ideology opposite to the explicit ideal of animals and the controlling spirits as gift givers.

11. *Social modes and the animal corpse*

When speaking of rules regarding the proper treatment for the slain animal, the idea which sums them up for the Cree is that respect should be shown, which is sometimes expressed as not making fun of the animal. From another perspective the illusion of a social relation between the hunter and the animal must be dissolved, and in its place a re-emphasis of the social relations between the hunter and both his commensal family and his hunting group takes place. Bringing home an animal means for the hunter not only the end of the hunting cycle, but the start of a domestic one. The presentation of the animal to the group, made in a period of silence, is the time when the hunter loses his position as a newly-arrived stranger and re-enters the group.[13] I would suggest further that the man-animal relationship has a distinctly sexual aspect, and that after the return the animal itself becomes a symbolic mediator in the starting, or the restarting, of sexual relationships in general.

My suggestion is based on a variety of evidence. To begin with there is the common metaphorical allusion to sexuality which occurs in divinatory dreams, in jokes, in male talk about hunting, and in the use of hunting terminology in descriptions of sexual intercourse. Secondly, when a young man kills the first animal of a major game species he is given a feast, and he is referred to as *usciiminhun*, meaning 'new marriageable person', and references are made to his readiness for sexual exploits the following summer.

During the period when game is displayed inside the tent most animals are laid on their backs with the hind feet towards the door, except in the case of those animals butchered before they are brought to camp. The women of the commensal family admire the animal at this time, and often stroke its fur. If the animal is considered an important kill, such as the first of a particular species killed in some time, women from the other families in the group will also gather around. At other times public contacts made across sexual lines are rare, particularly in the hunting group. As we have noted, an unmarried man may give his animal to a woman, although I only noticed cases of gifts to women within the commensal family.

There are also several references in myths to marriages between men and animals. Myth heroes also kill dangerous women, and women try to kill heroes, in both cases using hunting techniques. It is thus part of a pattern to find the corpse of a game animal used to symbolize both the contrast and the relationship between men and women.

Earlier in this chapter we noted the rules for serving, and the reasons for them given by informants. These rules apply only to the bear and the beaver (except for the serving of an animal's head), both animals which are brought back to the camp before butchering, and which are thus displayed by laying them out inside the dwelling. If we visualize the form of the bear being displayed within the social space of the two-family communal dwelling as given in Chapter 4, a new solution to the question of why the front legs are male and the rear legs are female, suggests itself (see Figure 15).

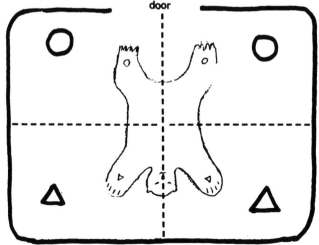

Fig. 15. The bear and the sexual division of domestic space

When the bear is laid in this position in the communal dwelling its
two front legs point to the male parts of the dwelling, and the two rear
legs to the female parts. Moreover, the head, which connotes honour,
is at the rear of the tent opposite the door, which is the same position
as the 'seat of honour' inside the dwelling (Paulson 1952). There is,
moreover, evidence that the two family communal lodge is a suitable
basic model on which to establish the symbolism of the bear. One of
the most common terms for a dwelling encountered in myths, and a
common term for a traditional feast tent, is *saaputwaan*, usually described as having two fires and two doors. Speck mentions an account
of a bear feast using a *saaputwaan*, a dwelling which was inhabited by
two families (Speck 1935:103). The standardized account of two fires
found in such descriptions of the *saaputwaan* indicates two families.

The significance of the laying out of the corpse of a major game
animal within the dwelling is underscored when we recall how the
structure of the animal corpse relates symbolically to various aspects of
the social organization of the hunting group. First, a personal relationship between the animal and the hunter, or the acquisition of the
animal's power, is achieved by the animal occupying the hunter's
personal sleeping space. Secondly, the corpse lying within the dwelling space symbolizes the social group as a whole, and this relationship
between the animal body and the group is, at a feast, maintained
during the meal by the way the body outline is at first preserved and
later divided by social categories. In particular, by providing separate
food for men and women, the beaver and the bear establish the
separate nature of men and women, and also makes possible the
relationship between the two. It is the animal, which is a combination
of sexual elements, which makes the establishment of sexual relations,
and therefore reproduction, possible.

12. Conclusion

With the proper disposal of the remains of the animal corpse the rites
of hunting come full circle, in the sense that this disposal established
the conditions for future production, in that it assures the continued
appearance of animals, and as we have just seen, it also assures the
conditions of human reproduction and the continuity of the hunting
group. In one particular myth the idea is put forward that animal
bones, given the proper treatment, become recovered with flesh as
new animals again. The more commonly-held belief is that the
inedible remains continue to be part of the species as a whole, and
their proper treatment is a way of avoiding giving offence to the
master of the species in question, and this enables hunting to
continue.

In terms of the initial problem with which this study began, we have
seen that the Mistassini Cree of today conduct their hunting production

in the context of an ideology which although undoubtedly changed from 'traditional' beliefs, is nevertheless a system of thought established primarily out of their life in the bush in the context of the natural elements of the environment and the animals, and in the social context of the hunting group. This is not, of course, the limit of Cree experience or the limit of Cree ideology, and in the introductory chapter and elsewhere I have referred to the part of the year spent at the settlement, and the relationship of the Mistassini with the agencies and the agents which dominate their conditions of existence, particularly the trader and the government officials. These factors, and the ideological context within which they are dealt with by the Mistassini Cree, are not, however, in conflict with the ideological systems we have described in this chapter and the three previous ones. The particular circumstances whereby this cultural ideology based on hunting continues relatively independently of the economic and political subordination of the Mistassini band is a major finding to which I wish to draw attention, and which I have suggested may be understood theoretically if we examine the total 'mode of production' by which those Mistassini who are engaged in the production of fur and subsistence meat are organized.

9
Mistassini Land Tenure

1. *The problem of ownership*

In this chapter I will discuss the question of how rights over land-based resources are distributed among the Mistassini, and the part played by religious ideology in this system. In doing so only a few references will be made to the long controversy that has raged between Algonkianists over the origin of land ownership among northern boreal forest hunters. The problem of ownership discussed here is, however, related to this debate, in that I attempt to resolve some of the contradictions which have arisen as these earlier discussions relate to the contemporary situation. I will begin with the point of view that ownership is, on the one hand, a system of controls whereby access to resources is enjoyed differentially, and on the other hand involves an ideological representation of this system of restrictions (Bloch 1976).

Some of the apparent contradictions in the data presented in this debate have arisen because it has sometimes been assumed that one could only speak about land as property in the restricted sense of a system in which a fixed relationship was held to exist between a person or group and the land itself. Speck's earliest descriptions of land tenure among the Algonkian hunters are of this type (e.g. 1915). Rogers has suggested that 'ownership of mobile resources such as fur-bearers must be associated with a defined area since wild animals cannot be marked to denote ownership' (Rogers 1963:83). However, instead of assuming ownership to be a relationship between a man and a defined area of land, I will include a broader definition which could include, for example, a relationship between a man and undefined land within a defined region (such as a vague area around a given central point) of a size suitable to his needs, or an area of a size he has occupied over a number of years. The land that is owned might be undefined as to exact location, except as having a fixed relationship to the location of that of surrounding neighbours. Where the ideology of ownership places the main emphasis on the relationship between the owner and other men, or between the owner and mobile resources like wild animals, the particular location involved may be of secondary importance. In the case of sedentary animal resources such as beaver, the area which includes the resources could be defined in terms of the locations of animals, at least in the short run. It seems inappropriate for us to decide and to define in advance that in order for hunters to have 'ownership' it must be a relationship of only one particular type. In the case of the Mistassini Cree the principle of territory ownership is not based on any attachment to land as such.

A similar problem of the special nature of Mistassini ownership arises in considering what resources in the area are owned, as well as who has what rights, and what is the order of priority, when the rights are shared. Rogers (1963:70-1) makes the observation that the hunting group only has exclusive rights to the resources which are used for trading purposes, while subsistence resources are free goods (i.e. available to anyone outside the hunting group). While this is correct, the significance of this distinction between types of resources is rather limited, and its purpose must be mainly ideological, since it has little practical everyday relevance. This is because the normal process of production involves the use of multi-family hunting groups, which exploit limited areas during the course of the winter, and to survive these groups must have access to both of the above kinds of resources. Thus, if a group was not able to exploit those resources used for trade in a particular area it would not be able to pass the winter there at all. At the most, the distinction would allow the group to make use of a few subsistence resources on a journey passing through such a territory to which it had no right to the market resources. Thus, despite the above distinction in rights, the hunting group in practice must virtually always enjoy exclusive use of all resources. But, at the same time, the ideology of hospitality, and the symbolically significant idea that game meat, as opposed to fur, is always subject to free distribution, is maintained.

The early historical data presents us with a contradictory picture of Algonkian land ownership, and other contradictions arise when we look at the present-day situation. For example, Knight, in looking at the contemporary situation at Rupert House, concludes that ownership of hunting territories would be unworkable for some hunting groups in the long run, due to conditions of ecological instability and of demographic change, so that the system would be forced to break down even during monopoly fur trade conditions (Knight 1965).[1] How, then, do we account for the fact that there is evidence of some sort of land tenure system in effect? Other contradictions appear when we question informants. For example, hunters will carefully point out the limits of their territories on a map, give detailed accounts of the histories of previous owners of the land over the past several generations from whom they claim to have inherited the land, and then add that anybody can and does hunt or trap wherever they wish.

There are at least two possible ways of explaining these contradictions in the evidence, and of determining how we are to understand the significance of hunting territories. One way would be to assume that the contradictions indicate a conflict within Mistassini society between a relatively new idea of land as property, which has yet to take hold firmly, and an earlier concept according to which all hunters had equal rights to hunt and trap wherever they wished. The problem with

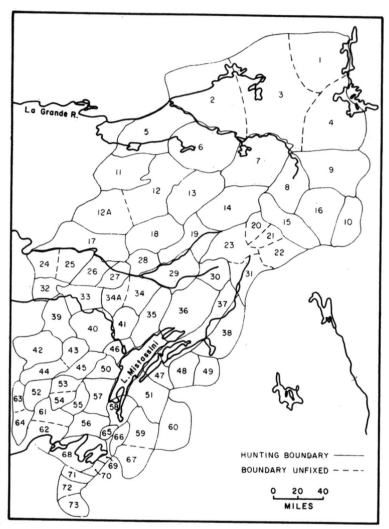

Map 4. Mistassini hunting territories

this assumption is that it means that we would have to assume that the two systems have continued to be in conflict over several generations, since, disregarding the disputed early historical material, we have good evidence for the existence of the hunting territories by at least the middle of the nineteenth century (Rogers 1963:75). The alternate approach is to assume that there is only one system of land tenure, but that it is not based on and is in conflict with European notions of fixed tracts of land.

If we begin with this approach as a working assumption, we see that

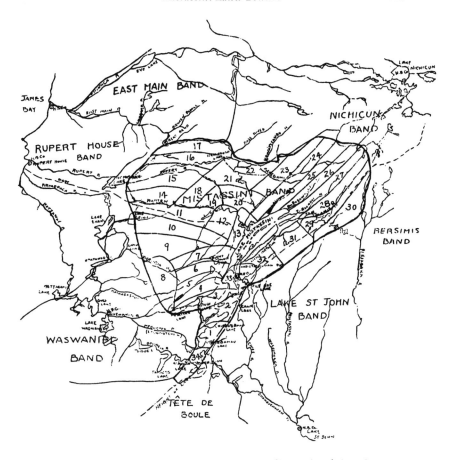

Map 5. Mistassini hunting territories according to Speck (1923)

most of the problems referred to above revolve around the question of the continuity of the system over the long run. If we regard the territories themselves as conferring the right of a group to enjoy, free from competition, the access to adequate resources in the places where they can be usefully exploited, for example in the areas around a group's set of winter campsites, we can see that a bounded territory could itself be, from the Mistassini viewpoint, largely an epiphenomenon. An alternate system which could fulfil the above conditions is the 'allotment system' (see Rogers 1963), but for a group to have a hunting area allotted to it each year would require a political authority over the whole of the band's territory. If we look at the operation of the Mistassini hunting territory system over the long run, it appears to be a mixture of elements of the hunting territory system and the allotment system. On the one hand Mistassini land tenure is a hunting territory ownership system in that there is a concept of 'title' which is inherited. On the other hand it is like an allotment system in that owners discuss their plans for the following winter at summer gatherings, so as not to overlap in their activities. Furthermore, they mark the position of only those traps placed at the edge of what they consider their territory as a warning to neighbours of their presence. These data suggest that there is a realization that people do not carry around a firm and fixed idea of boundaries in their heads.

My suggestion is that what people do carry about in their heads is (*a*) a knowledge of the areas which they and their neighbours have used over the past number of years. When committed to map form (see Map 4) this constitutes something like a snapshot of the hunting territory system, recording the distribution of property in land-based resources as they have been used over a limited period of time. People also have in their heads (*b*) an ideological and jural interpretation of resource use. These ideas include normative rules governing access to resources. These rules refer essentially to the conduct of social relations within the hunting group, plus rules governing relations with neighbouring groups. While membership in the hunting group may change from year to year there is a continuity of leadership, and the leader is identified with the area used by the group in such a way that we may speak of the leader having an overriding 'title'. However, in order to have this title generally recognized the leader must have a history of residence in the area, and a prestige built up on his demonstrated relationship with the animals, in the religious sense outlined in Chapter 7.

The hunting group, in one sense, may be thought of as existing for only one year at a time. Actual property relations in the context of this temporary social unit do not concern land. As with most hunters, the Mistassini Cree also have rules for defining the ownership of actual animals (see Dowling 1968). In some cases this ownership may be established even prior to the killing, as in the cases of the category of animals, like bear or beaver, which may be owned when they are first found, or when their homes are discovered. Moose and caribou are owned by the person who lands the first crippling shot. Most other animals are owned simply by the person who kills them. However, traps may be set on behalf of another person, for example a young woman, or a child who is at the time away in residential school, and the individual in whose name the trap is set owns any animal killed in that trap. The term 'ownership' is being used here in the sense of a 'title' which carries a certain priority, such that the animal is labelled as belonging to that person. This kind of ownership has little to do with how the animal is consumed, although for all species the owner usually has first rights to the hide, whether or not it is to be traded.

The 'ownership' of animals by individuals, usually hunters, is separate from the overall proprietorship enjoyed by the territory owner over the general area of land used by the group. The hunting group is a collection of families which emerges around the leadership of a senior man who has the right to use a particular hunting territory. The leader's position is largely one of prestige, shown by his receipt of largely symbolic prestations from others in the group. However, hunting group leadership and territory ownership tend to be both associated with religious leadership, such that, if the group has no other person with the reputation for superior religious power, the leader will be credited with the religious aspect of the material success of the group.

The structure of inequality between the leader and the other hunters in the group presents us with a paradox. On the surface, any such inequality is denied. In day-to-day activities no particular material preference is given to him, although guest hunters may sometimes present him with a few furs. His power to decide who should hunt in a particular place and when and where the camp should move depends on his overall prestige. He cannot openly show authority. But at the religious and juridical level, he exercises power over animals and has a property relationship with the land used by the group. In both these instances the inequality is symbolic, and is 'misrepresented', in the sense that the property relationship exists in the context of a flexible system of geographic movement and inheritance, such that the central qualification of an owner is the fact of his leadership of a hunting group, while his supposed power over animals is in part a reflection of the productivity of the group.

The relationship between the hunting group leader and the other families in the group appears to have been altered recently. The introduction of educational, welfare, health and housing services has resulted in a reduction in the proportion of young unmarried people and old people who spend the whole winter hunting. The unmarried men and women attend school, and, if they continue going to school after they are about seventeen years old, some of them are unable to go trapping after they leave, even if no alternative employment is available. The phenomenon of old people settling down at Mistassini Post, some for reasons of health, is also a recent development; in the past they would continue to spend each winter with a hunting group.

At the same time, the population of the band as a whole is rising dramatically. Since the unmarried men and old men, had they gone trapping, would have been 'followers' and not group leaders, the ratio between potential group leaders and other hunters has changed. Active hunters are a disproportionately middle-aged group. For this reason it is becoming difficult now for a mature and otherwise successful hunter with rights to land to put together an adequately-sized hunting group. This means fewer of the men who are potential leaders are able to lead their own groups every year. Since the population overall is rising this, however, has not meant a reduction in the number of groups. It is moreover doubtful if there is sufficient land to allow all the potential leaders to have full sized groups every year, even if there were sufficient 'followers'. What happens instead is that some of these men are now leaders only once every few years. It also means that the groups that are formed tend to be slightly smaller than in the past (see Table 14).

Table 14.　COMPOSITION OF THE MISTASSINI HUNTING GROUPS, 1969-1970

	Number of families per hunting group				*Total*
	1	*2*	*3*	*4*	
Number of groups	8	24	8	5	44
Per cent of the total number of groups	18	53	18	11	100

Formerly, hunting groups with only one commensal family were very rare, except during periods of severe game shortage, and for short periods during the winter, when members of a group might leave in different directions as family units and reassemble later. The possibility for a single family to stay alone for a whole winter has been enhanced by a lessening of the dangers of sickness and starvation in the bush. This danger is reduced mainly because of new roads which have been built in the southern part of Mistassini land, and because of the use of aircraft. In the areas which are some distance from Mistassini Post, aircraft have allowed the groups to take larger quantities of stored imported food, such as flour, when they travel to their hunting territories. Aircraft are also used by the H.B.C. to make two mid-winter visits to each camp. Moreover, not all groups stay in the bush as long as they did in the past. Instead of leaving in August or September and returning in June, some groups including some of those with only one family, may leave in October and return in March. In the case of owners of land with only a small beaver population, the introduction of beaver quotas may also lead to some reduction in the size of groups, although I have found no direct indication of this.

For the foregoing reasons, only a little over half the Mistassini hunting groups are led year after year by the same man, and only some of these even have the same followers year after year. For the rest there is an active period each summer to see who intends to be a leader, and which men will ask to go with him. In several cases in 1969 and 1970 leaders who would have preferred to have a larger group of followers were forced to leave without finding any more. Not all leaders prefer large groups, as this tends to crowd the area around the camp with trappers, and force the men to move further afield, and to spend nights away from camp more. But since they permit members to have a better social life in the camp, and to have more people available for cooperative tasks (moving, building camp, group hunting), a large group is thought to have advantages. Only in such large groups does leadership as a political force become an important factor.

This returns us to the question of the leader's function. Although the leader is called 'boss' (*ucimaaw*), the same term used for the Hudson's Bay Company manager, we have pointed out that in practice leadership consists largely in bringing the group together and coordinating group action. At the material level of social relations the distinction between leader and follower is small except that while the group as a whole must continue to act together and exchange labour and goods for the duration of the full winter season, the leader's contribution may outweigh the others, because of his skill. However, at the level of jural relations a small distinction does exist between owner and non-owner; small because it does not consist of the distinction between 'landed' and 'landless' person, but rather between the exercise of a different degree of a general right to use land. Finally, at the religious level, the differential between territory owner and non-owner is most marked, with the leader, or another older person, claiming a privileged position with respect to relations with the territory's animals. This relationship is held to exist between a man who has supernatural power and particular animals, or with a species, by means of divination, hunting magic, or through animal friendship, all points I have discussed in Chapters 6 and 7. These other kinds of 'proprietorship' have no effect, however, in determining who has access to resources within the hunting group.

The concept of a generalized 'ownership' of wild animals, in which an individual, usually an old man, is said to have something like an ongoing relationship with various species — a relationship which gives him preferential access to such animals as a resource — provides the ideological link between the short-term rules of access to resources within the territory and the group notion of a 'permanent' relationship which is said to exist between a group leader and the area he habitually uses. The relationship of hunters to the animals may sometimes be likened to having 'friends' or 'pets' among those animals which inhabit the particular region, but in relation to strangers, that is to people outside the potential members of the individual's hunting group, its relevance is, in effect, that of a relationship to the land area itself, and comes close to the general concept of land ownership.

2. *Hunting territories and government controls*

Most of the Northern Algonkian Indian groups of the boreal forest region of Eastern Canada have a system of land tenure which includes hunting territories. This feature has a number of general basic characteristics, while there are also important variations between different bands. Basically, the band's land is divided into tracts, each of which belongs to a family group, or, as is the case at Mistassini, to an individual who is leader of a group of several families. The owner or owners have usufructuary rights over a number of important resources in their own hunting territory. These rights are passed on by some sort of system of inheritance.

Hunting territory systems vary on the question of the degree to which the boundaries are fixed and marked, and on the rules over what specific resources a person outside the owner's group can or cannot use. In some cases there are firm rules which are enforced against trespass. There are also variations in the average size of a territory, due to differences in the productivity of the land. In those richer Algonkian areas to the south and towards the Great Lakes, the productivity results in territories small enough that all parts can be visited and exploited by one group each year. In the less productive regions to the north, on the other hand, the practice of rotational 'harvesting' of resources occurs, both within a single territory, and between several territories. In some cases the territory system and its rules explicitly deal only with the trapping of fur-bearing animals, and in such cases they have appropriately been called 'trapping territories' instead. There are also variations from band to band in the system of inheritance which is used.

The Northern Algonkian system of land tenure has undergone changes, most recently with the introduction by provincial governments of controlled harvesting of beaver, by means of a system of quotas. This wildlife management scheme has made use of the already existing system of hunting territories, so that quotas are assigned only to individuals who have rights in a particular territory, either as owners, or as members of the owner's hunting group. At Mistassini the provincial government established the whole of the band's land as a 'beaver preserve' in 1948, and at that time drew up a map of the individual territories, which they called 'registered traplines'. Since that time a few of these registered traplines have been officially sub-divided, as some territories were passed on to more than one person. On the surface there seems to have been a tacit acceptance by the Mistassini of these government regulations over their territories.

In reality, the system of registered traplines is based on quite different principles than is the Mistassini system of land tenure, and this has caused some friction to develop between the two. It has resulted in the operation of a largely fictitious system of 'game management' in which the Mistassini go through the motions for the benefit of government officials, and at the same time the continued operation of the Mistassini's own tenure system. The introduction of the government scheme has to some small extent altered this pre-existing system, and has introduced to the Mistassini some new concepts of land tenure, so that contradictions are now evident between the different descriptions of the system given by informants, and also between these descriptions, on the one hand, and the way the system can be seen to operate in practice, on the other.

The Government regulation of a sustained yield wildlife harvest is based, in the case of beaver, on a method of trapping which, stated in its ideal form, presumes that the trapper visits all his beaver lodges year after year, harvests only the annual production of each, and leaves behind in each lodge a sufficient number of animals in order that they may reproduce again and maintain the beaver colony for subsequent years. The annual production of each lodge is thus theoretically the additional number of beavers born in previous years which survive to be trapped as mature animals. Under the system of quota control, the trapper notes each year any new colonies since the previous year, and is required to submit to the government a map showing the location of all occupied lodges. A quota is then established, based on a theoretical rate of reproduction and survival of beavers in that particular region, and proportional to the number of occupied lodges shown on the map.

However, in Mistassini and other parts of the northern extremes of the boreal forest, an entirely different technique of beaver trapping is used. Beaver lodges in this northern region tend to be widely scattered, and territories are large, so that it is not possible to visit all lodges each year. Furthermore, because of the way resources are scattered in this region there can be little seasonal specialization of trapping production. In other words, because of the large distances which must be travelled by the hunters, it is most efficient for a group to move into a new region and then to intersperse the activities of hunting and fishing for food with various kinds of trapping activities, so that by the time they are ready to move to a new area, they have made use of all the different kinds of available resources.

The dilemma for hunters in the northern limits of the boreal forest may be expressed in terms of necessity to try to limit the expenditure of energy on travel for the amount that is produced. In the case of beaver we may speak of the mean number of miles of travel required to harvest each beaver. Where lodges are far apart it becomes more efficient for a trapper to reduce the amount of travel and to take *more* than the annual production of each lodge when he visits it, always leaving some animals behind, but to visit a colony only once every few years. For this method to work there must be sufficient land so that the group does not need to return to the same part of the territory again until several years have passed, and this is done by using some parts of the territory in rotation, and sometimes by leaving the territory entirely vacant for a year or more, while members of the group become guests of other groups.[3]

Thus when the leader of a Mistassini hunting group provides the
government with a map of the occupied beaver houses he has observed
it seldom relates to that part of his territory which he will be using
during the following year, and therefore it does not relate to the area
where the new quota will be harvested. In some cases a hunter will
make a scouting trip into a new section of his territory because he
intends to trap there at some time in the near future, and this may, on
a rare occasion, be done in the spring, after beaver trapping is
finished. But more often the hunting group leader chooses the section
of the territory which will be used in the following year from indirect
evidence, or from direct knowledge acquired some time prior to the
immediately previous year, and on the basis of this knowledge an
estimate is made of the current overall condition of the game resources.

Trappers must, at the same time, participate in the beaver quota
system, since only the government is permitted to buy beaver hides,
and each hide must carry an official seal. Each trapper is given the
same number of seals as his allotted quota. Since the game management scheme depends on the receipt of unverified information which
is voluntarily submitted by the trappers themselves, it can at best only
regulate any sudden increases in pressure on beavers. Any additional
control mechanism must lie instead within the overall land tenure
system, as it operates in the long run.

One effect of the introduction of the system of registered traplines
and fixed quotas may have been to lead trappers to emphasize, when
questioned, the flexibility of their own system over the long run, in
contrast to the fixed nature of the new government scheme. This is one
possible explanation for statements to the effect that before the introduction of registered traplines, anyone could trap wherever they
wished. These statements could be ideological correctives to what are
seen as the distortions introduced by the 'fixed' new system.

3. *Hunting territories and their recent history*

In 1971 seventy-six men of the Mistassini band were owners of hunting
territories. The boundaries of seventy-three territories are shown on
Map 4; three of these territories have been informally sub-divided,
although the owners had not yet decided on a firm boundary.[4]

The Mistassini territories cover an area of 59.354 square miles,
excluding the area of the two largest lakes, Lake Mistassini and Lake
Albanel, which are not considered to be part of any territory. The total
area of the territories may be further reduced by approximately 7,350
square miles, this being land which is unusable for hunting or trapping
as it is composed of bare rock and mountainous terrain. This leaves a
total area of usable land of about 52,004 square miles. The territories
thus average approximately 712.4 square miles. They range in size from
approximately 225 square miles to approximately 3,000 square miles.

The latter figure requires some explanation, however. It refers to the size of those territories located in the northernmost portions and also at the farthest limits of Mistassini land. The fact that a territory is located on the periphery of the band's land seems to introduce two kinds of additional factors, both of which tend to result in territories which are larger than they might otherwise be. In the first place, there is much more doubt among informants about where the far limits of such a territory are, since there is nobody else in the band who owns the territory on the far side. There probably exist some overlapping claims with owners from neighbouring groups, for example with those of the Waswanipi band whose land borders that of the Mistassini to the southwest. Secondly, the tendency for a group to extend a territory by moving their activities further and further into unused adjacent land has, in the past twenty years, become quite general along the northern and eastern boundaries of Mistassini land. The land to the east was formerly used by members of the Lac St. Jean band, and several groups of Mistassini who were trapping in this eastern region would in the past travel to Point Bleue, on Lac St. Jean, to trade. In the case of land formerly occupied by the Great Whale River band, to the north, the Fort George band to the northwest, and the Sept Iles band to the northeast, the feeling among the Mistassini is that because they no longer encounter hunters from these bands in these areas as they did in the past, the land is now free for their use.

Up to this point what we have been referring to as 'territories' are those areas pointed out on the map by a hunting group leader as being 'my land' (*nitascii*) or 'my hunting land' (*nitwaawhuuscii*). Apart from those territories located at the periphery of the band's land, just referred to, there is a high degree of agreement between owners of neighbouring territories as to where the boundary between them lies. At the same time seldom is any emphasis placed on an exact location of the boundary; both neighbours are content to express it approximately, in terms of broad geographic features (e.g. valleys, lakes and hills) which do not necessitate the fixing of an exact line. But although it can be seen that there is agreement on the location of the boundaries, we must also enquire whether the boundaries are always respected.

For the season of 1969-70 a check was made on this question by examining the exact locations of hunting groups. In that year there were approximately fifty Mistassini hunting groups, but the locations of nine of them could not be determined accurately. Of the remaining forty-one groups only eight were located in land not owned by a member of the hunting group using it. In these eight cases the leaders obtained the right to use the land; they had all hunted in the respective areas previously, and had the owner's permission. In all but two of these cases the owner himself was not using the land; in these other instances the owner had a hunting group of his own in one part of the territory, while the other man was leading another group in a different part of the same land. In both these cases this guest also owned land of his own adjacent to the territory being used. Some years previously, each of these lands had been included with the territory in question as a larger territory, which had then been sub-divided. As we will see when discussing the recent history of territories, it appears that even after many years land which has been nominally sub-divided sometimes continues to be treated as a single block, and over this whole block a group of owners may all exercise rights.

A check was also made for the 1971-2 season. In that year there were forty-five hunting groups active, not including another four groups from the Nemescau band which had joined the Mistassini band after the H.B.C. post at Nemescau closed in 1970. It was possible to determine the locations of thirty-four of the forty-five groups accurately, and all but eight of these were located on land belonging to the group's leader. Five of these eight groups were led by men who were closely related to the owner of the land they were actually using, and one other group was led by a man who owned land adjacent to the area where he was hunting that year. In the two remaining cases I did not discover on what basis the groups were using the land, except that it was not being used at the time by the owners.

These results indicate that, in the short run at least, the claims to ownership of land by Mistassini hunters are, in the main, recognized, and the land avoided by other hunters. A group's leader owns or otherwise has the rights to the land which the group uses. It also shows that it is possible for the rights to land to be shared between the nominal owner and another man, for one of the following reasons. In the case where the nominal owner does not use the land, the usufructuary rights may pass to a person or group who has in the past been a member of the nominal owner's hunting group. Where the nominal owner himself inherited his ownership by virtue of his membership in the former owner's hunting group other survivors of that group may also continue to exercise some rights over the whole area. Another likely person to obtain rights to unused land is someone who hunts on adjacent territory.

In the foregoing, where we have referred to the exercise of rights to land, we have been referring exclusively to the right to be the leader of a hunting group which may use the land in question. While it is clear that all members of a hunting group share the usufruct of the land they occupy we make the assumption that the leader has a 'proprietary' right, and that the other hunters in the group obtain their rights through him, in exchange for accepting his leadership. The reason for this rather over-formalistic way of dealing with the distinction between 'title', 'right', and 'use' of land is for analytical purposes, without doing violence to the ethnographic facts.

Having shown that, for the most part, the man who leads a hunting group has title to the land which the group uses, I must point out again that an owner may not use his land every year. In any one year several territories are left unused. For example, in 1969-70 only forty-four of the seventy-three Mistassini hunting territories were in use. Of the remaining twenty-nine unused territories fifteen of their owners hunted as guests in groups led by owners of other territories. In eight of these cases the host's territory was adjacent to that of the guest. In addition, fourteen of the owners of unused land remained in the vicinity of Mistassini Post, and either trapped part-time near one of the roads in the vicinity, worked for wages, or were ill. In 1971-2, forty-three territories were in use. Of the thirty owners of the remaining unused territories, twelve of them were guests on other territories, while eighteen either did not trap, or trapped close to Mistassini Post.

When a man who owns his own territory joins another hunting group for a single season it is usually said that he is giving his land a rest. Earlier in this chapter we explained the adaptive function of this system of exchange of hunting privileges. It sometimes becomes necessary to leave a territory unused for any of several reasons: it may have been over-hunted, it may have had a forest fire, or there may have been a local reduction in the animal population cycle. However, it is not to be assumed that all cases where the owner of one territory becomes temporarily the guest of another are due to shortages of resources. Among the Nichicun local band the number of territories left unused at different times in the ten years from 1960-1 to 1969-70, while the owners were guests of other groups, was such a high proportion of the total Nichicun territories that some additional explanation is called for. Table 15 illustrates the situation. It shows

Table 15.   EXCHANGE OF HUNTING PRIVILEGES, NICHICUN LOCAL
BAND, 1960-1 TO 1969-70

Owners	*Territories*							*Outside the Nichicun region*	*Total*
	Ta	*Tb*	*Tc*	*Td*	*Te*	*Tf*	*Tg*		
A	3	3	2	0	0	0	0	2	10
B	2	6	2	0	0	0	0	0	10
C	0	1	7	0	0	0	1	1	10
D	0	1	0	6	0	2	0	1	10
E	0	0	1	2	3	1	0	3	10
F	0	0	0	1	0	5	3	1	10
G	0	4	0	1	2	0	3	0	10

Note: Figures in the columns refer to the total number of years spent by each individual in each territory.

how many seasons each of the seven owners of territories in the Nichicun area spent on their own land, and on each of the other six territories. The letters A, B, C, etc. refer to the seven owners, while Ta, Tb, etc. refer to the territories of owner A, owner B, etc. [5]

One reason for the high rate of exchange of hunting privileges between territory owners in the Nichicun local band — a rate that appears to be higher than that practised among other Mistassini groups — may be the particular problem encountered by the Nichicun in forming adequately-sized hunting groups in their region. Because of the great distance from Mistassini Post it is not possible to hunt there on a part-time basis. Thus those members of the Nichicun band who follow a pattern of working for wages during part of the winter, and only hunting when no work is available (see Tanner 1968), are not able to join a Nichicun hunting group, and instead tend to join groups closer to Mistassini Post. Thus, while in the past twenty years there has been an expansion of hunting and trapping activities in the Nichicun area and an overall demographic increase among families of the Nichicun local band, the number of individuals who return each year to hunt and trap in this area has been stable, or is falling. With no shortage of land, a high proportion of adults are territory owners.

In order to form hunting groups of the preferred size, with several families, it is thus necessary to recruit men to hunting groups who are themselves owners of territories. An additional factor is that in the Nichicun region there is a group of three territories owned by one patrilateral extended family, an area which to some extent continues to be treated by the three owners as a single large territory.

Exchange of hunting privileges, while functioning to maintain the continuity of the hunting territory system in an unstable environment, also has important social implications, as does any other form of social exchange. The notion of 'exchange' in this context is purely a theoretical one, since informants deny that there is ever any obligation to make a return invitation to a host. Furthermore, an examination of the data, such as the ten-year record of movements of Nichicun owners which was the basis for Table 15, shows that there is no particular tendency in the short run for the host to make a return stay on his guest's territory. Any direct exchange which does occur takes place between owners of adjacent territories. Also the guest makes a direct return by acknowledging the host's leadership, albeit in subtle ways, and in common with all other members of the hunting group. But from a long-term viewpoint it can be seen that the systematic exchange of hunting privileges involves both direct and generalized exchange. In the case of a block of territories owned by several people who are united on the basis of kinship, where the owners regularly make use of each other's land, we may speak of a system of direct exchange of hunting privileges. In the case of the individual territory owners who periodically become the guests of other owners, the movements of these men amount to a system of generalized exchange.

For the 'blocks' of contiguous territories, exchange between owners is based on kinship, or common inheritance and on residential contiguity. The generalized exchange of hunting privileges also has its sociological basis, in this case with a preference shown to individuals who are close kin, former co-residents, or potential affines.

4. The inheritance of hunting territories

In this section we turn to the question of the continuity of the hunting territory system, by attempting to trace back the history of land tenure in various parts of the Mistassini territory for approximately two generations. Two sources of data on the past will be employed: most of the current territory owners were questioned about the history of the ownership of their land, and I have also consulted an article with a map by Speck, describing Mistassini territories *c*. 1915-20 (Speck 1923, see Map 5). Neither of these sources of data gives us precise knowledge of the exact locations of the territories of the earlier period. Speck's information was based on interviews with only a few of the actual territory owners, since he was able to interview only a handful of members of the Mistassini band while they visited Pointe Bleue, on Lac St. Jean, to trade during the summer. These were for the most part men whose territories were located on the eastern and southern borders of the Mistassini territory. Moreover, Speck had no accurate base maps with which to work, as the locations of only a few of the largest lakes and rivers were known to map makers at that date. Our own informants could only speak with certainty about the areas that they, their parents and their other co-residents, had hunted on during their own lifetime. In general genealogical material collected among Mistassini adults is only two or three generations in depth. Thus whatever baseline we have is not at all precise.

Given these problems my method will be to select a number of typical cases — but where the evidence happens to be the clearest — in order to show three kinds of conclusions: (1) there is a variety of kin and non-kin links by which land title passes from one person to another; (2) there is direct evidence that some of the present territories are in changed locations from the earlier ones; (3) there are cases of the existence of a group of contiguous territories which have remained together as a block, a block which has survived changes in the owners of the constituent territories.[6]

Case 1. In his map Speck did not include the Nichicun area, which he considered not to have been divided into individual territories (1931).

However, the present owners do trace back ownership for at least two generations. The large area to the north of Nichicun is associated with a man named *Waapusuyaan* (Wobsian — *Rabbitskin*), and his two sons, Jacob and Sam. Sam is remembered as the last chief of the Nichicun band, and was a shaman. This area now has nominally three or four owners, but is still considered one area by the government for the purposes of establishing beaver quotas. Jacob Wobsian married a woman of the neighbouring Great Whale River band, and he and Sam enlarged the area, since they found that the Great Whale River and Fort George Indians did not come as often to that region as they had previously. However, Jacob and Sam's hunting groups continued to meet the occasional group from neighbouring bands up till the 1940s. Jacob and Sam died in the 1940s, and Jacob's three sons, George, Abel and Samuel inherited the area. George died in 1963 and his eldest son, Williams, began to lead hunting groups in the territory. Abel died in 1966, and since his sons were in school and unable to inherit, Williams' brother Clarence is now spoken of as the owner. Clarence, however, seldom takes the role of hunting group leader and rather than claiming ownership says that 'only God could own the land'. Abel's sons, who have not hunted as adults, say they will claim the land in the future. Meanwhile the H.B.C. manager began to provide encouragement for trappers to use the northern Nichicun area more intensively. He built a warehouse for emergency supplies at Brisay Lake, and John Neeposh, whose father had a territory to the west of Nichicun, has hunted in the area regularly, starting in 1962. John Neeposh was at the time of my fieldwork considered an owner, in the sense that he had the right to be the leader of any hunting group using the most northerly section, but since then he has reverted to using the territory to the west, which had been used by his father.

Case 2. The territory in the vicinity of Lake Naococane, near Lake Nichicun, is owned by Sam Edwards, who inherited it from his father, William Edwards, who died in 1970. William's parents were from Rupert House, but trapped inland in the area near the Eastmain River. His father died and he continued to live with his mother, who continued to go inland with hunting groups. William was still a boy when his mother died while they were inland, and he was taken and looked after by a woman who was a member of a group that traded at the post at Nichicun. At the post he was adopted by the H.B.C. manager, William Iserhoff, who was part Indian. As the son of an H.B.C. employee he grew up hunting in the area around the post, and the southern part became his own hunting territory. He married Lizzie Longchap, of the Nichicun band, whose father, Pierre had his hunting territory adjacent to William's, to the east of Nichicun.[7]

Case 3. To the west and southwest of the present-day Nichicun territories, in the northwestern extremes of Mistassini land, are a number of territories owned by Ronnie Jolly, Charlie Jolly, Thomas Jolly, Sam Blacksmith, Boysee Blacksmith, Tommy Neeposh, and David Neeposh. Speck's map of this area shows Mistassini territories reaching at that time only as far north as the Eastmain River. The two Mistassini territories farthest to the northeast in this region belonged at that time to Albert Blacksmith, and to two other men with the surname Blacksmith. The eastern half of this area is now owned by Boysee Blacksmith, who says he inherited it from his father, Jacob, who in turn was the eldest son of Albert Blacksmith. This is a fairly clear case of simple patrilineal inheritance. At the same time, the territory immediately to the north of the two Blacksmith territories of Speck's time is now owned by Samuel and Billy Blacksmith, who say they inherited it from their father Charlie Blacksmith, who was another son of Albert Blacksmith.

While Albert Blacksmith and his descendants appear to have expanded northward, there has also been expansion into the same area by the descendants of Neeposh, and of Tommy Jolly, who at the time of Speck's enquiries was the Chief of the Nemescau band. On Speck's map Neeposh had the territory immediately to the south of the Blacksmith's territories just referred to. Nemescau land borders Mistassini land in the general area we are examining. The following diagram (Fig. 16) shows the kinship ties which link the present owners of territories in this area to the two former owners.

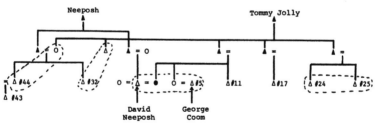

Fig. 16. Territories owned by the descendants of Neeposh and Tommy Jolly

The dotted lines in Fig. 16 indicate those individuals who often join the same hunting group. The numbers refer to the hunting territories, as shown on Map 4 (page 184). One of these groups has two members who are both owners of territories #24 and #25. This is a case of a territory which has been nominally sub-divided, and where the group usually alternates between the two divisions. In the case of the group which used territory #5, the ownership was formerly held by David Neeposh, until the death of his wife, a woman who was a descendant of Tommy Jolly. David stopped using territory #5 when he remarried, and the ownership reverted to a man who had married another descendant of Tommy Jolly, George Coom, a man who had earlier hunted on the land as part of David Neeposh's group.

Case 4. Speck shows a hunting territory to the south of Mistassini Post, between Chibougamau Lake and Lake Waconichi, as being owned by 'Little William'. This man was William Couchees, and his descendant Joseph began using the same area in the 1930s; Joseph continued to use the land, and as he got old he was looked after by Bally Husky, a man unrelated to him, but who had joined his hunting group. When the old man died Bally Husky inherited part of the land, while a grandson of Joseph Couchees, Phillip, took the other part. After Phillip died, leaving no other male descendants of William Couchees, his part of the territory reverted to Bally Husky, and it is now used by Bally's present wife's brother, and her son by a former marriage. These territories now have several roads built through them, and they are used both by hunting groups and by part-time trappers.

Case 5. On Speck's map there is one territory in the southwest part of the Mistassini land which was owned by Johnny Bosum. Today, in the same general region, there are six territories owned by this man's descendants. Burgess, however, notes that Johnny Bosum also acquired a territory northeast of Mistassini Post when he married his second wife, and that he moved his trapping activities at that time (1945:23). This would have been in the early 1930s, so that there must have been a gap of a few years before his grandsons began trapping in the area which he had vacated. These six contiguous Bosum territories have expanded the size of the area compared to that owned by Johnny Bosum in Speck's time. This has apparently happened in part by the taking over of some former Waswanipi land, or by overlapping with Waswanipi trappers in this area. It is possible that a readjustment of boundaries was made at the time the system of registered traplines was set up. The Bosum group of territories also appear to have expanded in a northeasterly direction. On Speck's map there were five territories in the area between Johnny Bosum's land and Mistassini Post, to the east. The owners were: John Stout, who died without sons; David Mianscum, whose grandsons François and George now own two territories in this same area; Charles Blacksmith and Robert Petawabeno, whose descendants now occupy land to the north of the area we are considering; and Albert Trapper, whose descendants moved to the Nemescau band, although many have since rejoined the Mistassini band. The area of five hunting territories of Speck's time has been inherited by only two of these five owners' descendants, and the other land has been expanded into a neighbouring group with a large number of male descendants.

Case 6. Another case where the patrilineal descendants of the past owner of a single territory now own a block of territories can be found in the territory which was owned by Gum Etienne on Speck's map, just north of Lake Mistassini. This man was born into the Lac St. Jean's band, but married a Mistassini woman, and Speck shows him as owning a hunting territory immediately adjacent to those of his wife's brothers, from whom, presumably, he obtained the land. At the same time Gum Etienne's sister married Joseph Metawashish, whom Speck's map shows to have had a territory in the same region. Gum Etienne had five sons, and now has at least ten married patrilineal grandsons. Five of them now own hunting territories in a single block which covers approximately the same area as the earlier ones of Gum Etienne, his two brothers-in-law and his sister's husband. The individual territories within the block are quite different in shape than the territories in the same block shown on Speck's map, even though it can be seen that there has been some continuity in the history of the tenure of the whole group of territories.

Case 7. The final example is of two territories shown on Speck's map for which the descendants of the two owners each have a territory today (#33 and #40) of roughly the same shape, dimension and spatial relationship to each other, but which are today some distance to the southwest of where Speck shows them. These are the territories which in Speck's time were owned by Solomon Voyager and Johnny Awashish, and are now owned by Sam Voyager and Isiah Awashish. While this apparent 'movement' of territories over time might be otherwise put down to the inaccuracy of Speck's map, both of the present owners volunteered the information that their fathers at one time used to hunt further to the north and east of their own lands. In fact, this case gives some confirmation of the usefulness of Speck's map.

The evidence from these recent cases of inheritance indicates that the Mistassini system of land tenure is flexible in the long run, and that hunting territories are not treated as fixed tracts of land.[8] In this case are we entitled to speak of a system of land ownership?

The underlying principle of Mistassini land ownership is that the owner has established by means of long term residence his rights in an area. Once an individual has satisfied the criteria he has a recognized proprietary title to the area for as long as the group he belongs to (and which he usually leads) continues to use it. Thus proprietary rights to land are held by individuals, and are exercised only by groups authorized by these individuals. This results in minimal overlapping in land use patterns by different groups. At the owner's death, or when he permanently moves away from the area, the rights to the land pass either to a descendant who has also used the land (usually a son, brother or son-in-law), or to another member of the former owner's hunting group, someone who has also thereby undergone a period of residence in the area. If no such person inherits, the abandoned territory can be taken over by others, usually by neighbouring owners who may expand their activities into the area.

In the realm of ideology, the concept of the hunting territory makes possible the ideological conclusion that within each hunting group there can be an individual who can exercise a special power over the animals in that limited area, by establishing a pseudo-social relationship with them. In other words, through the notion that the group is surrounded by its own land, and by its own animals, the religious ideology implies that the key relations of hunting production are not those between different hunters, or between men and women, but between men and animals, and thus it is the relations between the hunting group leader and the animals of the territory on which the prosperity of the whole group rests. The Mistassini do not see land in itself as an object of the property relationship. They often mock the European idea of men owning land, and claim that the land belongs to the animals, or to God. They also have no enforced rules of trespass. In reality, the individual or the family may join any hunting group, merely by making arrangements with the leader, and they may therefore hunt anywhere; but all hunting must be done in the context of hunting groups, and their activities are arranged and readjusted with respect to each other. The idea that a relationship can exist between a person and an object, land, is thus rejected by the Cree. But although the actual basis of property relations of resources in Cree society is to be found in the social relations between the groups and within the group, between the leader who has title because of his long-term residence in the territory and the other members who do not, Cree ideology proposes that property relations with respect to land are a matter of a mystical relationship with animals, while Cree social ideology suggests that it is a matter of inheritance.

10
Conclusion

1. *Introduction*

Mistassini is a society which is divided into two: a bush sector and a settlement sector. These sectors do not have distinct social groups associated with them; they are alternative social formations, and the Mistassini are able to move back and forth between them. Since each sector is associated with one of the two major seasons, for many people there is an annual cycle of movement back and forth between the two. Most Mistassini people spend the longer winter season in the bush sector, living in isolated groups of a few families, with their day-to-day activities centred around subsistence needs, and also producing fur for the market to the extent possible within the conditions of subsistence production. During the summer they reassemble to join others who live throughout the year in the settlement sector, where the day-to-day activities are shaped by the way cash income is obtained, through wage work, savings from winter fur production and government subsidies, and by the alternatives for spending money. The two sectors are kept separate, and the contrast between them is emphasized, but each is influenced by the existence of the other.

Given the existence of these two alternative social formations, when we compare Mistassini with other subarctic Indian communities — or even more specifically with other East Cree communities — we find that the bush sector is a comparatively important part of the total society. Subarctic Indian communities have been subject to many outside factors favouring change in recent years, and most of these factors have tended to strengthen the settlement sector and weaken the bush sector. In the first three chapters I considered some of the factors that would explain Mistassini as a special case where the effect of these factors has been dampened. In more general terms, since the bush sector is seen as a social formation, albeit necessarily linked to the settlement formation, I have taken the viewpoint that while the internal organization of the bush sector is flexible and can adjust to a certain degree of alteration in the settlement sector and in other outside factors, this formation as a whole has certain minimum interrelated conditions of existence, and that change beyond these limits would quickly see the collapse and transformation of the bush sector, as has already happened in other northern native communities. Moreover, I suggest that economic and ecological factors are not the only determinants of these processes of either adaptation or transformation. I am now ready to add to this discussion my conclusions on the other major kind of determination: ideology.

In order to take some account of this ideological factor I will look at present-day Mistassini society as the product of a process of social reproduction in which both the transformation and the repetition of familiar social forms take place simultaneously, often in debate with one another, so to speak. While this process of dialectical change follows ultimately from historical factors acting on the material base of society, these factors do not only act on the base directly, but also cause changes in the social formation. Given that the social formation can in this way have a changed relationship to the material base, then the existing cultural ideas and perceptions will expand or transform the cultural view of reality to one with new conceptions. The resulting understandings establish the perceived alternatives and the direction of social change.

In the context of Mistassini, the above model is partial, since it sees the community as totally isolated from the larger Canadian social and economic formation. In actual fact, many of the external change factors do not arrive for the Mistassini as individual elements, but are already related together in a system which itself is part of another social formation. For example, the opening of mines, a mining town, a railroad and roads, within fifty miles of Mistassini village has not only been an ecological factor which has limited the use of hunting territories in that area, it has also brought to the area a system of related innovations (that is, an industrial process of production, and the attendant social infrastructure) which have begun to change the character of the settlement sector, by making the village of Mistassini in many ways an economic satellite of Chibougamau. This has resulted in some Indians moving into a new niche in the overall regional economy. However, as I have shown elsewhere (Tanner 1968), most of those who have allowed themselves to be absorbed into this new economy have done so in a clearly arm's length, temporary way, one which does not force them to give up their options in the bush sector.

While recognizing the inadequacies of a model that does not emphasize the fact that Mistassini is part of a larger social reality (an inadequacy shared with many ethnographic studies in social anthropology), it should be pointed out that, at least until the announcement of the James Bay hydro-electric project, the Mistassini have been very much cut off from surrounding Canadian society. In addition to their physical isolation, the Mistassini's early involvement with the English Hudson's Bay Company, the Anglican Church, the Federal Government, and English language education, has resulted in a position of social isolation within Roman Catholic, French-speaking Quebec society. Moreover, within Canada as a whole since the 1920s Indian fur trapping communities have fallen into a period of irrelevance within the national economy. Mistassini has not seen serious outside competition for its trapping lands since the early 1800s and there are no reports to my knowledge of pressure in the area from

White trappers. Whether by the design of the Hudson's Bay Company or merely due to its physical and social isolation, Mistassini has been to a great extent cut off from the outside world, and most contacts with that world have been mediated to a large extent through special contact institutions, such as the 'putting out' system. This situation of relative social and economic isolation from, and irrelevance to, the larger Canadian social and economic formation — an isolation and irrelevance that is apparently coming to an end as Mistassini land is seen by the province as ripe for development of its mineral, forest and hydro-electric resources — allows me in my model to bracket out and pass too quickly over the question of the relation between Mistassini and Canadian society.

Historical change is responsible for contradictions (in the Marxist sense) at both the material and intellectual level. Moreover, there is no *a priori* reason to suppose that the intellectual level always gives an accurate representation of the determinant conditions within the infrastructure, or even that the contradictions that exist at the intellectual level correctly mirror infrastructural contradictions. The intellectual accounts with which a group explains its own behaviour cannot be accepted uncritically as final explanations in an anthropological investigation, since as Lévi-Strauss points out, along with many Marxist anthropologists, the purpose of these accounts is to obscure the underlying reality and thus to permit the social formation to continue to function and to reproduce itself (Lévi-Strauss 1963). To which perhaps should be added the recognition that some 'home made models' of society are utopian in nature, and designed to bring about change. However, in either case the fact that historical factors of change are relatively outside the control of ideology means that these attempts are never entirely successful, although the attempts themselves are part of the process of determination of the social transformation.

One of the difficulties we face in the discussion of intellectual factors in the social formation is that widely differing assumptions are made regarding the nature of 'ideology'. In order not to reduce the problem to one of semantics, I will try to take as broad an approach as possible, and look at my material with a view to accepting all intellectual activity as ideological, in so far as it feeds back, or attempts to feed back, on the level of social action. I will therefore first discuss the dialectical concept of ideology, and how this concept may apply to religious and symbolic material. Although my knowledge of the historical factors underlying the Mistassini situation is inadequate to the task of a demonstration, I assume that historical and ideological factors have combined in the production of consciousness, and ultimately of social change.

In much of Lévi-Strauss' work there is a tendency to lay aside native explanatory schemes at a certain point in the analysis, once he has identified the 'underlying' social reality. This is particularly the case in transformational studies, i.e. studies in which cultural or sociological data are seen as constituting an interrelated set, and where such a set is shown to have a relationship of homology with another such set of data, found either from another part of the same culture, from the same culture at a different historical period, or from an entirely different group altogether. Since in each set of phenomena there can be seen a transformation of the structure of the other sets, all can be analysed by models of the same type. This enables the level of content to be bypassed in favour of the structural level. However, having achieved this structural insight, the model can then be used to return to the level of the surface data and to re-examine the content of the particular ethnographic case. An example of this procedure can be found in his discussion of *mana* (1950), an appropriate example in the present context since it deals with a religious concept. Having looked at *mana* and a number of concepts like it which, following Mauss, are seen as central to the theory of magic, Lévi-Struass shows that the difficulty we have in understanding them comes precisely from the fact that their semantic role ' ... est de permettre à la pensée symbolique de s exercer malgré la contradiction qui lui est propre' (1950:2). If a theory of magic can establish the general nature of magical operations in the abstract, this perspective can be turned back on the ethnographic material to see more clearly how magic acts on particular social and material conditions. In the case of the present study, where we have chosen a single group, with little historical material to provide us with the possibility of analysing diachronic transformations, our procedure has been to remain at the level of the surface ethnographic content, while our structural analysis has had to take place simultaneously with the analysis of the particular determinants within the social formation. The point here is that structural analysis of religious thought does not have as its purpose the sweeping aside of the religious ideas themselves, but rather it can be used to examine their function as ideological elements in the reproduction of the social formation.

2. *Religious ideology*

When they are considered as a set, the rites, religious beliefs and myths of the Mistassini Cree constitute an intellectual tradition in the context of which there is a process of production of ideology, in the form of explanations, rationalizations and preparations for actions, as well as emotional predispositions which may help members of the group define some of their behavioural goals, especially during difficult circumstances. If we take the term 'ideology' to mean thought that effects social action, it might also be said that ideology is 'motivated thought'.

The term 'ideology' is often used to signify a mode of thought that stands in opposition to another mode of thought. This opposition may be in the context of at least two groups who have aims that are mutually incompatible, and where each group develops points of view that promote its own interest *vis à vis* the others. In the case of the Cree hunters, little religious ideology is used by particular structured interest groups. We have, it is true, made several references to differences of viewpoint between elders and younger hunters. The differences between these two groups, however, as reflected in their ideology and religious practice, and which have appeared in the analyses as the basis of explanations, form only a small part of the total content of religious ideas and practice. Most of what may be identified as 'motivated' religious thought is contained in beliefs and rites that are shared by all Mistassini hunters, and which cannot, therefore, be explained as elements in an ideology of opposition directed against other groups within Mistassini society.

Religious ideology refers to a particular kind of thought that is distinct and which is to be contrasted with other kinds. Religious ideology, consciously or not, feeds back on and modifies social action, and it is therefore relevant to situations of contention and indecision, or at least to times where there is the availability of alternatives. It thus contrasts with thought that is taken for granted and accepted by all without question. This kind of thought we may call 'common sense'. To employ Schutz's terms, we suggest that Cree religion would be found within a 'finite province of meaning', but not in the 'Paramount Reality' (Schutz 1945). This is not to say that 'common sense' reality has no effect on social action, and cannot have an ideological aspect, just as it is not necessary to presume that all aspects of religious thought are ideological.

For example, we have seen that hunters use divination to determine hunting success, but that this symbolic action is used at the same time as information about the presence of animals is collected by observing natural signs. Also, ritual activities intended to ensure good fortune in hunting exist alongside the careful use of skilled techniques for finding, stalking and killing animals. The conceptual opposition between the magical and the common sense methods of hunting are not drawn attention to in Cree thought. Some hunters have reputations for skill and success using non-religious techniques, others have a reputation for skill with religious techniques, but the two methods are not opposed antagonistically. There are not two groups of hunters, one of which follows one set of techniques and rejects the other, while the second group considers the first set of techniques unimportant, and rely on the second set. I had only one encounter with a Mistassini person who expressed opposition towards the idea of attributing success to the use of rituals in hunting. This man was a devout Christian. However, he did not dispute the efficacy of the rituals, but rather thought that in this day and age they should be replaced by Christian prayer.

A far more common attitude of ideological opposition held by some Mistassini individuals in the context of religion is to acknowledge that the Cree religious practice is itself made up of two parts, one legitimate, since it was used to assist people in their daily life (e.g. magic and divination used in hunting, trapping, fishing, weather control and health) and a second which is illegitimate, since it is used for personal hostility against others (i.e. sorcery). Since both activities use basically similar techniques a person with a reputation for skill in the use of beneficial techniques is more open to suspicion of sorcery, and for this reason religious practitioners tend to over-emphasize the harmless or recreational aspect of the legitimate forms. Thus, one aspect of the ideology of religion among the Cree is to emphasize its own legitimacy as a form of action.

To refer to ideology as 'motivated thought' means it is thinking in which the conclusions arrived at must be of a certain predetermined type, while any other possible interpretations, that is alternate ideological conclusions, must be rejected. Religious thought is not unrelated to the practical goals of everyday life, but it stands apart from 'common sense' thought, in that it offers quite separate techniques to produce these goals. We can characterize the ideology of religious action as distinct and separate from the ideological implications of the more common-sense methods used by the same group for achieving the same ends.

The religious practitioner accepts at face value the reality of the common-sense practical world, but refuses to accept this reality as an end point for speculation and action with respect to his interests. One might say that an underlying ideological message of all religious action is not to accept things at their face value, but to be prepared to live with additional levels of significant reality which are neither consistent with, but are not opposed to, the reality of the common-sense.

What, then, is the motivation that drives Cree religious ideology? At the most general level it is concerned with the question of 'totalizing'[1] the sense data that members of the group experience from their environment. Common sense and ordinary language divides this experience into discrete units. The common-sense viewpoint works within a framework of many discrete contexts, each defined by the specific and habitual tasks in which members of the group most often engage. Thus, in the context of the hunting of a particular animal species, or the trapping of a species, or the assessment of meteorological clues to the probable weather for the following day (to pick some common examples) the observations of the Cree hunter include many which when put together make immediate sense, in terms of a particular and limited task he has in mind.

This practical, task-oriented, context-bound relationship to the world, however, does not act as a limit to what is observed, nor does it limit attempts to make additional use of these observations. Moreover, these observations, which can also have significance beyond day-to-day tasks and goals, are not confined to the observation of the natural environment. To give examples at the social level, significance is attached to nuances in the way others in the group behave, especially in relation to the person doing the observing. Speculation about, or communication with, distant acquaintances, or people in nearby camps is discussed. Signs within the hunting group of interpersonal hostility (signs which are usually extremely subtly expressed in a Cree hunting camp) are taken note of. These events are significant for their implications as to the ongoing state of social relations, but as a result of such events each relationship is monitored and judged both in terms of the significance for the immediate practical transactions that must take place between people in day to day life, but also in terms of a larger and longer-term view. Moreover, it is just these observations and conditions which surround day to day tasks, in both the natural environment and within the social sphere, that are the primary subject matter reflected at the level of religious thought.

I have been careful to note at several points throughout this study the parallel existing between the various tasks in the productive process and tasks tackled in the religious domain (e.g. gathering information on game animals, paralleled by religious divination; the process of finding, killing and transporting the game, paralleled by hunting magic; and the process of bringing the meat to camp and distributing, cooking and eating it, paralleled by the code of respect to the animal victims). I have been less conscientious in pointing out the similar parallel that exists between various kinds of social interactions and the associated ritual activities. For example, great social importance is placed on the attainment of each new stage in the maturation process; relative age and relative attainment in activities which are taken to be important markers in the maturation process are accompanied by rites. The rites (e.g. the 'Walking Out' ceremony, 'First Kill' feasts, marriage), however, symbolize more than a mere public recognition of a new social status. For example, as I have just mentioned, during the winter period when the community is divided into small hunting groups, members of a group often focused attention on particular individuals who are not at the time members of the group, but who are in key positions in the social world of people who do make up the group. Frequent speculative conversations about how these people are doing take place within the group. Such absent people are often members of neighbouring hunting groups, due to the tendency for blocks of adjacent hunting territories to be used by closely related individuals. This everyday concern for absent friends is shown at the ritual level in the common occurrence of communication between distant persons whenever a 'Shaking Tent' is used, and in the common divinations that are made of the coming arrival of strangers to the camp. We might also mention the fact that personal hostilities — hostilities which apparently often also focus on physically distant persons — may be paralleled by sorcery, by charges of sorcery or by threats of sorcery. In both the production and the social spheres, then, practical action is paralleled by religious action. The rites are, moreover, specifically related to particular processes of material or social production (using the latter term to refer to the creation and maintenance of social relations).

We have seen that in its practice Cree religion has a direct relationship to the practical common sense reality of material production, and to the organization of social relations. However, the nature of this connection is neither that of a direct reflection of real practical problems of material and social production, nor is it merely a covering over of the realities and problems. Furthermore, it cannot be said that those aspects of material and social production which are most thoroughly accompanied by religious rites are necessarily those which are of most central significance to the functioning of the economic and social systems. For example, at the level of material production, bear hunting is economically marginal, but religiously it is the foremost activity. At the same time, other hunting rites appear to reflect more directly the economic importance of the animal species concerned. At the social level, I have argued in this study that the hunting group, centred around the hunting group leader, is the dominant unit in the coordination of both productive labour and economic exchange during the hunting and trapping season. The social rituals, however, reflect a far greater emphasis on status differentials than are directly related to material production, whereas the solidarity of the hunting group and the position of the leader is taken for granted, and underemphasized at the ideological level, and in the rites. We have also seen that while young men and young women become full producers while they are still in their teens, and reach their productive peak in their twenties and thirties, the religious ideology, to the contrary, gives the elders special 'productive' importance, and provides a rationale for them to be seen as responsible for production in excess of their actual economic contribution. These examples can be placed alongside many others contained in my analysis of religious rites in the previous pages, all of which affirm a relationship between the intellectual and material actions, but a relationship of homology, not identity, and one where the religious has a clearly separate domain, to some extent opposed to the common sense framework of material action.

3. *Symbolic action*

For the Mistassini their religion is a mixture of beliefs and rites derived from the Cree and the Christian traditions. However, little in the way of syncretic developments have taken place. The two traditions are not in conflict, since each has its own social context, the settlement sector for Christianity, and the bush sector for Cree shamanistic religion. For many years the settlement religion was missionary Anglicanism, in which local catechists played a large role in interpreting the moral teachings, and helping preside over major communal rites such as weddings, funerals, christenings and confirmations. As the settlement sector has expanded in size and complexity, and has become a full-time way of life for some people, religious factionalism has developed between the Anglicans and some fundamentalist sects, in particular with the Pentecostals. A central issue in this division is the acceptance or rejection of drinking alcohol. This development is quite recent, and has led to a division along these lines in the local political situation, e.g. in the elections of band council members. Although the White leadership of the fundamentalist sects are less tolerant of what they regard as 'devil worship' found in traditional Cree religious practices than the Anglicans, who treat it as mere superstition that will die out in time, we do not know if the fundamentalist converts, many of whom are members of families who are most attached to the bush sector, are abandoning their beliefs and practices any more quickly than before.

As far as the bush sector is concerned, the overall picture of religious practice that emerges is one in which various forces of nature are either seen as personified entities, or as indeterminate environmental forces. If we treat magic and religion as two techniques according to which humans can intervene in natural determinism, the former using direct intervention, the latter operating through the meditation of non-human persons, then the Cree make use of both approaches. Indeed, in this study I have not attempted to keep these kinds of actions separate, but have included both under the term 'religion', since I do not believe they are distinguished in Cree thought. Both are examples of actions derived from analogical thought. Religious actions involve the mediation of non-human persons. These persons are usually said to be located away from human habitation, in a far off land, under the water, on top of a mountain, or in the bush, and they usually tend also to appear in the myths. Those which play a role in hunting may also appear in the 'Shaking Tent'.

Much of the religious thought of the hunters is concerned with the state of the natural environment, with how the environment may be controlled, and with the reason for failure when hunters are unable to exercise that control. The task of material production is treated as if it were something akin to a series of friendly exchanges between the hunters and each of the animals' masters. Sometimes one side comes out ahead, and the other gives in with good grace. However, in times of shortage and starvation the whole exchange relationship with the animals breaks down. This viewpoint can be seen as an ideology which hides the contradiction between the use of a strategy of environmental control, in the form of hunting territories, rotation of land and exchange of hunting privileges, and the continual preparedness for starvation times and the consequent discontinuities in the land use pattern.

The natural environment of the Mistassini is characterized by few economic resources mainly in the form of animal species whose numbers tend to fluctuate independently of predations by hunters. The addition of fur as a market resource has not lessened the effect of this characteristic of the economy, rather it has intensified it, since fur is in addition subject to independent price fluctuations. It is an unavoidably unstable economy, and the key to this instability is animal population size and movements.

At the same time, the market sector of the economy is shifting away from the bush sector, due to increasing supplies of imported goods, which increases demand for cash, and increased income from the settlement sector. There has been a reduction in credit from the H.B.C., but the management of the market sector of the economy by the 'putting out' system has continued, with a shift from purely H.B.C. management and control of this sector to a combined control by the H.B.C. and government social agencies. As a result the cash sector of the bush economy remains as it was before government payments, relatively outside the control of the individual household. As in the past, the only means of direct control of this sector is by personal appeals to the powerful agents within the contact institutions.

The contrast between the religion of the bush and the religion of the settlement reflects this contrast between the hunting and the cash sectors of the economy. In the bush the hunter has a considerable degree of control over production, both technically and religiously, whereas in the settlement both economic and religious power rests at a great distance from the individual, and can only be influenced by pleading and through the intercession of power brokers. While there were such brokers in the aboriginal religious situation (i.e. the shamans) their role may well have been a small one in the hunting group, only coming to the fore at seasonal gatherings. Furthermore the shamans control the most quickly disappearing part of the traditional religion. Shamans who used to perform the 'Shaking Tent' have been displaced in the settlement by religious leaders who take the role of the catechist in the Anglican Church.

It is often assumed that religion and magic act to supplement actual control which a group has through its technology with a kind of illusory control, in those areas of human action where technological control is beyond its limits. For the Mistassini traditional religion, however, the ritual action parallels symbolically, rather than reaches beyond, actions performed at the physical level.

One problem for the hunter, at both the material and the

intellectual level, given an amount of uncertainty that may appear in an otherwise known and controlled context, is how can the continuity of cultural rules and understandings be maintained when his control over a situation is lost. Common sense, as opposed to habit, is continually monitoring and making allowances for new conditions, and modifying behaviour. In a situation of starvation no animals are to be seen, and there is no relevant environmental information to monitor. While this lack of information makes things difficult for the hunting strategist, to the religious philosopher, who uses a variety of other kinds of monitoring techniques, the process of understanding does not necessarily come to a halt. But eventually both practical action and religious understanding reach an abyss. Far from giving assurance in time of trouble, Cree religion merely says why things must be the way they are. For example, people who lived through the period when most food species except fish, rabbits and ptarmigan failed (about 1925-40 in the Nichicun region) told me that the disappearance of the animals had been foretold by the elders, but that they knew the animals would come back eventually. During that period they adopted a number of changes in their use of land: they broke up into very small groups (often single families), but located themselves within easy reach of one another, on lakes dependable for fish. Food was distributed between a number of these small groups within a district. With the return of larger beaver populations in the 1940s, and later with increases in the caribou and moose populations, the pattern of independent multi-family groups for the winter, and the use of hunting territories re-emerged. This lack of a specific religious interpretation of the general game shortage contrasts sharply with accounts of particular shortages or starvations which occurred in one area only, or for a short time only. Here the background causes and the specific supernatural entities believed responsible are usually known. There are, moreover, often as many versions of such explanations as there are informants. Material differentials are given explanations which transform them into symbolic differentials. Where such differentials disappear, such as when the situation of low animal populations in some locations and high populations in others changes to one of uniformly low populations, then it seems that Cree religious thought has difficulty in proceeding, which suggests that it is the differentials that make such thought possible.

From this summary overview we can see that to some extent the Mistassini religion is a natural philosophy which addresses the realities of their life both in the bush and in the settlement. However, it is not primarily a system of elaborate and explicit verbal explanations and exegesis. At the centre it is a system of symbolic action available for the individual to use or to ignore as he wishes. Because the bush religion is not passed on by formal instruction and is not surrounded in secrecy, it is approached very much as a set of environmental phenomena, much like the natural characteristics of the various animal species. Just as a growing boy is expected to show a curiosity first to learn and then to make use of knowledge about animal habits, so the culture gives rewards for those who assemble knowledge of religious ideas, symbolism and practice through myths, stories and through the observation of others, and who gradually develop self-reliance in the face of the world of unseen forces.

Ritual symbolism is not overtly aimed at the formulation of ideological messages but ostensibly at acting upon the environment, either directly or through the unseen entities. In this study I have attempted, nevertheless, to interpret the expressive symbolism of the rites, and perhaps in doing so have given the misleading impression that this ritual symbolism is a system of significances arbitrarily imposed on material elements and actions in the real world, in much the same way as language more or less arbitrarily imposes meaning on various sound formations produced by people (Sperber 1975). With language, however, the speaker experiences not meanings which are imposed on the sounds, but the existence of a ready-made system of relations between sounds and meanings, so that the sounds rather appear to impose their meanings on him; the situation is even more extreme with ritual. In language the speaker is still conscious that he is able to combine meanings and thus he has the apparent freedom to construct whatever meaning he likes. But this is not the case with ritual; the meaningful elements already have a complex significance as they appear to exist in an already given form. The ritualist who makes use of them is not merely using symbols as elements in a code to construct a message; rather he is actively intervening with the use of complex actions, without fully understanding how his actions work, in a pre-existing framework of action. To the Cree a meaningfulness is apparently already given in particular items seen in nature, which we call symbols, and which are apparently parts of total systems, which leads to the conclusion that men do not so much express themselves by means of symbols when they perform rites, as attempt to perceive nature through symbols. For the purpose of this understanding rites mark the special occasions when this perception can take place. Thus rites, by focusing all attention on the oracular messages that come from nature, and which express themselves in the symbols, establish an external validity to religious thought as a form of reality within nature. This reality at the same time becomes the object of attempts to control it, and these attempts follow the pattern used in the realm of material production. For the Cree hunter the production of ideology is part of the process of economic production. But he produces it, at least in part, from his interpretations of religious symbolism. Like the symbolism itself, this aspect of ideology is not verbally explicit, and is not standardized in the form of an exegesis. The symbols only offer a network of possibilities within which many ideological pathways and goals may be followed.

Notes

Chapter 1

1. This method can, however, in the right hands, produce extremely valuable insights into the winter regime. For example see Pothier, 1967.
2. There are, of course, many difficulties associated with the use of the concepts of ideology and religion. The significance of these concepts emerge as a central issue in the theoretical problems dealt with in this book. I will therefore leave to the final chapter the task of clarifying my use of these terms, where I will be able to make use of the results of the intervening analysis. In the meanwhile, let it be understood that religion refers to a class of beliefs and actions directly related to belief in supernatural (or non-ordinary) entities, while ideology involves ideas systematically formulated so as to provide an interpretation of empirical reality.
3. The following section is based on Rogers 1963; Tremblay 1968; Davies 1963; Pothier 1967; Cooke 1969.
4. In this brief account we have not included the role of Mistassini leaders in the fight to stop the James Bay hydroelectric project, since this did not begin until fieldwork was almost complete. See Richardson 1975.

Chapter 2

1. The name of the weather station uses the alternate spelling, 'Nitchequon.'

Chapter 3

1. Feit (1970) gives three seasonal periods of moose hunting for the Waswanipi Cree: early October, late January and early February, and late March and early April.
2. However, as canoes are replaced by other methods of transporting between the Post and the territory it will become possible to eliminate the pre-freeze up and the break up parts of the annual trapping season.
3. This practice of donating fur to the Church dates back at least to 1647, with the first mention of such gifts coming from Mistassini Indians in 1675 (Larouche 1972:151, 153).
4. Among the Naskapi of Labrador, who have had relatively little involvement in the fur trade compared to the Cree, competition for status and leadership by means of hunting success which enables a man to share meat generously, is pursued vigorously, and not in the surreptitious manner with which such competition is conducted among the Mistassini Indians (Henrikson 1973).

Chapter 4

1. See Chapter 7.
2. Rogers has noted an archaeological site in the area north of Lake Mistassini,

which has a lodge with a floor plan similar to that shown in Fig. 10, which he calls 'trilobate' (Rogers 1963b:224-225).

Chapter 5

1. The 'Walking Out' ceremony has some similarity to another, less formal initiation of the child. The first time the child is given a pair of snowshoes he or she is made to walk out of the tent door and onto the ice of the lake or river nearby. The snowshoes are then put on the child's feet and he or she is made to walk around in a circle.

2. This is one of a number of cases in which many Mistassini informants contrast their current Christian practices with the way things were done before contact with the missionaries. The earlier practice tends to be seen as unsophisticated. For example, another informant, who was also speaking of the Nichicun group before they were contacted by missionaries, stated that at that time children were not given *real* names; instead they were named after such things as animals.

3. Speck: 'The shaman also appeals to the "heart of the wood" to obey him' (1935:193).

4. Tobacco is also placed in or near rapids before they are negotiated, to prevent the canoe turning over.

5. This analysis can also account for the use of the squirrel by the Eastmain Indians, who burn the fur to produce *warm* weather. The squirrel is a summer animal, also found near the camp.

6. It is only during this time of year that birch bark can be properly collected; the heartwood, by releasing the sap, allows the bark to be removed. Birch bark, where it is readily available, is used for lighting the domestic fire, although in this case the bark need not be carefully removed, and can be taken at any time of the year.

7. Speck distinguished between the spiritual entity of the east wind (*waapinesuu*) and the spiritual entity of the 'day-sky' (*waapinuu*) (1935:241).

8. Rousseau states that when inside, he faces east, because that is where the spirits come from (1953:136). Vincent's recent data indicates that at Natashquan the spirits come from all quarters, good spirits from the southern sector, bad ones from the northern (ibid.:72).

9. Preston has referred to examples from Rupert House as 'ritual hangings' (1964).

Chapter 6

1. However, I was not there to observe it; I arrived a few days later, and was given a number of descriptions.

2. Feit (1971, personal communication) reports observing a 'Shaking Tent' recently among a Waswanipi hunting group on its way to the winter hunting territory. We would expect hunting divination, in the form of prognostications for the following winter season, to play a more important role in such cases.

3. Very little information on this concept could be elicited, and the term 'spirit' is used only to denote an immaterial natural force.

4. The same kind of observation was also made in a speculative way by

Speck himself, although in this case he was discussing the possibility of an aboriginal concept of a monotheistic Supreme Being, related to the present-day concept of *Cemantuu* (Great Spirit) (1935:38).

5. According to Speck, *Mistaapew* is located in a person's heart (1935:42).

6. Speck's 'Mistassini' informants were either, at the time he met them, part of the Lac St. Jean band, or summer residents at Lac St. Jean.

7. Several examples of dreams recorded at Mistassini are presented by Rousseau, with the implication that such dream reports are often used as public rationalizations for action (1952:195).

8. One of Speck's informants interpreted the noise made when the bone cracked during scapulimancy as a good omen (1935:144).

Chapter 7

1. All verbal accounts of events can be separated unambiguously into *tipaacimuun* ('historical events') and *aatiiyuuhkan* ('myths') (cf. Savard 1971:11-12).

2. Much of my material on this subject duplicates the findings of other ethnographers in the general region, starting with an article by Speck in 1917 (cf. Speck 1930; Speck 1935: Speck and Heye 1921; Cooper 1930; Rogers 1972; Rousseau 1954; Webber 1974).

3. Speck also speaks of the use of garters as charms, and shows examples of them made of beads (1935: facing page 207). This practice may be related to the so-called 'hunting ribbons' which are worn by the groom and the best man at weddings. In the recent past these consisted of ribbons of several colours attached to the upper part of each arm of the man's jacket. They now appear as rosettes worn on the lapel, giving the men the appearance of British political candidates.

4. Both of these items were mentioned by Speck (1935).

5. Informants also told of past use of many of the more elaborate practices which earlier ethnographers in the region have reported (e.g. Speck 1935; Skinner 1914; Hallowell 1926; Iserhoff 1925; Waugh, in Rousseau 1954). I was able to attend one bear feast, but I arrived in camp after the animal had been killed.

6. The pattern of moving the camp to the site of the kill (Rogers 1963:79) was not practised by the groups I observed. Reasons for the abandonment of this practice might be the increased importance of trapping, and the fact that in many cases moving camp is now a more arduous task than moving the kill.

Chapter 8

1. I have even observed tiny beaver foetuses no more than 2 inches in length which were carefully skinned before they were cooked and served.

2. In a Montagnais version of this myth collected at La Romaine, the giant hunts for porcupine, but will eat nothing but the lungs. Later when he and the child join a group of caribou hunters, he is given the caribou lungs to eat (Savard 1973:13-17).

3. An informant from Rupert House stated that the burnt beaver feast was held to assure success in bear hunting.

4. In this regard, as in others, the muskrat appears to play a role as the

humorous junior counterpart of the beaver. While the beaver head connotes honour to a hunter, the muskrat head is usually given with some mirth to a young boy who has not yet begun to hunt.

5. The idea of hat removal seems to be an extension of church practice. Feasts at which one of the senior men happens to be a catechist are often begun by this person saying a grace in Cree.

6. A Rupert House man told me of a similar practice in which the skin from under the caribou's chin is cut into strips, one for each caribou killed, and this is decorated and displayed outside the tent door on a pole at the end of a caribou hunt.

7. According to Webber, this term is used by the Naskapi of Davis Inlet to refer to a manufactured charm which is made following the dream instructions of a shaman, and worn secretly underneath the clothing (1975).

8. In the case of 'Shaking Tent', the polarities are reversed (the spiritual inside, and the physical outside), but the spatial structure is the same.

9. At Fort George I was told that women hunters would present animals they had killed to men. It was considered most proper if possible for a man to present to a woman a female animal, and for a woman to present a man with a male animal.

10. Versions of this myth were collected by the author from members of the Waswanipi and Rupert House bands. No attempt was made at an exhaustive collection of myths among the Mistassini, and, although I did not hear of this myth, we have no evidence that a Mistassini version of it does not exist.

11. As Lefebvre herself notes, the significance of this term *Ninimish* is difficult to establish. The word may be a dialect variant of the word *Namimsuu* which is used. A Rupert House informant told me that, in addition to the Animal Masters of the various game species, there is an Animal Master called *Naamins* which rules over all the animals. However the role of *Naamins* is unlike *Nanimsuu* in myths, since he acts as a benevolent leader of the other animal masters.

12. In some accounts of the feast the hunter who provides the feast gets no serving at all, or else the food is all distributed to others present, who then each donate a little of their servings to give to the hunter (see, e.g. Thwaites 1896-1901, Vol. 6:281).

13. Summer reunions between relatives begin with long periods of silence, or quiet weeping.

Chapter 9

1. In a critique of Knight's thesis I tried to show that at Mistassini the system need not break down, even though Knight's argument about the need of the system to adapt to change is perfectly sound. Land tenure can adapt to these changes because in practice the system does not, despite evidence to the contrary, consist of family groups restricted to using fixed tracts of land which are passed on to the next generation in a strictly patrilineal way. This 'fixed' account of the system is part of a complex folk ideology, but is not a functional description of the Mistassini tenure system (Tanner 1973).

2. This average figure of 2.2 commensal families per hunting group appears

rather low, since it includes several small groups hunting close to Mistassini Post, often close to a road. The average for the more typical groups that are isolated for the whole winter would be closer to 3 families per group.

3. This method of rotational harvesting was observed as early as 1893 by the geologist Low, while visiting Mistassini (1896:50).

4. In each of these cases of a sub-division of a territory being in process, the two new sub-divisions were not yet, in 1971, operating as independent territories, so that they will be treated here as single territories with joint ownership.

5. This designation is used to preserve the anonymity of my informants, since this information differs from the official record, as shown in the beaver quotas.

6. Elsewhere I have published an article containing a map in which the present locations of hunting territories has been superimposed on Speck's map of Mistassini hunting territories, and with a listing of the names of the present owners (Tanner 1971).

7. We find many cases among the Mistassini, where a man acquires a territory adjacent to that of his affines, and other cases of inheritance of land from affines.

8. These cases of territory ownership and inheritance are remarkable for the lack of instances of disputes over rights to land. As Rogers has pointed out, several cases of trespass, or accusations of trespass, were reported for the Mistassini group between 1820-1840, but few have been reported since the turn of the century (Rogers 1963:73; see also Lips˙1947). Further on in his account of the Mistassini hunting territories Rogers speaks of the system as having collapsed after the late 1800's. This change between the nineteenth and twentieth century form of Mistassini land tenure is a complex historical question which Rogers, among others, has analysed. Since the present study is not primarily historical, I have instead tried to show the ownership system as it now exists; that is, with flexible boundaries, with groups that are continually breaking up (the member families using other lands) and with ecological conditions of comparative plenty, due in part to economic subsidies. Thus trespass does not appear to be an important issue in the land use system, and this is itself in part due to the very flexibility in the way land rights are made available. It may be that this period of flexibility is temporary, and marks the re-emergence of the hunting territory system, after a period of decline due to game shortages in the first half of this century.

Chapter 10

1. For an extended discussion of the concept of totalization see Lévi-Strauss 1966.

Bibliography

Anderson, J.W. 1961. *Fur Trader's Story*. Toronto: Ryerson Press

Anderson, W.A. 1961. *Angel of Hudson's Bay: The True Story of Maude Watt*. Toronto: Clark, Irwin and Company

Baldwin, W.K.W. 1958. *Plants of the Clay Belt of Northern Ontario*, National Museum of Canada, Bulletin No. 156. Ottawa

Banfield, A.W.F. 1958. 'Dermoid cysts a basis of Indian legend', *Journal of Mammology*, 39:451-2

Bauer, G.W. 1973. *Tales from the Cree*. Cobalt, Ontario: Highway Book Shop

Bloch, M. 1975. 'Property and the end of affinity' in M. Bloch (ed.), *Marxist Analyses and Social Anthropology*, A.S.A. Studies No. 3. London: Malaby Press

Bouchard, S. and J. Mailhot 1973. 'Structure du lexique: les animaux indiens', *Recherches amérindiennes au Québec*, 3(1-2):39-67

Brody, H. 1975. *The People's Land*. Harmondsworth: Penguin Books

Burgess, J.A. 1945. 'Property concepts of the Lac St. Jean Montagnais', *Primitive Man*, 18:1-25

Clough, G.C. 1972. 'Observations on Beaver Populations and other Mammals along the Fort George River', James Bay Task Force, Indians of Quebec Association and Northern Quebec Inuit Association. Mimeo.

Cook, B.D. 1972. 'The Northern James Bay Hydroelectric Development Scheme: Its Implications for Vegetation and Related Fauna', James Bay Task Force, Indians of Quebec Association and Northern Quebec Inuit Association. Mimeo.

Cooke, A.G.R. 1969. 'The Ungava Venture of the Hudson's Bay Company, 1830-1843', Ph.D. thesis, Cambridge University

Cooper, A.E. 1942. 'Ecological Aspects of the Family Hunting Territory Systems of the Northeast Algonkians', M.A. thesis, University of Chicago

Cooper, J.M. 1930. 'Field Notes on Northern Algonkian Magic', *23rd International Congress of Americanists, Proceedings*, 513-18

——— 1944. 'The Shaking Tent rite among plains and forest Algonkians', *Primitive Man*, 17:60-84

Coutts, R. 1972. 'Small Mammals of James Bay and the Probable Impact of the Hydroelectric Development on these Mammals', James Bay Task Force, Indians of Quebec Association and Northern Quebec Inuit Association. Mimeo.

Davies, K.G. (ed.) 1963. *Northern Quebec and Labrador Journals and Correspondence 1819-35*, Hudson's Bay Record Society, Vol. 24. London

Denmark, D.E. 1948, 'James Bay Beaver Conservation', *The Beaver*, Outfit 279 (Sept.):38-43

Denny, J.P. and J. Mailhot 1976. 'The semantics of certain abstract elements in the Algonquian verb', *International Journal of American Linguistics*, 42(2):91-8

Dowling, J.H. 1968. 'Individual ownership and the sharing of game in hunting societies', *American Anthropologist*, 70:502-7

Dunning, R.W. 1959. *Social and Economic Change among the Northern Ojibwa*. University of Toronto Press

Ellis, C.D. 1960. 'A Note on Okima.ka.n.', *Anthropological Linguistics* 2(3):1

―――― 1973. 'A proposed standard roman orthography for Cree', *The Western Canadian Journal of Anthropology*, 3(4):1-37

Feit, H.A. 1969. 'Mistassini Hunters of the Boreal Forest: Ecosystem Dynamics and Multiple Subsistence Patterns', M.A. thesis, McGill University

―――― 1970. 'Cognitive Factors in Changing Ecological Adaptations: An Example from the Waswanipi Cree'. Mimeo.

―――― 1973. 'The ethno-ecology of the Waswanipi Cree: or, how hunters can manage their resources', in B. Cox (ed.), *Cultural Ecology: Readings on the Canadian Indians and Eskimos*. Toronto: McClelland and Stewart

Fitzhugh, W.W. 1972. *Environmental Archaeology and Cultural Systems in Hamilton Inlet*. Smithsonian Contributions to Anthropology No. 16

Flannery, R. 1939. 'Shaking Tent rite amongst the Montagnais', *Primitive Man*, 12:11-16

Friedman, J. 1975. 'Tribes, states and transformations', in M. Bloch (ed.), *Marxist Analyses and Social Anthropology*. A.S.A. Studies No. 3. London: Malaby Press

Godelier, M. 1973. *Horizon, trajets marxistes en anthropologie*. Paris: François Maspéro

―――― 1975. 'Modes of Production, Kinship, and Demographic Structure', in M. Bloch (ed.), *Marxist Analyses and Social Anthropology*, A.S.A. Studies No. 3. London: Malaby Press

Hallowell, A.I. 1926. 'Bear ceremonialism in the northern hemisphere', *American Anthropologist*, 28:1-175

―――― 1949. 'The size of Algonkian hunting territories: a function of ecological adjustment', *American Anthropologist*, 51:34-45

―――― 1955. *Culture and Experience*. Philadelphia: University of Pennsylvania Press

Hare, F.K. 1959. 'Climate and zonal divisions of the boreal forest formation in eastern Canada', *Geographical Review*, 40:615-35

Hare, F.K. and R.G. Taylor 1956. 'The position of certain forest boundaries in southern Labrador', *Geographical Bulletin*, 8:51-73

Harper, F. 1964. *Plant and Animal Associations in the Interior of the Ungava Peninsula*. Lawrence: University of Kansas

Henriksen, G. 1973. *Hunters in the Barrens: the Naskapi on the Edge of the White Man's World*. St. John's: Memorial University, Institute of Social and Economic Research

Hickerson, H. 1967. 'Some implications of the theory of particularity or "Atomism" of northern Algonkians', *Current Anthropology*, 8:313-43

Hind, H.Y. 1863. *Exploration in the Interior of the Labrador Peninsula*. London: Longmans, Green

Honigmann, J.J. 1964. 'Indians of Nouveau-Quebec', in J. Malarie and J. Rousseau (eds.), *Le Nouveau Québec*. Paris: Mouton

Hustich, I. 1949. 'On the forest geography of the Labrador Peninsula: a preliminary synthesis', *Acta Geographica*, 10(2):1-63

Iserhoff, S. 1925. 'Bear customs among Indians', *The Beaver*, Outfit 256 (Sept.):174-5

Knight, R. 1965. 'A re-examination of hunting, trapping and territoriality among the northeastern Algonkian Indians', in A. Leeds and A.P. Vayda (eds.), *Man, Culture and Animals*. American Association for the Advancement of Science, Publication No. 78

———— 1968. *Ecological Factors in Changing Economy and Social Organization among the Rupert House Cree*, National Museum of Canada, Anthropological Papers No. 15. Ottawa

———— 1974. 'Grey Owl's return: cultural ecology and Canadian indigenous people', *Reviews in Anthropology*, 1(3):349-59

Larouche, L. 1972. *Le second registre de Tadoussac 1668-1700: Transcription*. Montreal: Les Presses de l'Université du Québec

Larusic, I. 1970. 'From hunter to proletarian: the involvement of the Cree Indians in the White wage economy of central Quebec', in N.A. Chance (ed.), *Developmental Change among the Cree Indians*. Department of Regional Economic Expansion, Ottawa. Mimeo.

Leach, E.R. 1954. *Political Systems of Highland Burma*. Cambridge, Mass.: Harvard University Press

Leacock, E. 1954. *The Montagnais Hunting Territory and the Fur Trade*, American Anthropological Association, Memoir 78, Vol. 56, Part 2

Lefèbvre, M. 1969. 'Quand un récit m'était livré', *Interpretation*, 3(4):53-66

———— 1971. *Tchakapesh. Récite Montagnais-Naskapi*. Bibliothèque National du Québec

Lévi-Strauss, C. 1950. 'Introduction à l'oeuvre de Marcel Mauss', in M. Mauss (ed.), *Sociologie et Anthropologie*. Paris: Les Presses Universitaires de France

———— 1952. 'Social Structure', in Al Kroeber (ed.), *Anthropology Today*. University of Chicago Press

———— 1966. *The Savage Mind*. London: Weidenfeld and Nicolson

Lips, J.E. 1947. 'Naskapi law (Lake St. John and Lake Mistassini Band): law and order in a hunting society', *American Philosophical Society, Transactions*. New Series 37, part 4

Low, A.P. 1896. 'Report on explorations in the Labrador Peninsula along the East Main, Koksoak, Hamilton, Manicuagan and portions of other rivers in 1892, 1893, 1894, 1895', *Geological Survey of Canada, Annual Report*, 1895, 8, Pt. L. Ottawa

MacKenzie, M.E. 1972. 'The East Cree (Mistassini) Verb: Derivational Morphology', unpublished M.A. thesis, McGill University

Mailhot, J. 1975. 'Standardisation de l'orthographe montagnaise'. Mimeo

Mailhot, J. and K. Lescop. 1977. *Lexique montagnais-francais du dialecte Scheffeville, Sept-Iles et Maliotenam*, Ministère des Affaires Culturelles, Quebec

Martijn, C.A. and E.S. Rogers 1969. *Mistassini: Albanel Contributions to the Prehistory of Quebec*. Centre d'Études Nordiques, Université Laval, Quebec. Travaux divers, No. 25

Mauss, M. 1966. 'Essai sur les variations saisonnières des societés eskimos: étude de morphologie sociale', in M. Mauss (ed.). *Sociologie et Anthropologie*, 3rd edn. Paris: Les Presses Universitaires de France

Moore, O.K. 1957. 'Divination: a new perspective', *American Anthropologist*, 59:69-74

Murphy, R.F. and J.H. Steward 1956. 'Tappers and trappers: parallel process in acculturation', *Economic Development and Culture Change*, 4:335-55

Nekich, S. 1974. 'The Feast of the Dead: the origin of Indian-White trade ceremonies in the West', *Western Canadian Journal of Anthropology*, 4(1):1-20

Park, G.K. 1963: 'Divination and its social context', *Journal of the Royal Anthropological Institute*. 93(2):195-209

Paulson, I. 1952. 'The "Seat of Honour" in aboriginal dwellings of the circumpolar zone, with special regard to the Indians of northern North America', *The 29th International Congress of Americanists, Proceedings*, 63-5

Pothier, R. 1967. *Relations inter-ethniques et acculturation à Mistassini*, Centre d'Études Nordiques, Université Laval, Quebec. Travaux divers, No. 9

Preston, R.J. 1964. 'Ritual hangings: an aboriginal survival in a northern North American trapping community', *Man*, 64:142-4

⎯⎯⎯⎯ 1975. 'Cree Narrative: Expressing the personal meanings of events'. National Museum of Man, Mercury Series, Canadian Ethnology Service, Paper No. 30. Ottawa

Richardson, B. 1975. *Strangers Devour the Land*. Toronto: Macmillan of Canada

Rogers, E.S. 1963. *The Hunting Group-Hunting Territory Complex among the Mistassini Indians*. National Museum of Canada, Bulletin 195. Ottawa

⎯⎯⎯⎯ 1963a. 'The canoe-sled among the Montagnais-Naskapi', *Royal Ontario Museum Annual Report 1962*, 74-6, 125

⎯⎯⎯⎯ 1963b. 'Notes on lodge plans in the Lake Indicator area of south-central Quebec', *Arctic*, 16(4):219-27

⎯⎯⎯⎯ 1967. *The Material Culture of the Mistassini*. National Museum of Canada, Bulletin 218. Ottawa

⎯⎯⎯⎯ 1969. 'An ethno-historical account of the Mistassini Indians', in C.A. Martijn and E.S. Rogers (eds.), *Mistassini-Albanel: Contributions to the Prehistory of Quebec*, Centre d'Études Nordiques, Université Laval, Quebec. Travaux divers, No. 25

⎯⎯⎯⎯ 1972. 'The Mistassini Cree', in M.G. Bicchieri (ed.), *Hunters and Gatherers Today: a socio-econonic study of eleven such cultures in the twentieth century*. Toronto: Holt, Rinehart and Winston

⎯⎯⎯⎯ 1973. *The Quest for Food and Furs: the Mistassini Cree 1953-1954*. National Museums of Canada, Publications in Ethnology, No. 5. Ottawa

Rogers, E.S. and J.H. Rogers 1959. 'The yearly cycle of the Mistassini Indians', *Arctic*, 12:130-8

⎯⎯⎯⎯ 1963. 'The individual Mistassini society from birth to death', *Contributions to Anthropology 1960*, Part 11:14-36. National Museum of Canada, Bulletin 190. Ottawa

Romaniuk, A. 1974. 'Modernization and fertility: the case of the James Bay Indians', *The Canadian Review of Sociology and Anthropology*, 11(4):344-59

Romaniuk, A. and V. Piche 1972. 'Natality estimates for the Canadian Indians stable population models 1900-1969', *Canadian Review of Sociology and Anthropology*, 9:1-20

Rousseau, J. 1949. 'Mistassini Calendar', *The Beaver*, Outfit 280 (Sept.): 33-7

Rousseau, J. 1953. 'Persistances païennes chez les Indiens de la forêt boréale', *Les Cahiers des Dix*, 17:83-208

——— 1953a. 'Rites païens de la forêt Québecoise: la tente tremblante et la suerie', *Les Cahiers des Dix*, 18:129-56

——— 1954. 'De menus rites païens de la forêt canadienne', *Les Cahiers des Dix*, 19:187:232

Rousseau, M. and J. Rousseau. 1948. 'La Ceremonie de la tente agitée chez les Mistassini', *Proceedings of the 28th International Congress of Americanists*: 307-315

——— 1952. 'Le dualisme religieux des peuples de la forêt boréale'. *Proceedings of 29th International Congress of Americanists*, 2:118-26

Rue, L.L. 1964. *The World of the Beaver*. Philadelphia: J.B. Lippincott

Sahlins, M. 1971. 'The intensity of domestic production in primitive societies: social inflections of the Chayanov Slope', in G. Dalton (ed.), *Studies in Economic Anthropology*, American Anthropological Association, Anthropological Studies, No. 7

——— 1972. *Stone Age Economics*. Chicago: Aldine

Salisbury, R. *et al.* 1972. 'The use of subsistence resources among James Bay Cree of Fort George, Paint Hills and Eastmain', in J.A. Spence (ed.), *Not by Bread Alone*. James Bay Task Force, the Indians of Quebec Association and the Northern Quebec Inuit Association. Mimeo.

——— 1972a. *James Bay and Development: Socio-economic implications of the Hydro-electric Project*. Programme in the Anthropology of Development, McGill University, Montreal. Mimeo.

Sanders, D.E. 1973. *Native Peoples in Areas of Internal National Expansion: Indians and Inuit in Canada*. Copenhagen: I.W.G.I.A.

Savard, R. 1971. *Carcajou, et le sens du monde: récits Montagnais-Naskapi*. Bibliothèque Nationale du Québec

——— 1973. 'Structure de récit: l'enfant couvert de poux', *Recherches Amérindiennes au Québec*, 3(1-2):13-37

Schutz, A. 1945. 'On multiple realities', *Philosophical and Phenomenological Research*, 5(4):533-76. Also in A. Schutz, 1962, *Collected Papers I: the Problem of Social Reality*. The Hague: Nijhoff

Schwimmer, E.G. 1972. 'Symbolic competition', *Anthropologica*, New Series 14(2):117-55

Skinner, A. 1911. 'Notes on the eastern Cree and northern Salteau', *American Museum of Natural History, Anthropological Papers*, 9(1):117-76

——— 1914. 'Bear customs of the Cree and other Algonkian Indians of Northern Ontario', *Ontario History Society, Papers and Records*, 12:203-9

Speck, F.G. 1915. 'The basis of American Indian ownership of the land', *Old Penn Weekly Review*, 13:491-5

——— 1923. 'Mistassini hunting territories in the Labrador Peninsula', *American Anthropologist*, 25:452-71

——— 1924. 'Spritual beliefs among the Labrador Indians', *21st International Congress of Americanists. Proceedings*, 1:266-75

——— 1930. 'Mistassini Notes', *Indian Notes*, 7:410-57

——— 1931. 'Montagnais-Naskapi bands and early Eskimo distribution in the Labrador Peninsula', *American Anthropologist*, 33:557-600

——— 1935. *Naskapi, the savage hunters of the Labrador Peninsula*. Norman: University of Oklahoma Press

Speck, F.G. and L.C. Eiseley 1942. 'Montagnais-Naskapi bands and family hunting districts of the central and southeastern Labrador Peninsula', *American Philosophical Society, Proceedings*, 85:215-42

Speck, F.G. and G.G. Heye 1921. 'Hunting charms of the Montagnais and the Mistassini', *Indian Notes and Monographs, Miscellaneous Series*, 13-1

Sperber, D. 1975. *Rethinking Symbolism*. Cambridge University Press

Tanner, A. 1966. 'The Structure of Fur Trade Relations', M.A. thesis, University of British Columbia

———— 1968. 'Occupation and life style in two minority communities', in N.A. Chance (ed.), *Conflict in Culture: Problems of Developmental Change among the Cree*. Canadian Research Center for Anthropology, St. Paul University, Ottawa

———— 1971. 'Existe-t-il des territoires de chasse?', *Recherches Amérindiennes au Québec*, 1(4-5):69-83

———— 1972. 'The use of subsistence resources in the Kaniapiskau-Nichequon region', in J.A. Spence (ed.), *Not by Bread Alone*. James Bay Task Force, Indians of Quebec Association and Northern Quebec Inuit Association, Montreal. Mimeo.

———— 1972a. 'Name Mates and Name Sponsors among the Mistassini Cree of Quebec', paper presented at the Annual Meeting, American Anthropological Association, Toronto. Mimeo.

———— 1973. 'The significance of hunting territories today', in B. Cox (ed.), *Cultural Ecology: Readings on the Canadian Indians and Eskimos*. Toronto: McClelland and Stewart

———— 1975. 'The Hidden Feast: Eating and Ideology among the Mistassini Cree', in W. Cowan (ed.), *Papers of the Sixth Algonkian Conference*. National Museum of Man, Mercury Series.

Terray, E. 1972. *Marxism and 'Primitive' Societies*. New York: Monthly Review Press

Thwaites, R.G. (ed.) 1896-1901. *The Jesuit Relations and Allied Documents*, 73 Vols. Cleveland: Burrows Brothers

Todd, W.E.C. 1963. *Birds of the Labrador Peninsula and Adjacent Areas*. University of Toronto Press

Tremblay, V. 1968. *Histoire du Saguenay depuis les origines jusqu'à 1870*. La société Historique du Saguenay, Chicoutimi

Vallee, F.G. 1967. *Kabloona and Eskimo in the Central Keewatin*. Canadian Research Center for Anthropology, University of Ottawa

Van Stone, J.W. 1963. 'Changing Patterns of Indian Trapping in the Canadian Subarctic', *Arctic*, 16:159-74

Vincent, S. 1973. 'Structure du rituel: la tente tremblante et le concept de *mista.pe.w*', *Recherches Amérindiennes au Québec*, 3(1-2):68-83

Voorhis, E. 1930. *Historic Forts and Trading Posts of the French Regime and of the English Fur Trading Companies*. National Development Bureau, Canada

Webber, A. Podolinsky. 1974. 'The Healing Vision: Naskapi Natutschikans', *Arts Canada* (December 1973-January 1974):150-4

Wernstedt, F.L. 1972. *World Climate Data*. Lamont, Penn.:Climate Data Press

Wilson, L. 1952. *Chibougamau Venture*. Montreal: Chibougamau Publishing Company

Index

ISER BOOKS

Studies

Mailing address:

ISER Books
Memorial University of Newfoundland
St. John's, Newfoundland
A1C 5S7

Telephone: (709) 737-7474   FAX : (709) 737-7560
email: iser-books@ mun.ca
WEB site: http://www.mun.ca/iser/